784.932 Ley
Leyerle.
Vocal development through
 organic imagery.

The Lorette Wilmot Library
Nazareth College of Rochester

VOCAL DEVELOPMENT THROUGH ORGANIC IMAGERY

SECOND EDITION

REVISED AND ENLARGED

1986

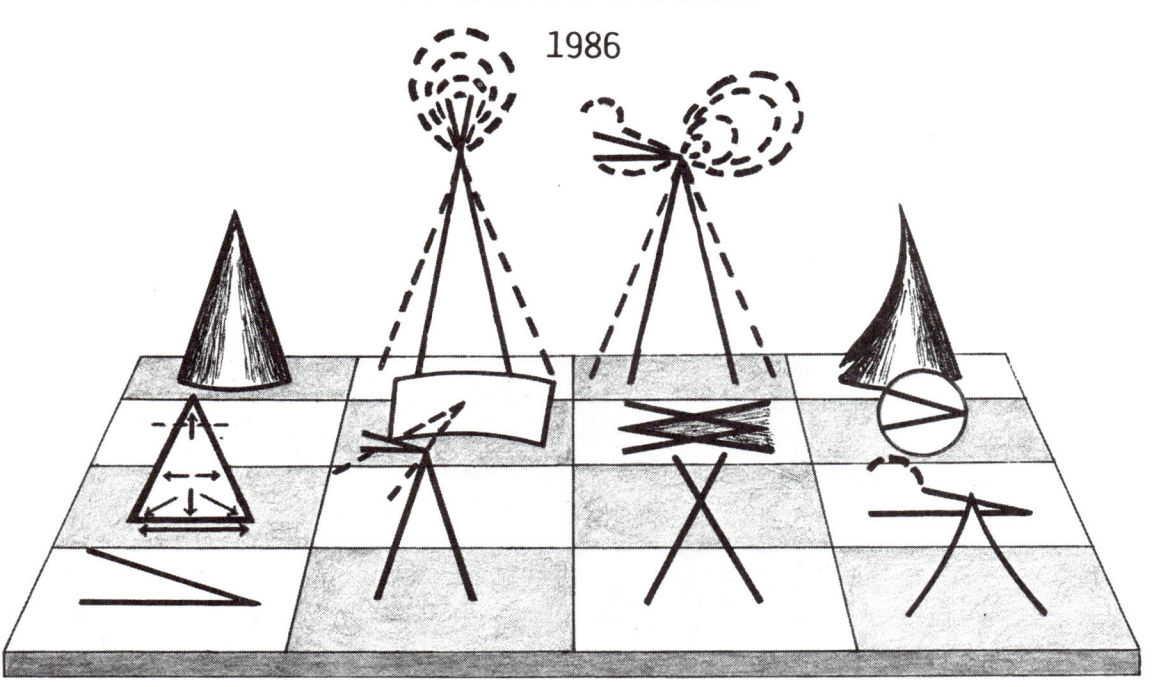

by

WILLIAM D. LEYERLE

STATE UNIVERSITY OF NEW YORK
COLLEGE OF THE ARTS AND SCIENCE
GENESEO, NEW YORK

VOCAL DEVELOPMENT THROUGH ORGANIC IMAGERY

First Edition Copyright © William D. Leyerle 1977

Library of Congress Catalog Number: 78-103579
ISBN 0-9602296-0-4

First printing 1977 College Printing Shop of the State University College at Geneseo, New York

Second printing 1978
Third printing 1980

Second Edition, Revised and Enlarged
© William D. Leyerle 1986
ISBN 0-9602296-6-3

No part of this publication may be reproduced, stored in a retrieval system or transmitted in any form or by any means, electronic, mechanical, photocopying, recording, or otherwise, without obtaining the prior written permission of the copyright owner.

LEYERLE PUBLICATIONS
Executive Offices
28 Stanley Street
Mt. Morris, New York 14510

Printed in the United States of America

Order directly from
LEYERLE PUBLICATIONS
Box 384
Geneseo, New York 14454

or from your local music dealer or bookstore.

DEDICATION

To my wife, Anne, for everything!

AN APPRECIATION

Slightly more than ten years ago, my friend, colleague, and mentor, Karl Trump, was proof-reading the prototype manuscript for VOCAL DEVELOPMENT THROUGH ORGANIC IMAGERY for content. As was his wont in moments of enthusiasm, he called me long distance to tell me of his delight with the book, even though he had only progressed through the fourth chapter. I prized this kind compliment, especially, from a man of Karl's artistic and literary tastes. But I had already grown accustomed to his ready generosity and enthusiastic willingness to help younger students and teachers.

We had first met, twenty years earlier, in Vienna's Akademie für Musik und darstellende Kunst (now known as the Staatliche Hochschule für Musik und darstellende Kunst). Karl was on his first sabbatical from the College of Wooster. He was registered at the Akademie in the German Lieder program and studied voice, privately, with Sergei Radamsky. I was there as a G.I. Bill student in the Opera Preparatory school and to study privately with Baron Hans Hugo Karg.

Karl was accompanied in Vienna by his wife, Ruth, and their two young daughters, Sally and Anne. I was there with my wife, Anne, who was also enrolled at the Akademie.

Anyone who is familiar with European schools knows that with their numerous religious holidays there are many three- and four-day weekends. This fact was not lost on the Trumps and Leyerles, who got together on numerous occasions for bridge, word games (including "Stinky Pinky"), luncheons, dinners, and trips (the Trumps had a Volkswagen) to the Burgenland.

It was during this year in Vienna that I was aghast at the overwhelming energy exhibited by Karl. Every time I saw him (about once a week) he had been to four or five concerts, recitals, or operas— not to mention an equal number of "Jauses" or other social events.

After our return to the states, Anne and I stayed in contact with Karl and Ruth, visiting them frequently in Wooster. It was on these visits that I learned what a busy voice teacher's schedule is *really* like. On one of my first Saturdays with Karl, he took me to a day's summer session in the neighboring Canton, Ohio, where he had twenty-one lessons (with a half-hour for lunch) in succession.

Karl maintained an "open" studio; so, on many other occasions over the years, I visited his studio at the College of Wooster. Although I never studied voice with Karl, I think I learned more from observing him teach than I did from most of my own voice lessons. Certainly, he is currently well-represented in New York City and in Europe by several of his former students, including Erie Mills, John Seabury, David Gordon, and Maggie Pettingill, to name but a few.

Karl was responsible for my joining the National Association of Teachers of Singing (NATS). During his second year as president of that organization, I attended their national convention in St. Louis. Anne and I were visiting relatives there at the time of the convention. Karl convinced me that I was adequately qualified to become a NATS member and became my sponsor for membership. I have never regretted that decision.

On December 5, 1976, the night before he was to have a routine checkup for his heart at a hospital in Canton, Karl called Anne and me to see if we planned to attend the NATS convention in Philadelphia (where Erie Mills was to be one of the finalists in the NATSAA competition). He also mentioned his and Ruth's plans for a trip to Sweden and other parts of Europe that following summer. It was one of the saddest days of my life to hear the very next day that Karl had died suddenly of a heart attack during his examination at the hospital.

I am sorry that we could not enjoy Karl's presence with us for many years to come; but, in a real sense, he is with us all the time, still offering his words of confidence and guidance. Thank you, Karl.

Death cannot turn off such a light!

CONTENTS

INTRODUCTION.. ix

CHAPTER I POSTURE.. 1

    A. Placement of feet... 1

    B. Alignment of spine.. 1

    C. Position of shoulders and chest... 3

    D. Position of chin and jaw.. 3

    E. Cranial flex of the spine... 4

    F. Position of hands... 4

CHAPTER II RESPIRATION... 6

    A. The Respirators.. 10

        1. Channels... 10
        2. Receptacles.. 10
        3. Machinery.. 10

    B. Inspiration.. 11

        1. Diaphragm.. 11
        2. External Intercostals.. 11

    C. Expiration... 12

        1. Abdominal Muscles.. 12
        2. Internal Intercostals.. 12

    D. Coordination of Inspiration and Expiration............................. 12

CHAPTER III PHONATION.. 19

    A. The Larynx... 19

    B. The Open Throat.. 22

        1. A low larynx.. 23
        2. A forward tongue.. 25
        3. A lifted palate... 26
        4. A dropped jaw... 27
        5. Correct breathing... 27

    C. Focus.. 28

    D. Coordination of Respiration and Phonation.............................. 31

CHAPTER IV RESONATION.. 36

    A. The Resonators... 36

        1. The Pharynx... 37
        2. The Nasal Cavity.. 37
        3. The Mouth... 37
        4. The Sinuses... 38
        5. The Larynx and Esophagus.. 38

    B. Coordinated Resonance.. 38

        1. Mask Resonance.. 39
        2. Head Resonance.. 42

C. Coordination of Phonation and Resonation........................ 44

　　　　　1. Coupling... 45
　　　　　2. The Attack... 45
　　　　　3. Vowel Dualism.. 46
　　　　　4. Vowel Migration.. 47
　　　　　5. Registration... 52

CHAPTER V REGISTRATION.. 54

　　　One Register Theory.. 55
　　　Two Register Theory.. 55
　　　Three Register Theory.. 55

CHAPTER VI ARTICULATION... 73

　　　A. The Articulators... 73

　　　　　1. The Tongue... 73
　　　　　2. The Lips... 74
　　　　　3. The Teeth.. 74
　　　　　4. The Hard Palate.. 74
　　　　　5. The Alveolar Ridge... 74
　　　　　6. The Velum.. 74
　　　　　7. The Pharyngeal Wall.. 75
　　　　　8. The Glottis.. 75

　　　B. Classification of Consonants................................... 75

　　　　　1. Basic Classification of Consonants........................... 75

　　　　　　　a. Voiceless.. 75
　　　　　　　b. Voiced... 75

　　　　　2. Descriptive Classification of Consonants..................... 76

　　　　　　　a. Plosives... 76
　　　　　　　b. Fricatives... 76
　　　　　　　c. Nasals... 76
　　　　　　　d. Glides... 76
　　　　　　　e. Trills... 77

　　　C. Coordination of Phonation, Resonation, and Articulation........ 77

CHAPTER VII COLORATION.. 80

　　　Overtones.. 81
　　　Chiaro-Oscuro.. 84
　　　The Snerd Synthesizer.. 85
　　　The Snerdometer.. 86

CHAPTER VIII VOCAL PROBLEM SOLVING...................................... 90

　　　A. Technical Problems... 90

　　　　　1. Tone... 90

　　　　　　　a. "Breaking" Voice... 90
　　　　　　　b. Breathiness.. 91
　　　　　　　c. "Chesty" or "Belty" Voice................................ 92
　　　　　　　d. Covered Tone and Hooking................................. 92
　　　　　　　e. Excessive Compression.................................... 94
　　　　　　　f. Falsetto... 94
　　　　　　　g. Intonation... 95
　　　　　　　h. Nasality... 97

    i. Stridency... 97
    j. Tremolo... 98
    k. Vibrato... 98
    l. Wobble..100
   2. Intensity...100
    a. Volume..100
    b. Amplitude...101
    c. Projection..101
     (1) The "small voice"................................102
     (2) The "large voice" that does not project...........103
   3. Miscellaneous...104
    a. Breath Flow...104
    b. Breath Control......................................104
    c. Humming...106
    d. Position..107
    e. Range...108
    f. Timing..109
    g. Trills..109

 B. Health Problems..112
  1. Physical Health..112
   a. Rest..112
   b. Diet..112
   c. Physical Training...................................113
   d. Morality..114
   e. Maladies and Afflictions............................114
  2. Psychological Health....................................115
   a. Confidence..116
   b. Ego (Self-Image)....................................116
   c. Excitement..116
   d. Lethargy..116
   e. Motivation (Enthusiasm).............................116
   f. Nervousness (Fear, Stage-Fright, etc.)..............117

CHAPTER IX THE WHOLE ELEPHANT....................................118

 A. Balanced Directions..119

 B. Metaphysical Concepts..120

 C. Characterization...122

 D. Mirrors, Tape and Video Recordings, and Recordings...........123

 E. Imagination..123

CHAPTER X USING THE IPA..126

  Broad Transcription...127
  Narrow Transcription..127
  Phonetic Symbols..129

CHAPTER XI VOCALIZATION..135

 A. Warming up the body..135

 B. Warming up the voice...136

 C. Extending the range..137

    D. Extending breath control.................................139

    E. Developing flexibility..................................139

    F. Extending dynamic control..............................143

    G. Developing articulation................................143

    H. Developing chromaticism................................145

    I. Developing a floating tone.............................146

CHAPTER XII THE APPOGGIAMETER.....................................148

    The Instrument...149
    The Support Column.......................................151

APPENDICES..154

    I International Phonetic Alphabet[I]......................155

    II International Phonetic Alphabet[II]...................156

    III Voice Classification.................................159

    IV Vowel Focus Exercises................................163

    V Vowel Migration Charts.................................165

    VI How To Study A Song...................................166

    VII Imposto..167

    VIII Register Coordination Exercises.....................168

    IX The Blind Men And The Elephant........................170

BIBLIOGRAPHY..171

INDEX...173

INTRODUCTION

It has often been said that one cannot learn to sing by reading a book. This is true to an extent, but it might also be said that one cannot learn singing from a teacher.

If this be true, where does that leave the student?

For this, he needs guidance. Both teachers and books can provide *some* of the guidance a student may need during the course of his development.

I hope this text will provide some insights into singing which will prove beneficial to the reader at his present stage of vocal development. It was written originally as a basic text on voice production for class voice students and for voice majors on a college or university level. The concepts included herein are valid, however, for *all* singers, including high school students who are sufficiently mature to pursue vocal study and for choral singers who wish to gain more knowledge about their voices.

More technical information may be included in this manual than is necessary, or possible, for voice classes to assimilate in one semester. My approach to class voice during the first semester is to cover the material in the manual, emphasizing basic technical development and using songs as a medium. The second semester I reverse the emphasis, giving more attention to repertoire and applying technical considerations as needed. The manual should be used as a text for the first semester and as a reference guide thereafter, except in such cases where the material cannot be covered at a comfortable rate in one semester's time.

I suggest the reader scan this manual in order to gain a feeling for its general content. Then he should proceed in a more deliberate manner with Chapters I through VII. The first seven chapters are the heart of the manual, and should be covered thoroughly by both voice classes and individual students. Chapters VIII through XII and the Appendices may be used to supplement the first seven chapters as needed.

It is not necessary for singers to memorize all the bones, muscles, and cartilages enumerated in these pages. They are included here as reference material and as an aid to the reader for gaining a physiological over-view of what is involved in voice production.

The class voice student need not necessarily learn the phonetic symbols for foreign languages, as they are presented here principally for voice majors; but all voice students should learn the International Phonetic Alphabet (IPA) for English. It is an efficient and effective tool for solving problems in diction and tonal imagery. While this is not a manual for English or foreign language diction, the IPA will aid immeasurably in the study of diction as needed for technical aspects of vocal development. If, at some later time, the student should take diction courses, he will have an immense advantage by already knowing the IPA.

Imagery has long been a popular and effective device for helping teachers communicate with their students when words seem inadequate. Some of these images take strange and fantastic forms. While I applaud their use in general, I also feel that imagery can be logical and progressive, based on a firm, physical foundation. That is the reason I have developed the concept of *Organic Imagery*. (See p. 14)

x VOCAL DEVELOPMENT THROUGH ORGANIC IMAGERY

Organic Imagery is not a radical vocal concept. Every phase of it, as presented in the following pages, conforms to accepted vocal practices and to the correct physiological functions of the vocal mechanism. They say, "A picture is worth a thousand words." The efficiency and effectiveness of Organic Imagery will attest to the validity of that statement. I have been both gratified and surprised with the consistent response of the hundreds of my students who have used Organic Imagery as a part of their vocal development. It works!

I must state again that this manual is designed principally for voice production. It is a guide to aid the reader in understanding the medium of vocal technique. A sound technique is the first prerequisite for a singer who wishes to progress into the more mysterious realm of vocal art.

Technique, then, is only a "door opener" which will allow the student to proceed to the ultimate goal of singing— expression. Before he can reach that goal, he must open the door.

PREFACE TO THE SECOND EDITION

The preceding introduction is virtually the same as it appeared in the first edition almost ten years ago. Only a few references to chapter and page numbers have been changed to conform to this enlarged edition.

In an effort not to betray the trust of those teachers who are still using *VOCAL DEVELOPMENT THROUGH ORGANIC IMAGERY* as a text for their voice classes, I left the first five chapters relatively undisturbed. The changes which were made reflect various refinements which are inevitable during ten years of constant classroom use. Because Chapter IV (Resonation) grew so large in revision, it spawned an additional Chapter V (Registration); thus the old Chapter V (Articulation) became Chapter VI, etc.

Instead of seven chapters, the volume now has twelve; and, although there are still nine appendices, two of the former ones have been incorporated into the main body of the text: Former Appendix VI (Vocalises) is now a complete Chapter XI (Vocalization). Former Appendix VII (The Snerd Synthesizer) now constitutes a substantial part of Chapter VII (Coloration).

Those readers who are familiar with the first edition will note that one of the previous chapter titles, *Et Cetera*, has been changed to *The Whole Elephant*.

Some readers may question the placement of Chapter XII (The Appoggiameter) as the last chapter in the book, rather than introducing it with Respiration or Phonation. I must admit that my original intention was to include it as an appendix when the idea was a simple "invention"; but, as I started committing the idea to manuscript, it grew beyond what I consider a wieldy appendage to be. Further, as the opening paragraph will indicate, the concept works quite well as a "culminating activity" after the student has had ample time to experiment with the other basic concepts prerequisite to support.

Those teachers who believe that Support is the "first cause" in vocal technique may not wish to wait until Chapter XII to broach the subject, however. In this case, Chapter XII can be transposed to any other position in the text where the teacher believes it to be more appropriate.

PREFACE TO THE SECOND EDITION xi

Practically all new chapters are: V Registration, VII Coloration, X Using The IPA, XI Vocalization, and XII The Appoggiameter. Other significant additions and improvements to the new edition include: numerous illustrations, all of which are numbered for convenient reference; a larger format with more legible text; Smyth-sewn signatures, which should add many years to the physical life of the book; and a bibliography.

One new feature of the revised edition is, of necessity, on the negative side. For almost ten years the price of the first edition remained the same— $6.95— in spite of spiraling inflation, which struck with unreasoning force against the paper industry. Against the advice of well-meaning colleagues, I resisted the suggestion of increasing the price over the ensuing years. But, with the inclusion of about fifty-six additional pages, while paper and production costs are still undeclining, there was no choice. Even without the enlargement and improvements, *reproduction of the old volume* would have cost almost as much as the revised edition. Therefore, it seemed a suitable time to make the revision.

In regard to one aspect of the writing style adopted for this volume, I would like to quote a footnote from the introduction of Lehman Engel's book, *GETTING THE SHOW ON*:

> "...The masculine gender used throughout the book has been chosen simply to obviate the "he/she" and the "his or her" awkwardness that can often arise in attempts to avoid sexist language. Unless otherwise specified, both males and females are implied..."[1]

At no time do I wish to exclude the ladies from consideration of any part of this book. (Some of my best friends are women!) I have wrestled with the gender problem in coping with magazine articles in the past. The most acceptable solution, I found, was to resort to a constant use of plurals; but this also becomes tedious to write and more so to read. Further, my English teachers had enough difficulty drumming the prevalent rules for grammar and usage into my head. Blame the system! Perhaps, sometime in the near future, grammarians will find themselves able to adopt and to agree upon an absolutely new word for a uni-sex pronoun which will roll trippingly off the tongue and not be offensive to anyone. At such time, I will be its most enthusiastic advocate.

In regard to differentiation of various octaves throughout this book, I have adopted the Helmholtz method, rather than that of the U.S.A. Standards Association. (See below)

C_1 C   c c^1 c^2 c^3 c^4

---

[1] Engel, Lehman; *GETTING THE SHOW ON*; Schirmer Books, New York; Collier Macmillan Publishers, London; 1983; p. xi

CHAPTER I
POSTURE

Posture is the first phase of vocal technique, and its importance cannot be overstated. Good singing posture provides the foundation of all subsequent technical considerations.

The rules for good posture are few and easy to master. We shall group them into six divisions:

A. Placement of feet
B. Alignment of spine
C. Position of shoulders and chest
D. Position of chin or jaw
E. Cranial flex of spine
F. Position of hands

A. Placement of feet

The feet should be placed with one heel slightly behind the other at about a 60 degree angle:

a. Correct   b. Incorrect*   c. Incorrect   d. Incorrect

Fig. 1

The reason for standing with feet at a proper angle is to facilitate balance (Fig. 1a). If a singer stands as illustrated in Fig. 1b, he might sway from left to right during the heat of performance. *However, this position is acceptable, and sometimes *preferable*, for some women because of their pelvic construction. In Fig. 1c, in addition to being rather uncomfortable, he might sway forward or backward.

The weight of the body should favor the balls of the feet and not the heels. This will give the singer a more dominant and aggressive stance. The weight on the balls of the feet should be distributed equally on the right and left feet.

Fig. 1d is generally incorrect for concert performances and most stage performances, as it is considered brash and vulgar. The exception would be, of course, if the characterization calls for a brash or vulgar personality.

B. Alignment of spine

A performer must never be off-balance. If his feet are firmly planted at the correct angle and if his weight is forward, a straight back will give him a feeling of potency and energy. His entire body should feel like a plumb line. All his weight from the top of his head to the balls of his feet should feel as if in a straight line downward.

2 VOCAL DEVELOPMENT THROUGH ORGANIC IMAGERY

Achieving a straight back for singing is often difficult for students unused to such a position. If a person is naturally sway-backed, it may be impossible for him to straighten the back entirely. For all other singers, not so afflicted, the process may still take some effort.

One way of checking if the back is sufficiently straight is to stand with back, head, buttocks, thighs, calves, and heels firmly against a wall. If the small of the back is pressed firmly against the wall so that one's hand cannot be inserted between the small of the back and the wall, then the back is straight.

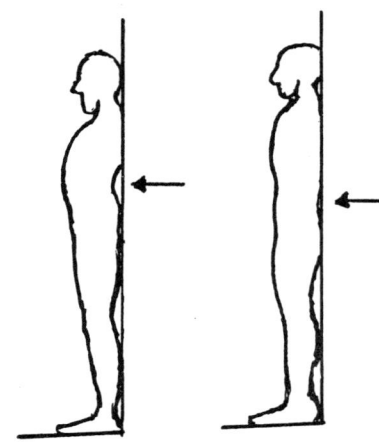

a. Incorrect   b. Correct

Fig. 2

This will seem an uncomfortable position to those unused to it. If it is too uncomfortable and is detrimental to singing, it should be modified or discontinued until such time as the position can be strengthened and made comfortable.

One means of getting the small of the back against the wall is to <u>tilt the pelvis forward</u>, as in the "bump" of a burlesque dancer's "bump and grind." This is called "<u>tucking</u>." Singers with dancing experience are often much quicker to realize success in this position.

A student can also lie flat on the floor and try to flatten the small of the back against it by slowly bending the knees toward the chest. The trick, then, is to lower the knees to their original position without allowing the back also to curve to its original position. The additional relaxation inherent in this latter position may elicit more rapid progress than standing against a wall, although not necessarily. In either case, the student should never lock the knees.

After some degree of success is realized in the wall or floor position, the student should practice standing away from these props. From that point, he should strive to make it a natural and spontaneous part of his singing posture. It should become habitual.

One word of warning: Some singers become so adept at keeping their backs straight that they continue to maintain the tilted pelvis position when they are not singing. This might lead, eventually, to the problem of not being able to bend the back in a swaying position. Normal exercise should preclude this happening, but one should be alert to the possibility of becoming inflexible.

C. Position of shoulders and chest

The correct position of the shoulders should be backward and down. The chest should be held high.

Francesco Lamperti stated that a singer should "...hold himself erect, with the chest expanded and the shoulders easy— in a word, in a position of a soldier."[1]

William Vennard states "...The high chest implies that the shoulders go back, but they should relax and be comfortable. There should be no straining like a soldier on parade..."[2]

At first glance, there would seem to be a discrepancy in postural concepts between Messrs. Lamperti and Vennard. This is not the case. The key to the apparent discrepancy is the word "soldier." In all other respects, the gentlemen agree. Perhaps the Italian army is more lax than the American army, lending a certain ambiguity to the analogy of the singer and the soldier.

As the student reads more and more books on various aspects of singing, he will probably discover, if he has an open mind, that many points of contention among vocal pedagogs is a result of ambiguous terminology, rather than actual fact. One of the goals I hope to achieve in this text is a conciliation of concepts by various factions. A teacher or singer who rules out certain ideas in favor of others because of semantical hairsplitting may be missing an important part of his development.

More will be discussed about chest position in the next chapter on Respiration. There are good reasons for maintaining a high chest, best explained at that time.

While the chest should be held high at all times, the shoulders should never be raised during vocalization.

It is a common occurrence for beginning or untutored singers to raise the shoulders while reaching for high notes. This is a compensatory act which serves no useful purpose except to point out that something is wrong in other quarters. This is true of *all* compensatory acts.

D. Position of chin or jaw

The chin and lower jaw are parts of the same mechanism. While the lower part of the jaw is not actually parallel or horizontal with the floor, it is often helpful to the singer to feel as if it is. The reason for this will be discussed in the chapter on Phonation.

As the upper jaw is relatively stationary, it poses no particular problem in regard to posture. One exception to this might be the tendency for untrained singers to throw their heads backward when singing high notes; but this would violate the principle of keeping the spine straight, as has already been established. After the singer's basic technique has been firmly developed, it is helpful to incline the head slightly backward for the high notes, but in such a manner that it will not disturb the spinal alignment.

---

[1] Lamperti, Francesco; *THE ART OF SINGING*, translated by J.C. Griffith; G. Schirmer, Inc., New York; p. 10.

[2] Vennard, William; *SINGING, THE MECHANISM AND THE TECHNIC*, revised ed. 1967; Carl Fischer, Inc., New York; p. 19, §79.

4 VOCAL DEVELOPMENT THROUGH ORGANIC IMAGERY

E. Cranial flex of the spine

We have already mentioned that the spine should be straight as a fundamental necessity for good posture. We may now add to this the concept of "cranial flex," which will help to insure that the spine is straight. A simple device for achieving the cranial flex has been used by voice teachers all over the world and for several centuries.

Imagine a string being attached to the back of the skull, and that the singer is suspended from that string as a puppet. The sensation is one of stretching the back side of the cervical vertebrae, or the neck portion of the spine. In other words, the singer will feel as if he has a longer neck and a straighter back.

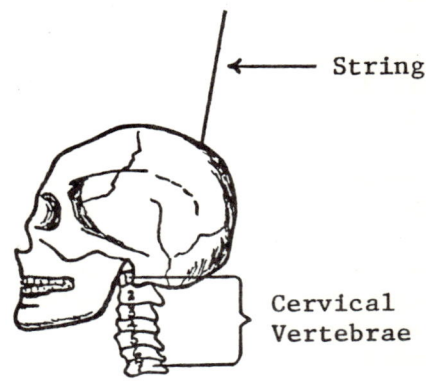

Fig. 3

Not only will the spine be straighter as a result of applying this concept of suspension, but the singer will be more able to feel the logical connection with the breathing apparatus, which we shall discuss in the next chapter. In addition, he will feel more noble, psychologically, and will have a strength of comportment that he would not have otherwise. This will allow him to stand or move with an authority and grace which is lacking in too many performers.

It is easy to teach a nobleman how to slouch. It is not so easy to teach a sloucher how to stand nobly.

F. Position of hands

For beginning singers, the hands are to posture what the tongue is to phonation and articulation— "unruly members." Invariably the untrained performer will instinctively feel he must do something with his hands; and, just as invariably, he will do the wrong things.

Many teachers advocate three acceptable hand positions:

1. Lightly clasped in front and above the waist line, the back of one hand in the palm of the other
2. One hand held in front, above the waist line, while the other is dropped and relaxed at the side
3. Both hands dropped and relaxed at the sides

Of these three possibilities, the third is preferable— at least for the beginner. It is the simplest, most appropriate, and the least obtrusive; but it is also the most difficult to habituate.

The probable reason for this is that most beginners are either nervous or uncertain of their images, or both. Inappropriate hand movements or positions are certain signs that the performer is not in control of the situation. The singer realizes this unconsciously and tries to "do something" with his hands. Unless he has been taught to realize that the hands should be in a position appropriate to the mood of the song, or that any movement whatsoever should only help to intensify the intent of the text and music, then he will surely do something to detract from the performance.

Therefore, the safest position is with the hands at his sides.

As the singer gains more confidence, he will discover other hand positions for purposes of variety or heightened expressiveness. The means for achieving this are dependent upon his involvement in and understanding of both music and text.

There is some disagreement among voice teachers in regard to gestures on the concert stage. Some believe the hands should be used as an actor uses his— with gestures. Others believe that the general posture and facial expressions are adequate to convey the message. Either is acceptable as long as the performer does it convincingly and in good taste.

Whichever style the performer adopts, a helpful guideline might be the old adage of the theatre, "Less is more."

Early in this chapter I said that the rules for good posture are few and easy to master. This is true. However, it has been my observation that many students seem to forget what they "mastered" after their initial efforts. For many of them it seems to take five minutes to explain and five years to enforce. This is due, in part, to the diversions created by the graduated complexities of developing a first-rate vocal technique and applying it as an artistic performer. Therefore, each serious vocal student should ask his teacher to call any kind of bad posture to his attention, if and when he falls out of form, because he will never develop a truly first-rate technique or artistic performing ability with bad posture.

CHAPTER II
RESPIRATION

Breath is the fuel for sound. It is the motivating force.

The proper term for the breathing process is *respiration*. This includes breathing in and breathing out. Breathing in is called *inspiration* or *inhalation*. Breathing out is called *expiration* or *exhalation*.

There are two basic types of respiration:

1. Breathing for the life processes
2. Breathing for work

Respiration for sustaining life is an unconscious act. Everyone does it and without training, except for that first slap on the backside one gets immediately after birth. Since this instinctive type of breathing requires no particular study, we need not discuss it further.

Respiration for work is something which *can* be improved through a better understanding and application of concepts. It is this type of breathing with which we are concerned because singing requires work. It should be mentioned that inefficient breathing requires more work than efficient breathing. Therefore, our object will be learning to breathe as efficiently as possible in order to eliminate as much unnecessary work as possible.

THE RESPIRATORY MECHANISM

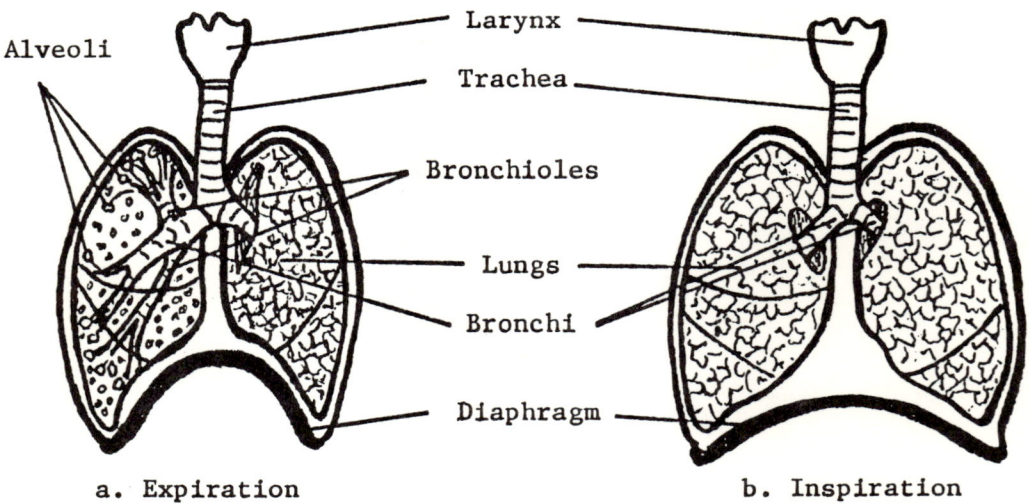

a. Expiration b. Inspiration

Fig. 4

RESPIRATION 7

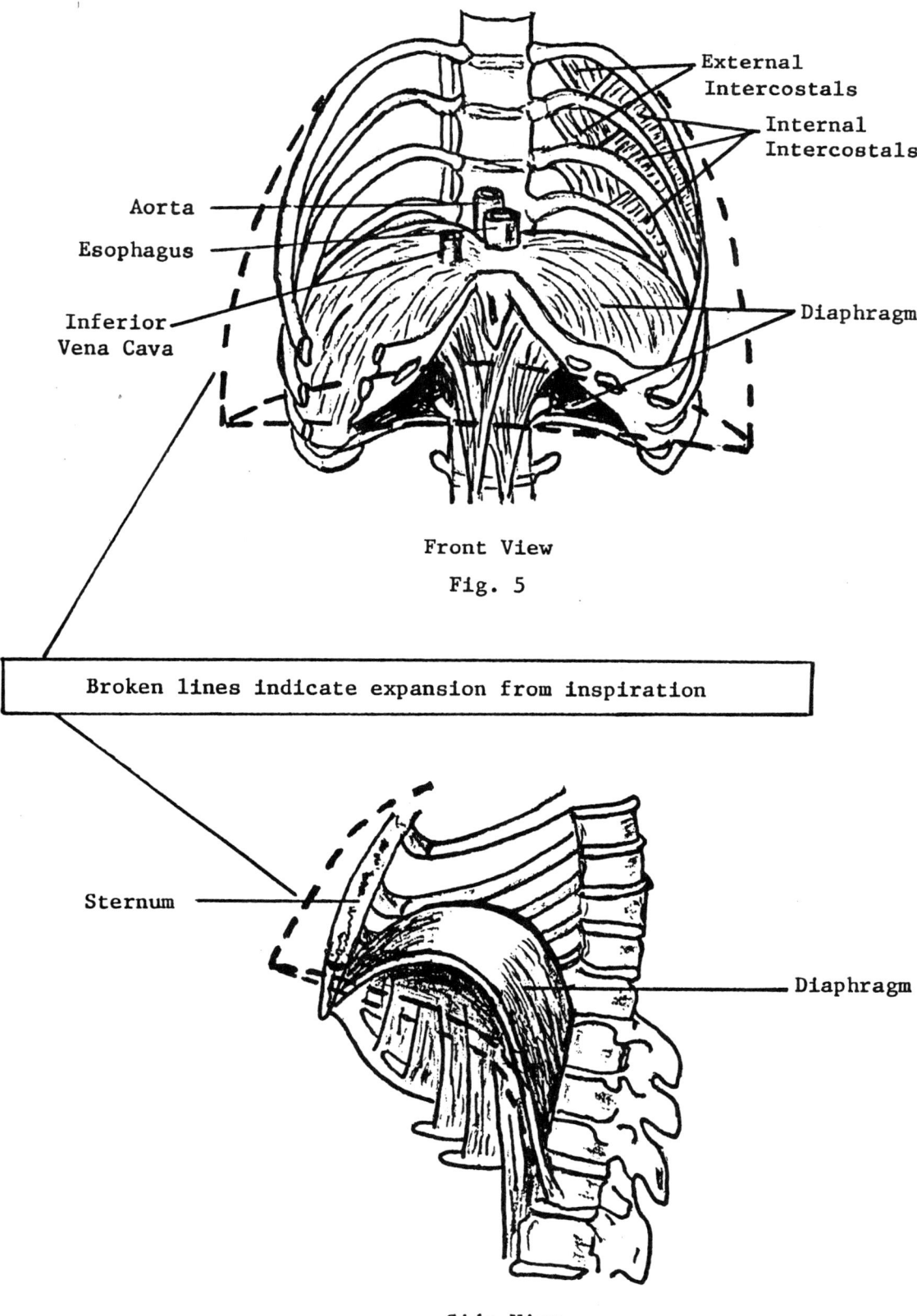

Front View
Fig. 5

Broken lines indicate expansion from inspiration

Side View
Fig. 6

8 VOCAL DEVELOPMENT THROUGH ORGANIC IMAGERY

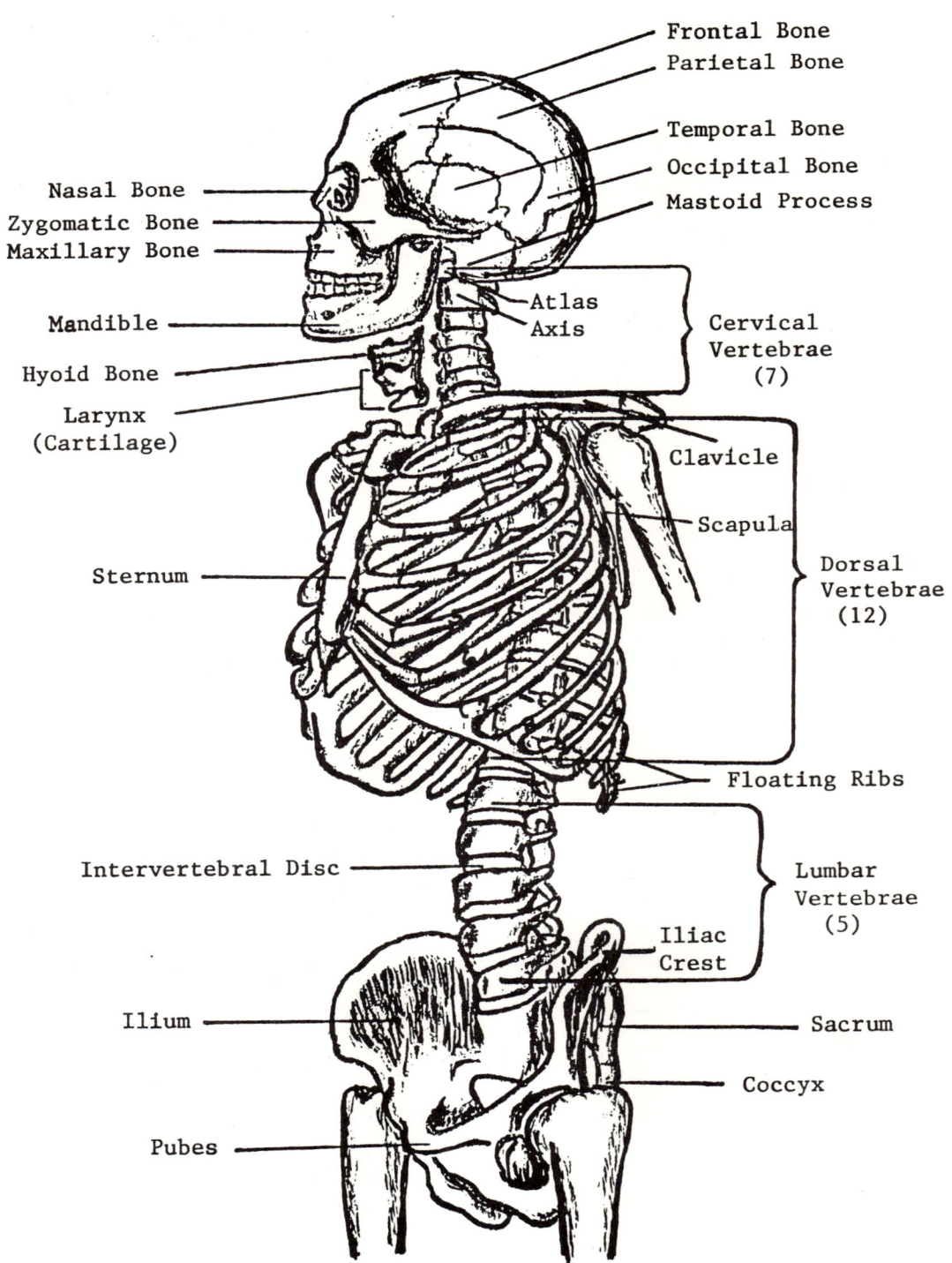

Fig. 7

RESPIRATION 9

ABDOMINAL MUSCLES

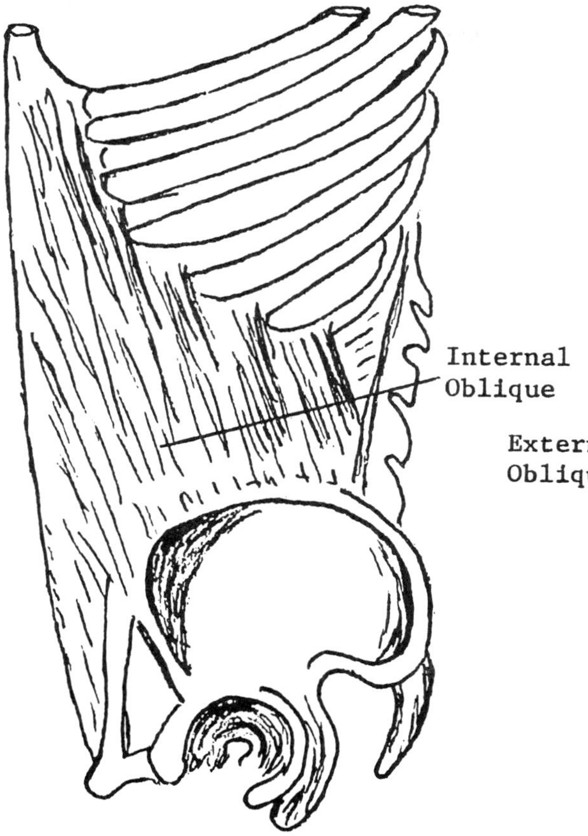

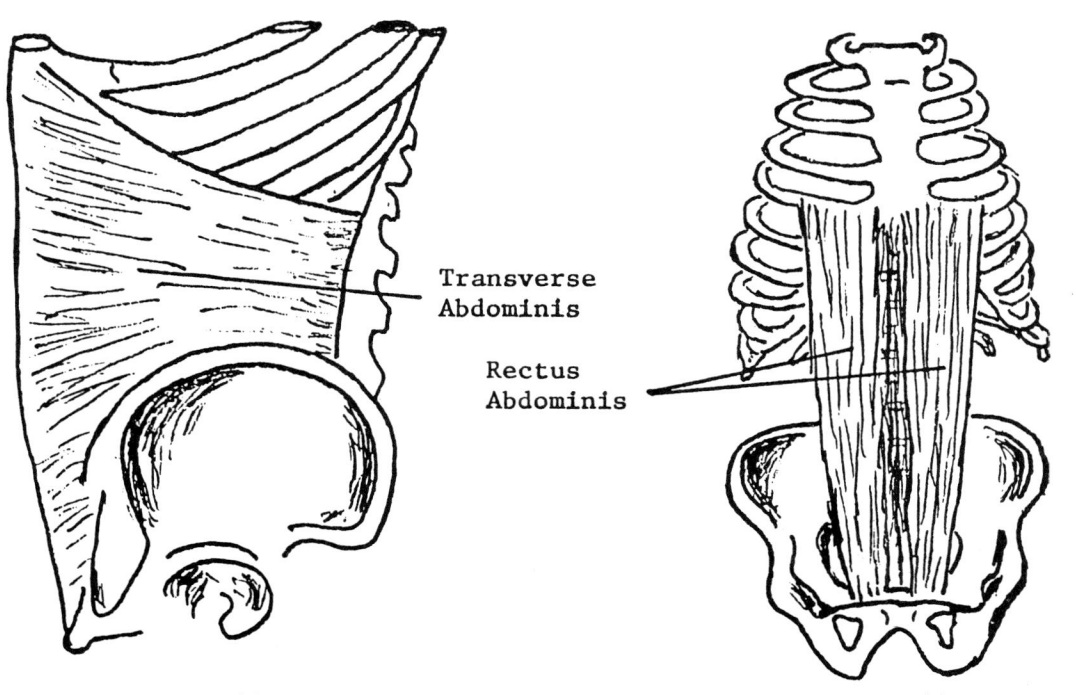

Fig. 8

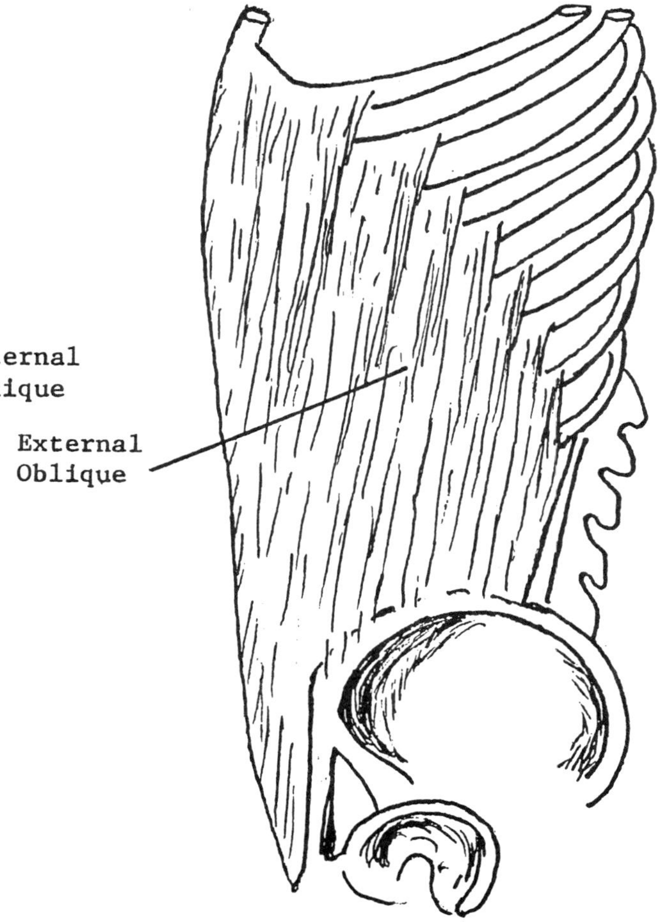

Fig. 9

Fig. 10

Fig. 11

Internal Oblique

External Oblique

Transverse Abdominis

Rectus Abdominis

10 VOCAL DEVELOPMENT THROUGH ORGANIC IMAGERY

A. The Respirators

The respirators, or breathing mechanism, can be divided into three general sections in relation to function:

1. Channels
2. Receptacles
3. Machinery

1. Channels

The channels through which the inhaled air goes to be utilized are:

    a. Mouth and Nose
    b. Pharynx
    c. Larynx
    d. Trachea
    e. Bronchi
    f. Bronchioles

The function of these channels is obvious, so we need not dwell on them.

2. Receptacles

    a. Alveoli
    b. Lungs

a. Alveoli

The first receptacles for the breath, after it has passed through the bronchioles, are the alveoli, or air sacks. (See Fig. 4a) The alveoli are like hundreds of tiny balloons which fill during inhalation and collapse during exhalation.

b. Lungs

The lungs contain not only the alveoli, but parts of the bronchi and the bronchioles as well. The right lung has three sections and the left lung has two sections. After the air fills the alveoli, it filters into the spongy parts of the lungs; then oxygen is taken into the blood stream where it performs the necessary biological functions.

3. Machinery

The machinery for the breathing apparatus are those parts of the anatomy which actually do the work. This machinery consists, in large part, of the following bones, cartilages, and muscles:

    a. Ribs and Vertebrae
    b. Diaphragm
    c. Abdominal Muscles
    d. Intercostal Muscles

a. Ribs and Vertebrae

The ribs and vertebrae form the boundary for the lungs. The lungs expand only so far as the space provided by the ribs will allow. We shall consider the vertebrae as being part of the ribs.

b. Diaphragm
c. Abdominal Muscles
d. Intercostal Muscles

The diaphragm, abdominal muscles, and intercostal muscles will be discussed in greater detail in the following section of this chapter.

B. Inspiration

Respiration involves many muscles. A trait of any muscle is that it performs one function only— to pull or flex in one direction. It cannot, after pulling in one direction, pull in another. After flexing, it can only relax and allow an opposing or antagonistic muscle to do the opposite task.

Although several muscles, or sets of muscles, are involved in inspiration, two are thought to be of extreme importance. They are the diaphragm and the external intercostal muscles.

1. Diaphragm

The diaphragm is said to be the most important of all the muscles of inspiration. It is the boundary between the chest and the abdomen. (Refer to Figures 4, 5, and 6 on pages 6 and 7.)

As the illustrations show, the diaphragm is a large, dome-like muscle, slightly higher on the right side than the left. It forms the floor of the rib cage.

For the purposes of this text, we shall not become overly involved with a detailed anatomical study of all the facets of the diaphragm. It should be sufficient to know its general size, shape, location, and basic function for singing. If the reader wishes to pursue the subject further, a reputable book on anatomy will provide the details. Also, William Vennard's excellent book, *Singing, the Mechanism and the Technic*, is enlightening. (See bibliography.)

During the act of inspiration, the diaphragm starts in the high position and flattens to a relatively low position, pushing the stomach downward. (Refer once more to Figures 4, 5, and 6.) The diaphragm also pulls the ribs upward and outward at the front and sides. This allows more room for the expansion of the lungs as they fill with air. Indeed, it is this space which allows the air to enter the lungs.

It is a common misconception that we suck the air into the lungs. Instead, we make room for the air by opening the throat and lungs and the air pours into the body by atmospheric pressure.

2. External Intercostals

The intercostals are those muscles between the ribs (*inter* = *between*; *costae* = *ribs*). See Fig. 5, page 7.

The external intercostal muscles are for inspiration. They are believed to assist the diaphragm in pulling the ribs upward and outward.

It is not yet known just how much the external intercostals aid in inspiration. The diaphragm does most of the work. Some researchers in vocal anatomy suggest that all the intercostals do is simply hold the ribs together as the diaphragm expands them. If this be true, then the intercostals may not be as important for respiration as many voice scientists believe.

Even so, the singer may benefit by presuming the intercostals are important for psychological reasons, as their proximity to the expanded rib cage *feels* logical.

C. Expiration

Expiration involves two basic groups of muscles, as does inspiration. These muscles are the abdominal and the internal intercostals.

After the air has entered the lungs by means of the lowered diaphragm and expanded rib cage, the abdominal muscles and the internal intercostals reverse the process. They expel the air by contracting the space for the lungs.

1. Abdominal Muscles

The abdominal muscles exert an upward thrust, pushing the stomach and diaphragm back into the rib cage. The abdominal muscles are the natural antagonists to the diaphragm. The importance of this fact will be apparent when we discuss coordination of inspiration and expiration. (See Figures 8, 9, 10, and 11 on page 9.)

2. Internal Intercostals

The internal intercostals are the muscles between the inside section of the ribs, opposite the external intercostals. (See Fig. 5, p. 7.)

If the external intercostals *do* actually play a vital part in expanding the rib cage, then it must follow that the internal intercostals are just as important in contraction, as they are the opposing muscles.

D. Coordination of Inspiration and Expiration

The coordination of inspiration with expiration is the basis for *breath support* and *breath control*.

Breath support is the motive force or impetus for vocalization. It is to singing what gasoline is to an automobile engine.

Breath control is the degree of facility by which breath support is utilized. It is to singing what the accelerator pedal and foot are to acceleration.

No matter how much or how little support a singer needs to accomplish his singing objectives, the principle of balanced breath support remains constant. Fidelity to this principle will determine the measure of the singer's facility.

We have discussed the physiology of the breathing mechanism. Now we must train the antagonistic muscles for each phase of respiration to cooperate for maximum efficiency.

Many teachers believe that correct use of the breath is the most important part of singing. It has been said that "He who breathes well sings well." If we again use the analogy of the automobile, no one can deny the importance of gasoline; but the gasoline would be less than effective without an engine.

Actually, no *one* phase is *most* important to the over-all act of singing. It requires the entire mechanism. But efficient use of the breath is definitely important.

The relative importance of breath to singing is indicated by the amount of time given to the subject by various teachers. Some teachers devote many hours of exercises to help their students develop their breathing. Others barely discuss the subject.

The important thing is that the singer learn to do what is necessary. No matter how much emphasis he devotes to the breathing process, he must find the proper balance. How does one achieve this balance?

The first stage is for the singer to become increasingly aware of the physical sensations attendant to inhaling and exhaling. He might go about it in the following manner:*

1. Take a deep conscious breath with the mouth closed.
2. Take a deep conscious breath with the mouth open.
3. Take a deep conscious breath through both the mouth and the nose simultaneously. (It might require some practice.)
4. Contrast the results of 1 and 2 with 3, and repeat steps 1 through 3.

> At this point, the singer should be aware that mouth breathing is more effective than nose breathing. He should realize that mouth and nose breathing simultaneously is preferable. He will also have noted the high chest position, as well as expansion at the sides of the ribs and in front, immediately below the sternum (breast bone).

5. Breathe gently through the mouth and nose on the count of three (one second for each count), and hold the breath without compression for three seconds.
6. While holding the breath, notice the physical sensations; then expel the breath.
7. Repeat step 5; and, with the lips pursed as if around a thin drinking straw, gently expel the breath on the count of three. *Do not let the ribs collapse*.

> During step 7, the singer should note that, on expiration, he will have the sensation of *holding back the breath* and *not holding the breath*. He is balancing inhalation with exhalation.

8. Repeat step 7, but on the count of six, instead of three.
9. Extend the time count, one second at a time as far as is comfortable. *Never* exert tension by compressing the breath more firmly than is comfortable. This is dangerous!

---

*It should go without saying that the singer must maintain a proper singing posture while doing these exercises; otherwise, everything discussed in chapter I will be useless. In order to derive maximum benefit from this text, the reader should think of each chapter as being prerequisite to the next.

14 VOCAL DEVELOPMENT THROUGH ORGANIC IMAGERY

We have discussed how the rib cage expands and rises during inspiration. The ribs attach in the back to the spine (vertebrae). In front, they are more flexible. The upper ribs are attached to the sternum by small sections of cartilage. The lower two ribs on each side (numbers 11 and 12) are completely detached in front. They are called "floating ribs." (See Fig. 7, page 8.)

Because of greater flexibility in front and at the sides of the rib cage (movable) than in the back (stable), the singer *should* be aware of more stability at the back than in front during inspiration. This stable feeling in the back is the result of the expanding lungs meeting with more resistance at the back than in the front. This sensation indicates that the singer is taking a complete breath, known as "back breathing."

Unfortunately, not all singers have this sensation because they do not use the full capacity of their lungs. Oftentimes this results when a teacher tells the student to support from the diaphragm while the teacher points to the front of the abdomen! The student may get the impression that he should feel the support in front, and does not develop the back support.

The singer may be assured that, if he feels the support at the small of the back, everything will still be all right in the front portion. Both frontal and back support are vital.

How can a singer stabilize the concept of back breathing as a habitual function?

Most teachers rely on some form of imagery for inducing automatic and indirect control of the singing mechanism. William Vennard describes imagery as "Figures of speech to express concepts which are difficult to understand literally."[1]

Imagery may be more than figures of speech, however. They may be actual mental pictures of a literal or figurative concept.

Some approaches to imagery might include the *metaphysical, psychological, transcendent, physiological, fantastic, super-impositional, substitutional, transpositional, geometric,* and *spatial,* or various combinations of these.

Quite frequently I use a term which I have coined as "organic imagery." This is a combination of four of the varieties above: The physiological, super-impositional, geometric, and transpositional.

The process of organic imagery is the utilization of a mental geometric picture, easily conceived, based on physiological reality, super-imposed over the singer's physique, but sometimes transposed from its actual location for purposes of approaching the subject indirectly.

The value of organic imagery is that it is an effective objective device for helping students activate and maintain functional concepts.

How may we apply organic imagery to respiration?

If we super-impose a triangle over the back of the torso in the following manner,

---

[1] Vennard, William; *SINGING, THE MECHANISM AND THE TECHNIC*; Carl Fischer, Inc., New York; 1967; p. 261, § 952.

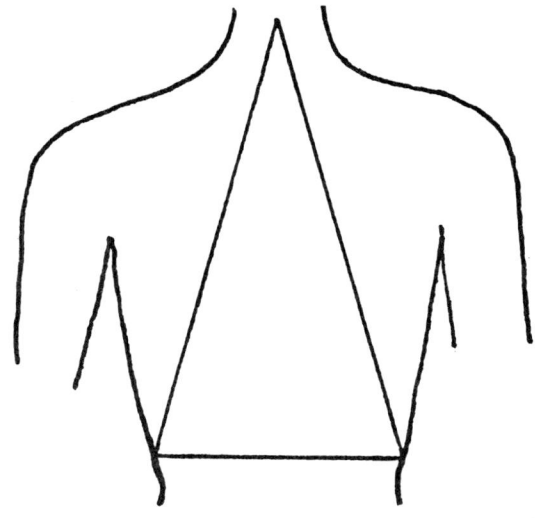

Fig. 12

we may use this simple geometric image for almost any application of breath control.

Now that it is understood where the triangle fits, we can dispense with the illustration of the torso for purposes of simplification.

The apex of the triangle represents the direction of breath flow— upward to the back of the neck.

The base of the triangle represents the lower boundary of the expanded lungs. It is here that we are most aware of the sensation called *breath support*. Since the base of the triangle is the widest part, we have the feeling of building our breath support on a firm foundation. Later, we will transpose the base of the triangle a bit lower— to the belt line— where it will include the abdominal muscles. For the moment, it is better to keep it at the base of the ribs.

The sides of the triangle represent the sidewise expansion of the lungs. It helps if one conceives this expansion as having a downward direction, as well as sidewise. With these ideas in mind, our image takes the following form:

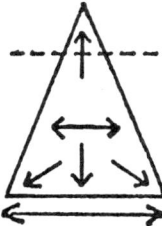

Fig. 13

All arrows below the broken line are active sensations. The one arrow above the line, representing breath flow, is a passive sensation— at least until we connect the breath with phonation in the next chapter.

16 VOCAL DEVELOPMENT THROUGH ORGANIC IMAGERY

This same figure may be compared to the action of a fireplace bellows:

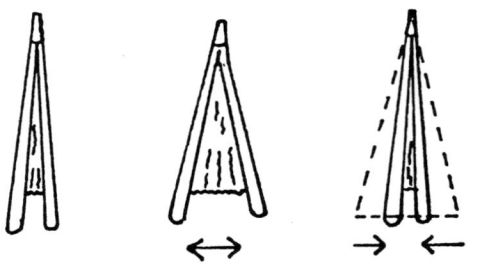

a.   b. Inspiration   c. Expiration

Fig. 14

The principal difference between the bellows and the triangle as an analogy to breath support is that for exhalation the bellows must close to expel the air after it has been taken in, whereas the triangle does not. The triangle should remain extended throughout exhalation or even increase in width at the base in order to maintain a balance of inhalation with exhalation. The abdominal muscles will push the air out of the lungs. The diaphragm will keep the ribs expanded.

One of the very best physical sensations for maintaining the expansive position results from the concept of "inhaling" the tone while singing.

The old Italian singers used the term "drink the voice," which is quite effective, but might be confusing to singers who have been told *not* to use the swallowing muscles while singing. The adverse effects of the swallowing muscles used while singing will be discussed in the next chapter. The advantages of *inhaling* or *drinking the tone* will be discussed in chapter V, Registration.

We know the voice sounds or "speaks" on exhalation and not on inhalation; therefore, the exhalation muscles must dominate the inhalation muscles. If the singer develops the sensation of inhaling while he is actually exhaling, he will have a reliable objective device for helping make the balance of respiration automatic.

An important adjunct which accompanies balanced respiration is a feeling of *elation*. Elation is an effect, but the singer can feel it as a cause. Long before I realized why I felt so good when I sang *properly*, I called this sensation my "happy feeling." If I did not have it when I walked on stage, I knew I was in trouble.

It is possible to relate the feeling of elation to stage-fright as a means of "harnessing" the wasted energy of stage-fright and turning it into a positive force. If a singer can convert the "butterflies in the stomach" to "ecstasy in the back," he can retrieve victory from the jaws of defeat. He should learn to capitalize on this sensation, making it another habitual component of his over-all vocal technique. I often encourage my students to induce stage-fright for themselves in the practice room in order to learn how to cope with it. They can accomplish this by imagining a large audience is listening to them, or by actually inviting friends to observe their practice.

An image which has been helpful to many of my students in activating the *happy feeling* is:

The Smiling Back

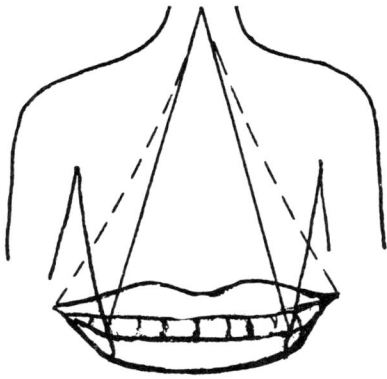

Fig. 15

We may now add a third dimension to the organic imagery triangle, as follows:

   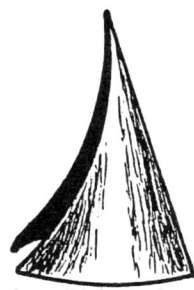

a. Back view   b. Side view

Fig. 16

Note that the base of the triangle is no longer limited to the back, but that it wraps around the sides in an ever-widening circle from top to bottom. If we extend the implied boundaries of this figure to their logical conclusion, we no longer have a triangle, but a cone:

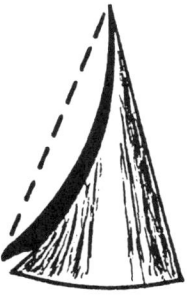

Fig. 17

It should be stated that, in the beginning of vocal training, most active physical sensations should have a downward and backward tendency. When a singer needs greater support, demanded by a higher range or a crescendo, however, he will become aware of a forward push against the belt line which eventually extends downward to the pubic bone. This expansion is caused by the abdominal muscles. (See p. 10, Figs. 8, 9, 10, and 11) Since seventy-five to eighty percent of a singer's effort does not require such strong support, he will be more aware of his back support than of the frontal abdominal support, although he should main-

18 VOCAL DEVELOPMENT THROUGH ORGANIC IMAGERY

tain a constant contact with these frontal muscles (three of which extend to the sides and back, as well).

Frequently a student will have difficulty in expanding the lower back part of his torso during inspiration. It is always interesting to me to note the large number of students, some of whom have sung for several years, who have never heard of this concept. *Telling* these singers to expand the lower back during inhalation is often not enough. A simple device for helping the singer find this sensation is to have him bend over comfortably, with his back reasonably parallel with the floor and his arms dangling loosely:

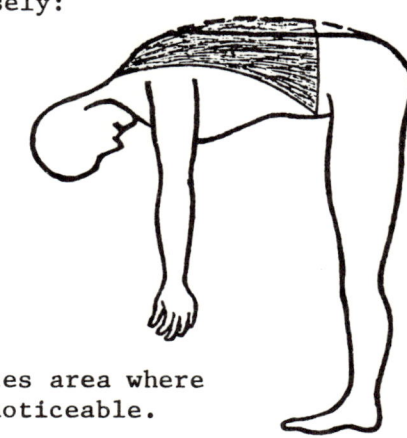

Broken line indicates area where expansion is most noticeable.

Fig. 18

After he is in this position, he should inhale slowly and positively. In this position he will feel the lower back expand noticeably. (Shaded area, Fig. 18) He will also notice a natural expansion of the lower front part of the abdomen. He should expel the breath and repeat the inspiration two or three more times. It is often helpful to have someone clasp his hands firmly around the singer's waist so the singer can feel the pressure.

WARNING: It is not unusual for dizziness to occur during this exercise. In such case, the singer should stand or sit for a few seconds or minutes to regain his composure before resuming the exercise.

After the singer develops a feeling for back expansion in the bent position, he should stand erect and attempt to feel the same sensation in that position while he inhales. Some students are not able to duplicate the expansion when they stand, even after several attempts. Rather than expanding the lower back, the shoulders keep rising. Eventually— sometimes after several weeks— most students learn to expand the backs.

Another popular device for feeling back expansion, and one which allows the singer to stand erect, is to drop the jaw without opening the lips and then to suck air through the closed lips. The student may be temporarily disconcerted by a buzzing sound at the lips and a slightly ticklish sensation; but he will also note a powerful expansion in the back.

Ultimately the singer will rely on this sensation, in combination with the frontal downward movement to the pubic bone, as the basis for breath support. A curious thing happens when he reaches this stage: the back support will feel more like resonance than support, and he will feel as if the abdominal muscles are the actual support. This will allow him to free the throat and neck muscles. The big muscles of the diaphragm and abdomen should do the big work.

CHAPTER III
PHONATION

Phonation is the production of sound. It occurs when the breath meets resistance at the vocal folds (vocal cords), which are set into vibration. The frequency of these vibrations determines the pitch (relative highness or lowness of the tone.)

A. The Larynx

The organ of phonation is the larynx. The larynx is comprised of muscles and cartilages. The muscles of the larynx cannot be directly controlled. For this reason, the following information is presented for general anatomical understanding only.

Whereas a student cannot learn to sing by understanding the function of the larynx, it might prove to be somewhat embarrassing for him to go through life not knowing the names of the various parts of his instrument or having at least a general idea of their functions. I know more than one professional singer who pronounces *larynx* as *larnyx* and *pharynx* as *pharnyx*.

PARTS OF THE LARYNX

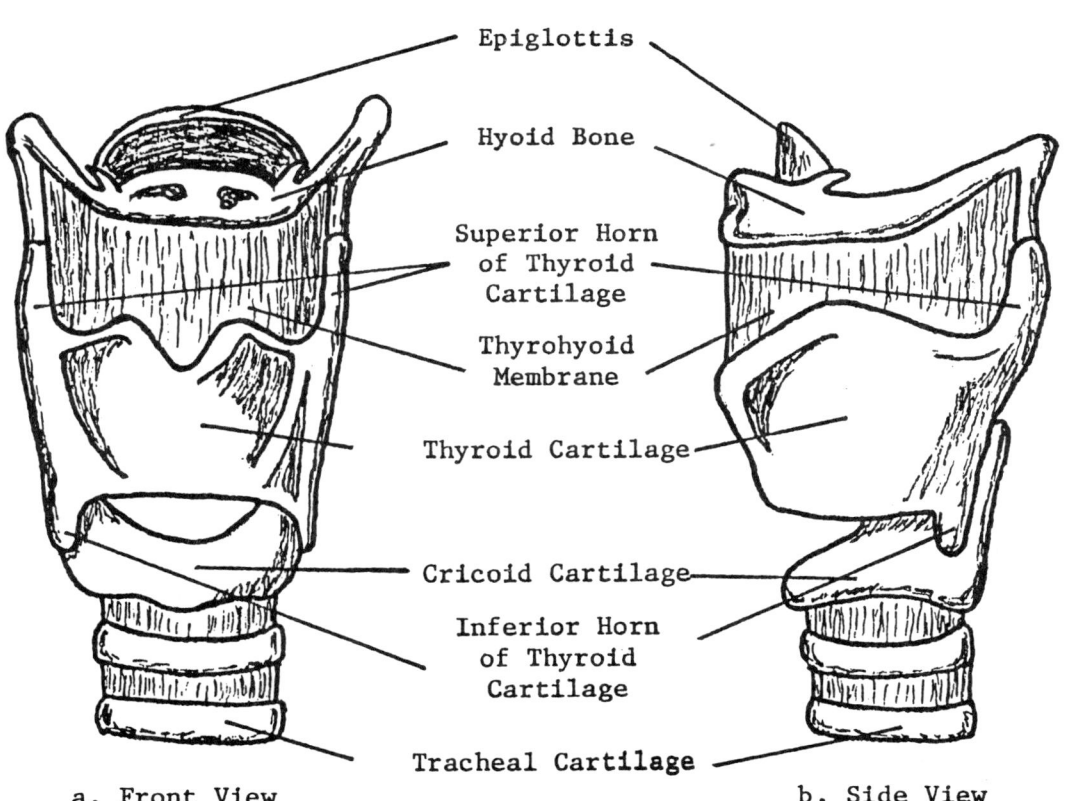

a. Front View   b. Side View

Fig. 19

20 VOCAL DEVELOPMENT THROUGH ORGANIC IMAGERY

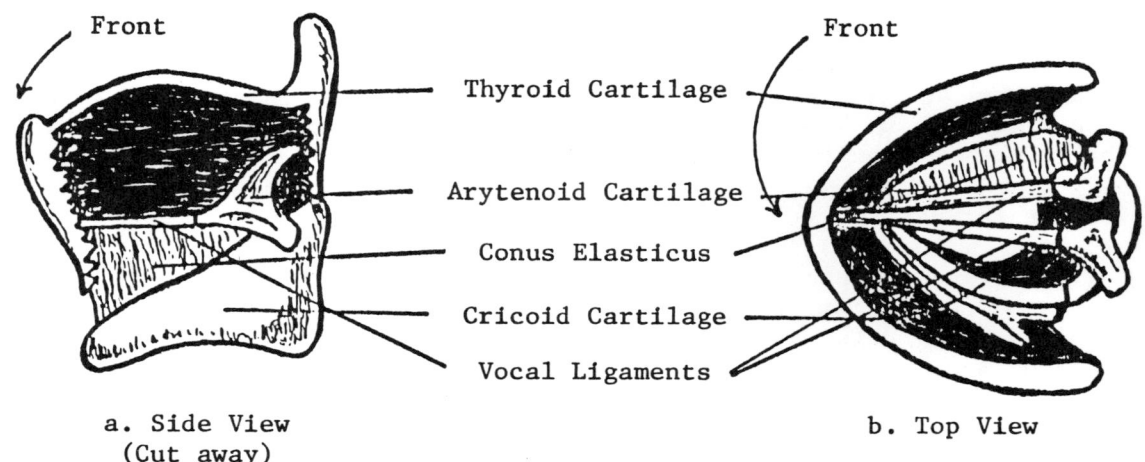

Fig. 20

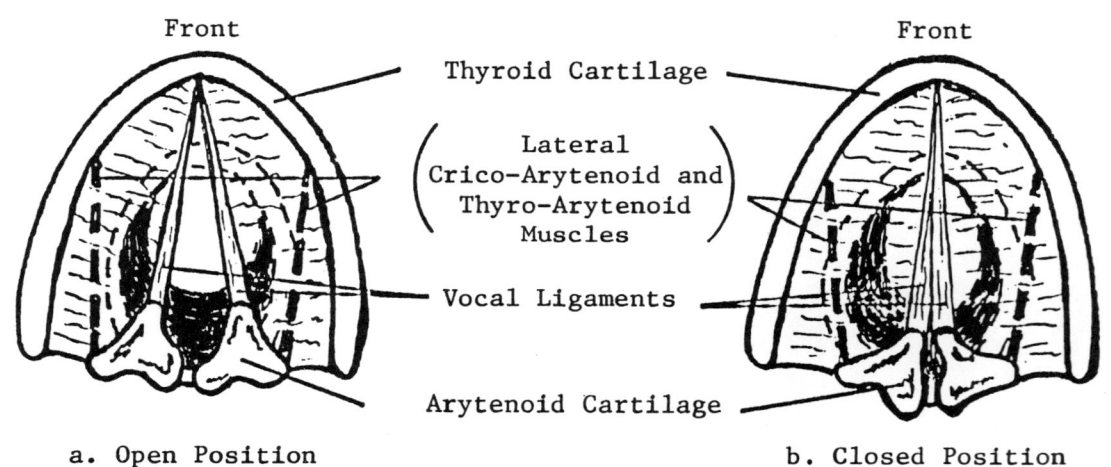

Fig. 21

Fig. 19 does not show the arytenoid cartilages, as they are covered by the thyroid cartilage.

In figures 20a and 20b the reader will notice that the arytenoid cartilages are attached to the upper back sides of the cricoid cartilages. Attached to the front ends of the arytenoids are the vocal ligaments, or vocal cords. These vocal ligaments continue to the front of the larynx, where they attach to the thyroid cartilage. The front of the vocal ligaments are stable. They do not move at the point of connection with the thyroid cartilage.

The back of the vocal ligaments are movable because the arytenoid cartilages, to which they are attached, are able to pivot, hinge-like, at their points of connection with the cricoid cartilage.

When the lateral crico-arytenoid, transverse arytenoid, and oblique arytenoid muscles (latter two not shown here) flex, they cause the arytenoid cartilages to pivot and rock in such a manner that the vocal ligaments are brought together. (Fig. 21b) Only when the vocal cords are together, or in the closed position, will they be able to vibrate sufficiently to cause projective sound.

Sound is caused when the column of air from the lungs passes between the closed vocal cords. The air pushes the elastic cords open, allowing a small puff of air to escape. The cords close again immediately, and the process is continued. Each time, pressure builds up before the air gains enough force to push through the cords. After the air is through, there is a sudden drop in pressure. These high and low pressure areas cause waves of tension and release, which the ear drum receives and translates as sound. However many of these cycles are made each second determines the pitch of a given tone. For example, 440 cps (cycles per second) produces the A above middle C.

The preceding description explains the myoelastic theory of vibration, which is basically a muscular approach (*myo = muscle; elasticus = to drive*). A more recent theory is the aerodynamic theory, exemplified by the *Bernoulli Effect.*

Daniel Bernoulli (1700-1782) was one of a distinguished Swiss family of scientists and mathematicians. His most important work was *HYDRODYNAMICA* (1738), which dealt with the theory of statics and motion of fluids and their practical applications. His theory was simple: When a liquid is in motion, it exerts a less than usual pressure against its surrounding environment. The same theory applies to gas and air, as well. Although Bernoulli's research was done in the early 18th century, his theory has been applied to aerodynamics and singing in the 20th century. Robert Taylor, William Vennard, et al, have written in detail about this phenomenon in relation to singing.[1]

In essence, the emission of air through a narrowly open glottis causes a suction that draws the cords together; more air emission displaces the glottal closure and the cycle is repeated. Taylor maintains this phenomenon should relieve excess muscularity of the vocal cords. Therefore, the singer should emit a bit of air before actually sounding the tone. The trick is to prevent the audience from hearing a breathy attack. When the singer's timing is correct, this can be accomplished. The combination of the myoelastic and aerodynamic theories is desirable in the complete vocal technique.

In order to change the rate of vibration, or pitch, of the vocal cords, the cords must be stretched or slackened.

Stretching the vocal cords is accomplished when the thyroid cartilage rocks forward on its hinges (inferior horns) connected to the cricoid cartilage. Since the fronts of the vocal cords are attached to the thyroid cartilage and the backs are attached to the arytenoids, the forward rocking of the thyroid pulls the cords forward, causing the pitch to rise. When the thyroid cartilage rocks backward, the vocal cords slacken and the pitch lowers. (See Fig. 22)

---

[1] Large, John, editor; *CONTRIBUTIONS OF VOICE RESEARCH TO SINGING*; College Hill Press, Houston, Texas 77035; 1980; pp. 48-57. Reprint of an earlier publication from *The NATS Bulletin* (Now *The NATS Journal*), Feb. 1961; pp. 8-12.

22 VOCAL DEVELOPMENT THROUGH ORGANIC IMAGERY

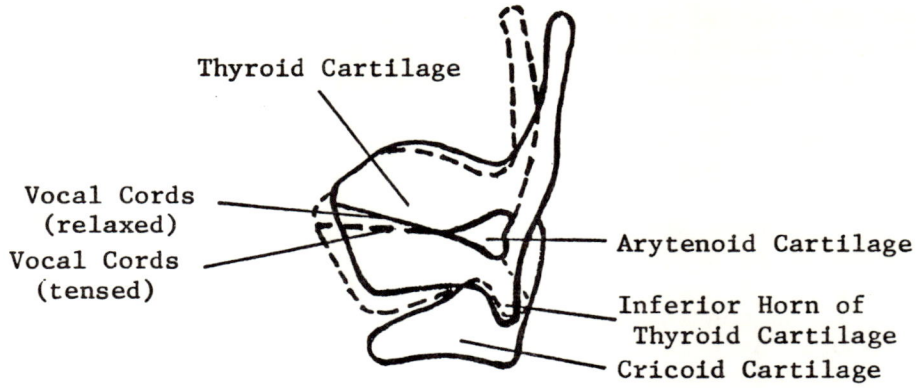

(Broken line indicates forward rocking motion of thyroid cartilage.)

Fig. 22

What has been presented here concerning the larynx are the bare essentials for understanding its structure and function. We shall go no further than that. The reader should realize that the larynx is a complicated organ comprised of many more muscles than we need know about in order to sing. However, in the next chapter (Registration) more will be said about the musculature of the larynx.

If the reader plans to teach, or is simply interested in knowing more about the physiology of the larynx, he should avail himself of any competent book on human anatomy, such as *ANATOMY OF THE HUMAN BODY* by Henry Gray, published in Philadelphia by Lea and Gebiger, 1950 (many other companies now publish this book inexpensively), or *THE MECHANISM OF THE LARYNX* by V.E. Negus, published in St. Louis by C.V. Mosby Co., 1949.

B. The Open Throat

Briefly stated, the open throat is a large pharynx.

To be more specific, when the throat is said to be open, the pharyngeal tract is wider and/or longer than when closed and, most particularly, in the laryngo-pharynx. (See Fig. 37, p. 36.)

Several conditions allow for optimum efficiency in opening the throat. The more important ones are:

1. A low larynx
2. A forward tongue position
3. A "lifted" soft palate
4. A jaw dropped loosely from its hinges
5. Correct breathing (dependent upon correct posture)

The value of the open throat cannot be exaggerated. If the singer maintains this position throughout his entire singing range, it is virtually impossible for him to damage his vocal apparatus. Indeed, this should be the first objective of all singers in developing a sound vocal technique. *Safety First* should be one's guideline.

Most of the devices voice teachers use are designed to achieve an open throat, whether directly or indirectly.

Undoubtedly, the most common method for inducing an open throat is through the simple device of the yawn [*beginning of* yawn]. Everyone has experienced this sensation and can readily identify with it. When a person yawns, he automatically activates the five conditions enumerated above.

Unfortunately, a few other conditions accompany a good healthy yawn which are *not* desirable for healthy singing. The more insidious ones are:

   a. The larynx usually goes *too* low, causing the condition known as "depressed larynx."
   b. The entire circumference of the neck expands outwardly, particularly in the front and sides.
   c. The base of the tongue is depressed.
   d. Many other muscles involving the throat, tongue, and larynx become rigid, making them less flexible and free than they should be.

Concerning the open throat, Edgar F. Herbert-Caesari states:

> "...To increase the volume of a sound the pharyngeal tube should be adequately dilated, on the principle of the yawn..."[1]

He states in a footnote to the above:

> "That is, the mere beginning of a yawn, not a developed or complete yawn which stiffens the entire vocal machinery."[2]

To reinforce the importance of Mr. Herbert-Caesari's statements, I quote Hermanus Baer:

> "...I believe the automatically opened throat is one of the most important conditions for any singer, but the consciously opened throat is one of the most harmful..."[3]

1. A low larynx

In light of the foregoing, the yawn should be used *only* as a *primer* for inducing a low laryngeal position, and then discarded as a direct method. Eventually, any mechanical device for actuating vocalization must be made automatic and habitual; otherwise, it undermines its own usefulness and does more harm than good.

Priming devices or mechanical devices are often useful, but must be utilized judiciously. Many voice teachers avoid these "gimmicks" as the plague, and not without some merit.

I prefer to take an occasional calculated risk, however, leaving it to the student's ability to discern what is mechanical and what is automatic as he feels his development from one toward the other. The teacher must insure that the student *does* progress from one to the other.

---

[1] Herbert-Caesari, Edgar F.; *THE SCIENCE AND SENSATION OF VOCAL TONE*; Crescendo Publishing Co., Boston; Fifth printing, 1971; p. 114.
[2] Ibid.; p. 114.
[3] Baer, Hermanus; "Establishing A Correct Basic Technique For Singing"; *The NATS Bulletin*; Chicago, Illinois; Vol. XXVIII, No. 4; May/June 1972; p. 12.

The more obvious advantage of taking a mechanical approach to singing— at least in the beginning— can be seen through the analogy of learning to drive a car. To give the analogy more emphasis, let us take a car with a standard gear shift.

When one sits behind a steering wheel for the first time, every move he makes is monumental. Yet it is extremely important that the inexperienced driver learn one step at a time and that he have specific instruction in how to accomplish it.

It is probably unnecessary to enumerate these specific steps. Suffice it to say that, as the driver progresses from starting the engine to using the clutch as he changes the various gear positions, while rolling cautiously along the road, he must concentrate intensely on every phase. With experience, he eventually learns to relax, using only the correct amount of concentration needed to get him to his destination. The process of changing gears, acceleration, braking, steering, etc. becomes second nature to him. It becomes automatic.

For a voice teacher to tell a student to sing without telling him how to lower his larynx is like asking a new driver to drive without explaining gear changes to him. The driver and the instructor will *know* when the process is correct and when it becomes automatic.

Let us return to the yawn as a learning device.

Most beginning students of voice sing with high larynges— especially as they ascend the scale. The higher they sing, the higher the larynges go, until the throat is almost completely closed. When this happens, the voice "breaks." This phenomenon exists, incidentally, not only with beginning singers, but with many misguided experienced singers.

It is often helpful to discover the polarities of technical possibilities in order to achieve balance.

Whereas the yawn will lower the larynx to one extreme, swallowing will raise it to the other. Swallowing is necessary for eating and drinking, but certainly not for singing. When one swallows, his larynx rises for a very good reason. It enables the epiglottis to close the windpipe so the food or drink will go through the esophagus to the stomach, and not through the windpipe to the lungs.

On the other hand, when we sing, we *want* the air to come directly from the lungs through the windpipe and vocal folds to be converted to sound and continue through the mouth and/or nose.

The more the throat is open (without tension), the fuller and freer will be the resultant sound and ease of production. A *medium-low larynx* helps accomplish this. Many scientific studies have confirmed this, as have astute, but unscientific, observations; so we need not belabor the point.

The yawn-swallow exercise will enable students to follow the moving larynx in order to find its medium-low position. Most singers can see the larynx ("Adam's apple"), move up and down by looking in a mirror. Many women (and some men), however, cannot see this movement because of fleshier neck tissue. Also, after puberty the female larynx is smaller than the male's. Although they will have a more difficult time finding the larynx, they can feel the movement by placing thumb and forefinger loosely on each side of the area where they suspect the larynx may be, and then by practicing the yawn-swallow. It is much safer to put the thumb and forefinger on the sides of the larynx than to place a finger on top of the larynx. The latter could be quite painful if the singer should accidentally swallow, locking the finger between the thyroid cartilage and the hyoid bone.

2. A forward tongue

Another important means of opening the throat is keeping the back of the tongue forward, except when necessary to pronounce vowels that demand tongue backing.

The tongue is capable of wreaking havoc in many different ways. It is the most important organ of the singing mechanism for producing the proper vowels (Resonation) and certain consonants (Articulation). It is also extremely important for achieving proper phonation. This triple function causes much of the confusion in voice production because of misapplication of one function for another. Some of the more frequent of these abuses will be discussed in the section of chapter IV— Co-ordination of Phonation and Resonation.

For the moment we need only consider the tongue's relation to the open throat.

Because of the structural relationship of the tongue to the larynx, when the tongue is depressed in the back, it forces the epiglottis backward and downward, covering or partially covering the glottis and trachea. Instead of opening the throat, as those who depress their tongues think they are doing, they are actually closing or narrowing the part of the pharynx which needs to be open the most. They are sacrificing an open throat for a bigger mouth cavity. (See figure 23, below.)

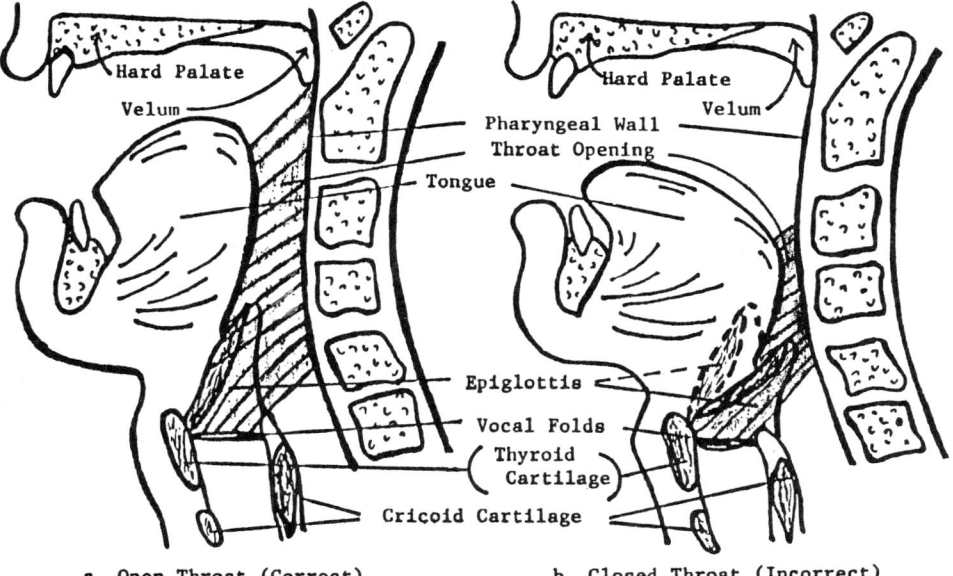

a. Open Throat (Correct)   b. Closed Throat (Incorrect)

Fig. 23

The complete yawn may be partially to blame for this unfortunate exchange. One of the undesirable side effects of yawning, as mentioned earlier, is that the tongue is depressed. (See Fig. 23b) Knowing this, a student can practice yawning without depressing his tongue and will be much better off for it.

It should be noted that, in figure 23b, the important factor in terms of "openness" is the tilted epiglottis, not the nearness of the back of the tongue to the pharyngeal wall. Indeed, for the [ɑ] vowel, the tongue is actually that close to the pharyngeal wall! In this sense, "openness" is a relative term, depending on which vowel is being sung.

Another contributing factor to tongue depressing can be traced to the admonition of some voice teachers to keep the tongue down.

Again, this results from a slight misunderstanding. The tongue has a front, middle, back, sides, and bottom. Certain vowels and consonants demand elevation of the tongue in varying degrees and varying shapes as one sings a song. For example, when one sings the word *too*, the tip of the tongue must go up in front for the *t*, but it should come down immediately for the *oo*. The back of the tongue should be relatively undisturbed, or else the throat will fluctuate excessively in size and shape. This is not to say the back of the tongue should be all the way up in back. It should be relatively low and very relaxed, but not extremely low and depressed. When a student is told to lower his tongue, he usually goes all the way with it if he is conscientious; and who wants to work with a student who is not conscientious? The effective teacher must be diligent in combating this sort of confusion.

Most teachers tell their students to keep the tongue, when not articulating, on the floor of the mouth, with the tip gently touching the lower teeth. This is good *general* advice but should not become a fetish. Many first-rate singers do not abide by that advice. Robert Weede was one notable example. Nothing in singing should become a fetish, as it is certain to upset the balance of the over-all singing process. As the reader will discover, if he has not already, balance is all-important in effective vocalization.

I must confess that I prefer to maintain contact of the tip of my tongue against the lower teeth, firmly but without stiffening, because it gives me a sense of proportion for the rest of my tongue. That is, it makes it easier to feel the relationship of one vowel to another, thereby allowing for greater consistency.

3. A lifted palate*

A third device for keeping the throat open works in tandem with the lowered larynx. This is the stretched soft-palate, or velum. Although it is possible for those who are very well-coordinated to stretch the palate without lowering the larynx or vice-versa, it takes more effort and concentration to do so than to do the preferable thing: to stretch the palate and lower the larynx simultaneously.

*Actually, the palate moves backward until it contacts the back of the pharyngeal wall. *Lift* means *stretch*. It stretches backward more than it lifts upward; however, the sensation of lift is quite important to the singer.

Stretching the palate accomplishes three things which are vocally advantageous:

a. It creates slightly more mouth resonance space.
b. It makes the surface of the velum more firm, which inhibits damping (muffling) of the resonance of the mouth area.
c. It allows for a more natural function of the lowered larynx and the forward tongue.

Letters a. and b. above are more appropriate to resonance than phonation; but one eventually arrives at that point where incorporation is expedient, if not unavoidable.

4. A dropped jaw

A fourth method for achieving an open throat is to open the mouth by dropping the jaw from its hinges. A certain portion of the British population seem to have a particular penchant for this. Any singer would do well to cultivate the habit, but within discriminate boundaries.

Rather than open the mouth by dropping the chin, the singer should feel that the lower back portion of the jaw, just as it curves upward, drops about half an inch or more. After doing this, he can feel with his finger a hollow cavity at the posterior side of either hinge (Condyle of the Mandible). During this drop, the jaw should move slightly backward— *never forward!*

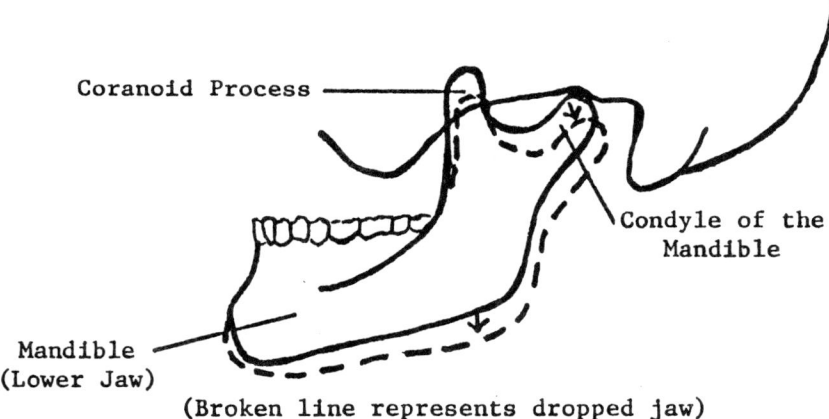

(Broken line represents dropped jaw)

Fig. 24

Dropping the jaw in the above manner accomplishes at least three things:

a. It has a relaxing effect on all adjacent muscles.
b. It reinforces the feeling of openness of the throat by adding a sensation of width, as well as depth.
c. It establishes a position which facilitates greater balance with with other aspects of phonation (to be discussed more thoroughly with Focus and Mask Resonance).

5. Correct breathing

A fifth throat-opener *may be the most important*, although not as immediately obvious as the previous four. This is correct breathing.

Hermanus Baer states "...There are sets of muscles extending from the larynx to the sternum and from the larynx to the back. As the distance between the chest and back is increased, these muscles will naturally pull the larynx downward."[1]

Our imagery for back breathing will help accomplish the above process; but, before we will be able to see the complete picture, we must first discuss *focus*.

C. Focus

In singing, the term *focus* is almost universally used when speaking of resonance. Many teachers do not accept the term at all because they do not believe a singer focuses a tone anywhere; but everyone knows what the word implies.

Focus, as used herein, will be a radical departure from the standard application of the term. Rather than thinking of focus as *forward placement*, as it is usually conceived, we shall use it in relation to phonation, or *backward placement*.

Focus is too good a word not to use at all. When applied to resonance, it is misused; but it seems to me to be most appropriate when applied to phonation.

Originally, focus was a Latin word for *hearth*, or a central point of heat. Later, it was adopted by the field of optics. We have always focused our vision to bring objects into clearer view. With the advent of cameras, motion pictures, and television, focus became a familiar term in those media. In the case of motion picture projection, it is *always* the lens of the projector which is adjusted for clarity— *never* the motion picture screen!

A standard definition of focus is: *The point where rays, as of light, sound, heat, etc., meet*. If we think of the vocal folds as being the center of sound production, it is quite logical to convert this definition to read: *Point at which the vocal folds converge*.

The standard terms for bringing the vocal folds together are *adduction, impingement,* and *approximation*. The efficiency by which this is accomplished might well be the single most important aspect of voice production as far as eliminating vocal problems is concerned.

In focusing the vocal folds, the singer adjusts that mechanism for clarity of tone, just as the eye and camera lens adjust for clarity of vision. This is the heart (or hearth) of phonation. It embraces such areas of vocalization as registration, timbre, quality, range, dynamics, and flexibility. Proper focus of the vocal folds simplifies the processes of breath support (respiration) and resonance. A thorough understanding of this fact can do much to untangle the confusion which plagues singers. It is the most direct means of separating *cause* from *effect*.

[1] Baer, Hermanus; "Establishing A Correct Basic Technique For Singing;" *The NATS Bulletin*; Chicago; Vol. XXVIII, No. 4, 1972; p. 13.

The vocal folds may be thought of as *resistor* to the breath. The principal problem of teaching or learning to focus the resistor lies in the nature of the larynx. The larynx is comprised of intrinsic muscles (muscles entirely inside the larynx) which are controlled completely involuntarily. This means that the singer must learn how to make the proper adjustments *indirectly*. He cannot consciously manipulate the muscles of the larynx, as I mentioned earlier.

How, then, can a singer learn to control this organ of sound?

Again, we can utilize organic imagery:

    a. Start with an open throat, as already discussed. The open throat can be imagined to look like an almost completely empty neck.

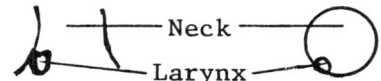

3/4 Profile   Top (looking down)

    b. Imagine a thin, sharp unbreakable steel wire being stretched in front of the neck, directly in front of the larynx.

    c. Sing a breathy vowel *a* (as in father) on middle C (women) or an octave lower (men).

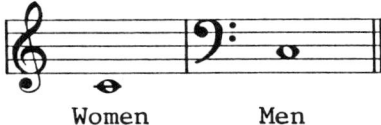

Women   Men

    d. Imagine the wire as cutting slowly through the neck.

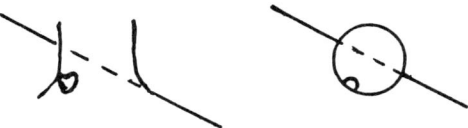

    e. As the wire cuts through the neck, the vowel should become more intense and *ringy* until the wire cuts through to the back of the neck.

    f. The tone should now be as intense as the singer can make it, without forcing or straining.

Fig. 25

30 VOCAL DEVELOPMENT THROUGH ORGANIC IMAGERY

The results of this exercise have always proved to be effective to some degree on the first or second attempt. Repetition brings improvement rapidly in a few successive attempts.

During each stage of the above, after phonation begins, the singer should listen to the sound as it becomes gradually firmer, and remember the attendant physical sensations. The firm sound is focused. (See Appendix IV, Vowel Focus Exercises, pp. 163-164). He should also note what happens to the belt line support when he focuses the tone.

After the singer achieves success in singing the *a* intensely, he should convert the image to one more functionally symbolic, and considerably less grisly, as follows:

a. Side   b. Top

Fig. 26

Now the singer can relate the point of the triangular wedge to focus, rather than the more complicated steel wire image. The broad front of the triangle represents the breathy tone, and the point of the triangle represents a vibrant, ringy tone.

At this stage, the singer should strive to produce all sounds on the point, and *never* in front of the neck.
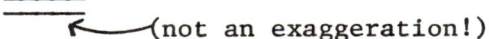
(not an exaggeration!)

This device has proved to be effective not only with individual students but with voice classes and choral groups as well.

After the student achieves proficiency at starting the tone at the point, on a single pitch, he is ready to apply the technique to intervals, beginning with a major second, slurring from the first to the second tone and back again. Frequently, the *a* (as in *may*) or the *e* (as in *me*) vowels are more effective; but, in the beginning, *a* (as in *father*) is better, as a general rule.

Fig. 27

From this point, the student should extend the range scalewise until he can no longer maintain an open throat *and* intensity of tone, produced with ease.

An image which illustrates the most common problem encountered at this stage is:

a. Side   b. Top

Fig. 28

The point should connect with the back of the neck, but it does not. In addition to loss of intensity in the above instance, the singer will probably feel as if the front of his neck is becoming *bottled up*, incresingly, as he ascends the scale. This is a certain indication that the throat is closing and that the air cannot get through properly.

In his excellent book, *THE SINGER AND THE VOICE*, Arnold Rose calls focus "the edge."[1] This term is especially good, as it describes directly what is happening at the vocal folds: The edges come together with the proper degree of firmness, eliciting what older writers called "steel" or "metal" in the voice. Mr. Rose takes a more direct approach to the subject, however, than our concept of organic imagery will allow, as our concept is designed to manipulate the vocal folds by *remote control*, and this action must be felt at the back of the neck, rather than at the glottis.

D. Coordination of Respiration and Phonation

Now that we have isolated the areas of posture, respiration, and phonation, it is time to coordinate these elements into one functional unit. We have yet to cover the areas of resonation and articulation in detail; therefore, what we do coordinate will have to be with the understanding that the resultant coordination will still not be complete.

Again, by using organic imagery, we begin to get a clearer idea of what we are trying to achieve.

By taking the symbol for breath △ , and adding

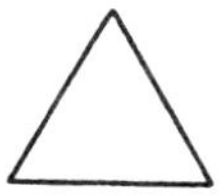

focus ━━━━━ , we get the following picture:

a. Side View   b. Back View

Fig. 29

---

[1] Rose, Arnold; *THE SINGER AND THE VOICE*; St. Martin's Press; New York; 1962, 1971; pp. 152-167.

32 VOCAL DEVELOPMENT THROUGH ORGANIC IMAGERY

By superimposing the above image over the human torso, we have:

a. Side View

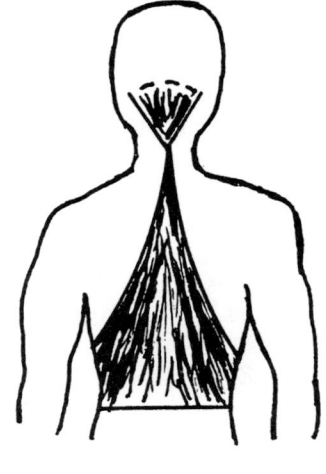
b. Back View

Fig. 30

For the sake of simplicity and convenience, let us use the back view of this superimposed figure and think of it as an "X", the upper section being proportionally smaller than the lower:

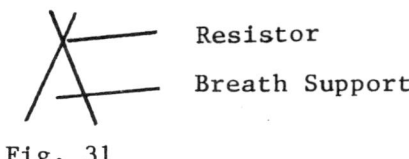

Fig. 31

"What happens when an irresistible force meets an immovable object?" This question has been pondered for centuries.

If we consider the breath as being the irresistible force and the resistor as being the immovable object, probably no sound would be forthcoming. But, if the resistor became only *slightly* movable, that would be all that is necessary to have a tremendous amount of phonation. This would be the ultimate in phonational intensity or vocal energy. The point at which force and resistance meet would be the focal point.

Obviously, the breath support that a human being is capable of producing is limited, thus, not irresistible. Likewise, his resistor is also limited. But the principle is still valid in terms of voice production: A maximal amount of breath converging at an *almost* maximal amount of resistance will produce maximal phonation, or vocal *buzz*.

It must be noted that a singer should *never* use maximal phonation. It is important only that he know what that extremity is and how to achieve it. In this knowledge, he will understand his limitation in that direction. His subsequent challenge would be to explore the *minimal* possibilities of effective phonation, which is more difficult and comes much later in vocal development.

*Note that the symbol for focus is now raised so the point converges at the nape of the neck. Hereafter, we shall consider it to be at that location, rather than being horizontal with the larynx.

PHONATION 33

Developing a feeling for the most and the least his voice is capable of producing will teach the singer a most important concept: *directional tendencies*.

It should also be noted that the best way to explore extremities is from the standpoint and starting point of *moderation*.

Many studies have been made concerning the relative effectiveness of dynamic levels of singing. The most efficient and productive dynamic level is mezzo forte (*mf*). This is the ideal level at which to begin the study of voice production.

Singing too loudly can overtax the voice and destroy its efficient coordination. Singing too softly inhibits the use of the *complete* vocal mechanism, therefore, certain areas cannot be coordinated at all. Mezzo forte allows the best of both worlds.

The same may be said of range. A singer should never begin at the high and low extremities of his range, but in the middle. The proper direction is from the middle and gradually progressing both higher and lower, while never compromising the integrity of correct vocal production.

In coordinating breath support and focus, the singer should note the following tendencies as the musical scale ascends or as the tone cresscendos:

   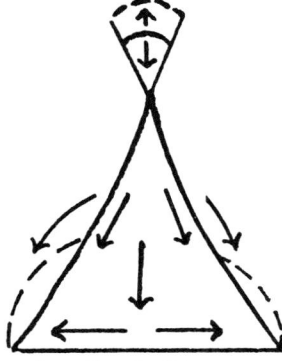

a. Front View   b. Back View

(The broken lines in this figure indicate expansion.)

Fig. 32

On the descending scale or on a diminuendo, the reverse of the process indicated in Fig. 32 holds true, to a degree. The singer will be more aware of these tendencies, while ascending the scale or while crescendoing, than in the reverse process, however, as the former seems more active and the latter more passive. This phenomenon should not lure the singer into the pitfall of letting go of the intensity of the tone. If any one factor may be said to be more important than another in this respect, it would be the backward focus:

Fig. 33

Too often, as a singer descends the scale or diminishes, the direction of focus moves forward  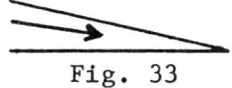 , blunting or detaching almost com-

Fig. 34

completely from the point of contact with the breath, as follows:

34 VOCAL DEVELOPMENT THROUGH ORGANIC IMAGERY

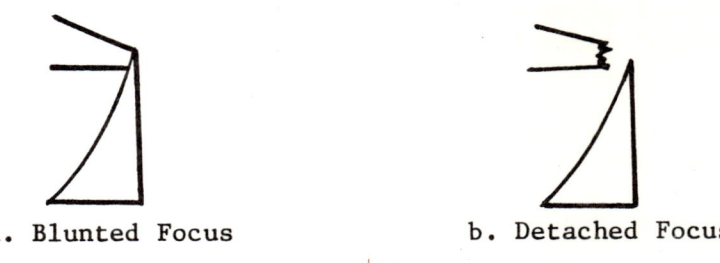

    a. Blunted Focus   b. Detached Focus

Fig. 35

This is the principal reason why a singer should not begin his lessons by trying to sing softly. He does not maintain enough energy or intensity to retain contact between breath and resistor. Consequently, the tone is breathy and weak. The *core* of sound is lost. As a result of this, all sorts of compensatory efforts are brought into play to the detriment of both tonal quality and the singer's well-being.

Another frequent occurrence which accompanies premature efforts to sing softly is failure of the breath support mechanism to maintain its own balance— that is, balance of inhalation with exhalation.

A guideline for avoiding this problem is three fold:

    a. The breath should always maintain contact with the resistor.
    b. The breath should flow freely, except for the desired amount of balanced impedance of the resistor.
    c. There should be neither more nor less breath compression than is necessary to do the job required.

In other words, separation of breath from resistor must be avoided during phonation, and a balanced breath should meet a balanced resistor.

We mentioned earlier that certain muscles for respiration connect with the larynx, enabling respiration to control phonation by *indirection*. Perhaps this is only a *seeming* indirection, as there is a direct connection.

Another concept which has proved most helpful to my students for coordination of breath support and phonation is the following:

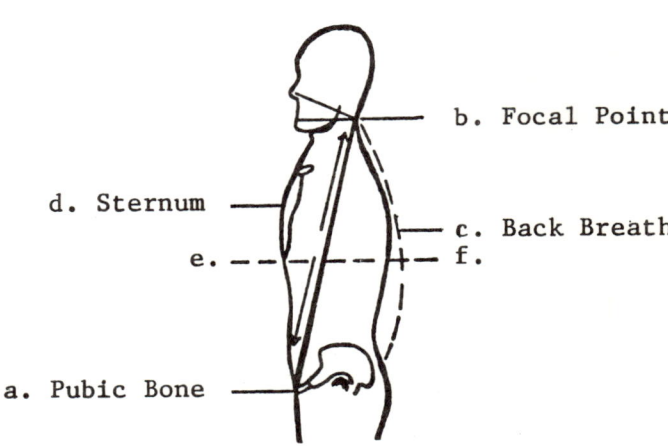

Fig. 36

The diagonal line from a to b simplifies all previous images and gives the singer an *energy line* which is most effective. While he takes his back breath, he should activate the sensation of pressing down on the pubic bone. The degree of support required determines the proportion of pressure needed. This is an action, or cause. This action will allow the singer to minimize all pressure above the rib cage (line ef). There should be *no feeling of compression* above that line. Furthermore, he will feel a direct connection from a to b (Focal Point) which will seem like an *electric charge* at the focal point. This is a reaction, or effect.

The singer should be cautioned not to allow the abdomen to become rigid; otherwise, he will not be able to center the support narrowly down on the pubic bone. When the diagonal line is properly utilized, the singer will feel as if the back breath support becomes a wall of resonance, which will aid him further in releasing all undesirable pressures.

In addition to the downward direction of support toward the pubic bone, the singer will feel an outward pressure against the belt line. The belt line should never feel static, or locked into one position. As the singer ascends the scale or crescendos a tone, the abdominal muscles at the belt line will move outwardly. As he descends the scale or diminuendos, the belt line will move inwardly. Some singers mistake holding or locking the abdominal muscles for support. This is counterproductive, resulting in the muscles fighting themselves rather than cooperating with one another. Locking these muscles is the main cause of abdominal fatigue and contributes, in turn, to shortness of breath.

One recurring problem with some beginning students is the tendency to hold the breath in a misguided attempt to control it. However, breath is like money. It has to circulate to be useful. The breath is also like love. "The more one gives, the more one has."[1]

Because many aspects of Phonation are closely intertwined with Resonation, we will conclude this chapter, prematurely, and procede to a discussion of Resonation in Chapter IV.

---

[1]Leyerle, William D; Pedagogical Opinion: "Organic Imagery and Technical Vocal Priorities;" *The NATS Bulletin*; Volume 37 No. 5, May/June 1981; p. 32.

CHAPTER IV
RESONATION

Resonance is the reinforcement of vibration (phonation). If the resonator is *in tune* with the frequency of the vibrator, the resultant tone will be superior in size and quality.

The size, shape, and texture of a resonator determine the best tuning for any given frequency. In singing there is one best size, shape, and texture of the resonators for each vowel, timbre, pitch, and intensity.

The singer's object is to find that ideal resonance position throughout the entire vocal range.

A. The Resonators

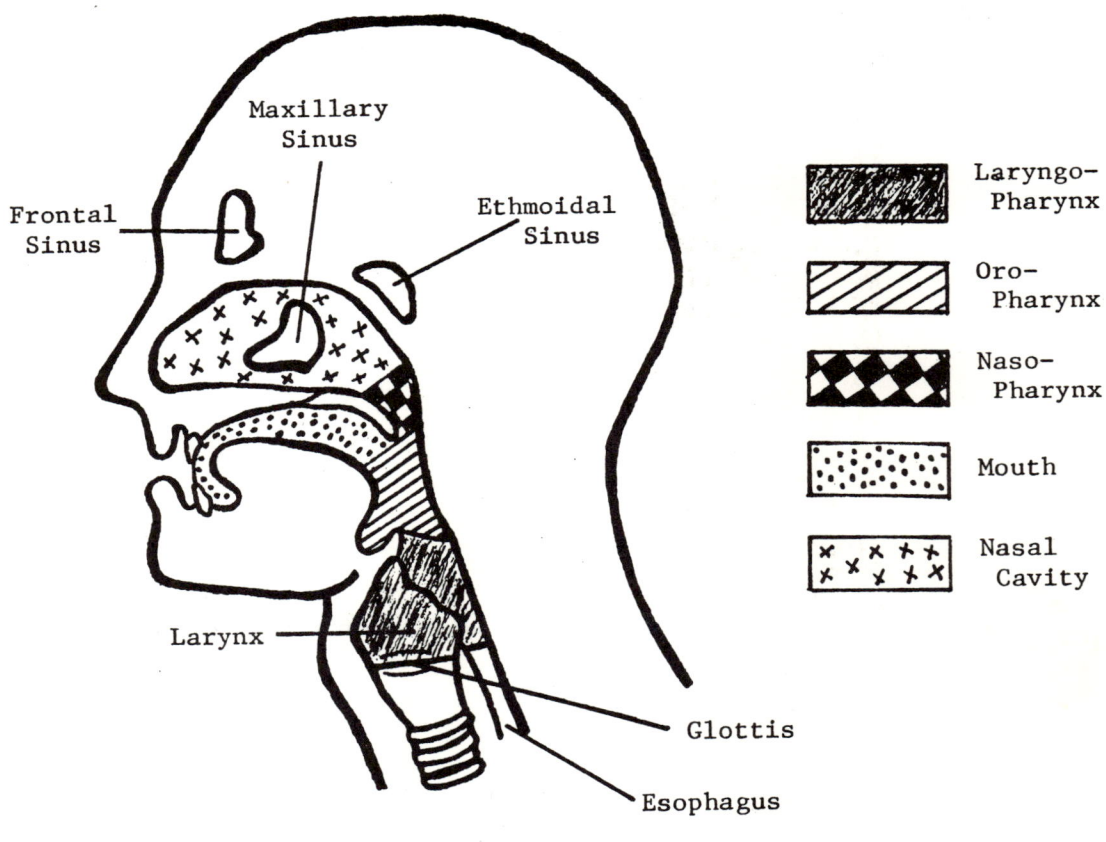

Fig. 37

Resonation is determined by the five principal areas as shown in Fig. 37. The throat, or pharynx, is divided into three parts, named because of their locations. The laryngo-pharynx is above the glottis and behind this upper section of the larynx. The oro-pharynx is adjacent to the oral cavity, or mouth. The naso-pharynx is at the opening before (under) the nasal cavity.

1. The Pharynx

   The lower two-thirds of the pharynx (laryngo- and oro-pharynges) is the most important of all the resonators. The naso-pharynx is important, but only for nasal resonance, which is used for a much smaller portion of the over-all singing time.

   Resonation and phonation are so closely related that it is difficult to separate the two.

   For example, we have discussed the open throat as a part of phonation; but, by examining the illustration in Fig. 37, it is obvious that the open throat *is* the laryngo- and oro-pharynges.

   As this chapter progresses, it will become apparent that resonance is, more or less, a passive phenomenon; whereas phonation is an active one. In other words, *how* we open our throats is more in the realm of phonation. *What* we open is the resonator. This distinction is quite important.

   If we consider the resonator simply as a cavity, the only things we have to change while singing are the size, shape, and texture of that cavity. This will help us avoid the pitfall of confusing resonance with tone production.

   As a case in point, I reiterate what I stated earlier about *tone-placement* in terms of resonance. If we open the resonating cavity correctly, the tone will simply pour into that space. We do not have to push, pull, or point the tone in that direction any more than a clarinetist has to direct the tone to the resonator. The clarinetist, or *any* instrumentalist, has only to set the vibrator in motion. The clarinet, trumpet, drum, piano, or violin has its resonating position built in. Of these instruments, the drum and piano have not only built-in resonators, but their built-in phonation positions, as well. They need only the motive force to produce the tones.

   When the resonating cavity is correctly shaped, the proper vowel will be produced, or vice-versa. If the resonator is not properly shaped for a given pitch, intensity, or timbre, there will be an immediate adverse effect on the larynx (phonation). Therefore, when a singer is asked to "place" the tone, he is really being coaxed into finding the correct vowel position. This movement feels like the vowel is being pushed or urged forward, up, down, or backwards. Since musical instruments do not pronounce vowels, their resonation is much simpler than that of singers, although good instrumentalists use vowel positions for tone color.

2. The Nasal Cavity

   The nasal cavity is dependent upon the velum, as is the naso-pharynx. If the velum is raised and pressed against the back wall of the throat, the nasal port is closed, and the phonated sound cannot reach the nasal passages. This resonating space is used only for the nasal consonants, [n], [m], [ŋ], and [ɲ], and certain nasal vowels, such as the *i* in the French word *vin* and the *en* of *encore*. Only when the velum is lowered are these nasal sounds possible.

3. The Mouth

   The second most important resonator is the mouth.

38 VOCAL DEVELOPMENT THROUGH ORGANIC IMAGERY

The most important element in changing the size and shape of the mouth is the tongue. The position of the tongue is the single most important factor in defining vowels. The *purity* of the vowel is the best indication that the mouth resonator is correctly opened. The *quality* of the vowel is a combination of proper resonation and phonation. The vowel is the end product of complete vocal production.

The jaw plays an important role in both mouth and pharyngeal resonance. Opening and closing the jaw, naturally, changes the size and shape of these resonators.

The lips must also be considered in resonation— especially for the [o] and [u] vowels and their close relatives. The lips are only a refinement in vowel production, however. Rounding the lips, alone, will not produce the ideal [o] and [u] positions. The proper mouth and pharyngeal shapes must accompany the lip positions. It is quite possible to sing an [o] or [u] with the lips in *any* position, but why fight nature?

4. The Sinuses

The sinus cavities (See Fig. 37), which were formerly thought to have great importance in resonation, have been found to be virtually useless for that purpose. They probably contribute more to the *sensation* of resonance than actual resonance.

5. The Larynx and Esophagus

The larynx and esophagus are not as significant to resonation as the pharynx, mouth, and nasal cavities. It is possible that their significance also lies in the realm of sensation, due to the effect of sympathetic vibration.

B. Coordinated Resonance

If we take the image for focus: ———————>, we can now apply it to both phonation and resonation, *but* with certain reservations. The pointed portion represents the backward focus. The open portion represents the *direction* of resonance.

We know, however, that the pharynx is behind the mouth and that we need more vertical space in the back of the mouth than in front. Thus, in reality, the image would logically be reversed for resonation, like an inverted megaphone, as follows:

Fig. 38

Consequently, the *pure* combination of resonance with phonation, as organic imagery, would look more like this:

Fig. 39

In order to keep our imagery simple, one image should suffice for both focus and resonance, considering the *direction* of resonance, rather than the *shape* of resonance, as follows:

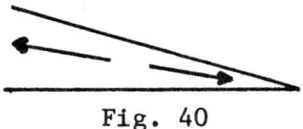

Fig. 40

1. Mask Resonance

It seems appropriate at this point to consider the term *mask resonance* or *masque resonance*, as it is frequently spelled. This phenomenon has probably contributed more to the concept of *forward placement* or *tone placement* than any other.

As mentioned previously, most of our sensations of movement in voice production, until now, have been in a backward and downward direction. Now comes another exception. It is closely allied to the forward direction of resonance, except that the direction of resonance is a passive sensation and mask resonance seems to be more active.

At one time mask resonance was considered to be *nasal resonance*. Many teachers continue to use the term and the concept with good results. But, if we examine the reality of the situation, we find that, except in the cases of nasal vowels and consonants, mask resonance is *not* nasal resonance, but only a sensation of it.

The reason why mask resonance is not nasal is due to the well-documented fact that, during phonation of all but the nasal vowels and consonants, the nasal port is closed off from the breath stream. This closing is accomplished when the velum (back portion of the palate) stretches to the back wall of the throat:

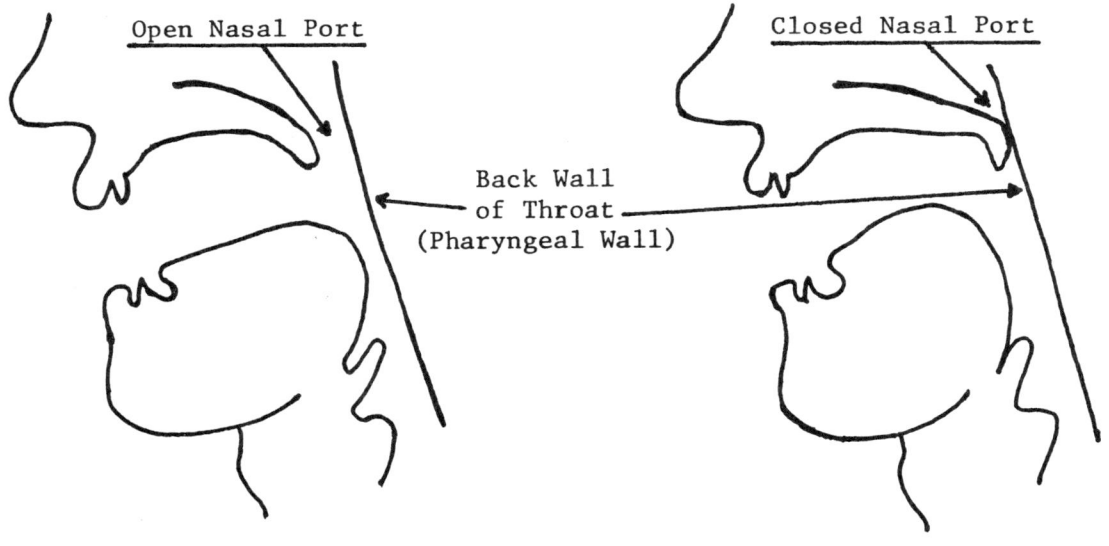

a. Lowered Palate   b. Raised Palate

Fig. 41

40 VOCAL DEVELOPMENT THROUGH ORGANIC IMAGERY

A simple test should convince even the most skeptical of this truth: Hold the nostrils closed with thumb and fore-finger, while singing a non-nasal vowel, such as *a* in *father*. Once the tone is established, the nostrils may be opened and closed intermittently while the tone is sustained. If the tone is well produced, there will be no compression at the point of closure at the nostrils. All the sound will go out the mouth. Neither the vowel nor the tonal quality will change character during the intermittent opening and closing of the nostrils.

A further test would be to hold the hand over the mouth and try to sing the same vowel. The singer will find that he no longer has an *a*, but only a hum. Only the nasal consonants can be sung with the mouth closed off completely. The nasal vowels can only be effective when *both* the mouth *and* nasal port are open.

How does all this apply to mask resonance? If mask resonance is not nasal resonance, what is it?

Possibly the best answer is that mask resonance is the physical sensation a singer feels at the forward section of the hard palate, both above and below, which is due to sympathetic vibrations caused by phonation. It is a reaction, not an action. It is an effect, not a cause. We do not place or point the tone there.

All this is not to demean the validity of the sensation as an aid to singing.

The great tenor, Jean De Reszke, summarized his vocal success by attributing it to "singing in the nose." Almost every professional or amateur singer who warrants being heard has experienced this sensation and uses it to advantage. Rosa Ponselle, America's pre-eminent spinto soprano, described the sensation as follows: "You get the feeling your face is going to come off." [from the vibrations][1]

When a singer feels that he does more than *sense* mask resonance, the chances are strong that whatever he *does* to accomplish the sensation has more to do with phonation than with resonation.

Because the sensation of mask resonance is often felt above the hard palate, as well as below it, the singer has the impression that nasal resonance is activated. This sensation can be consciously heightened by lifting or stretching the muscles and tissue around and above the nasal bone, as the broken lines indicate in Fig. 43 on the next page.

If the singer thinks of a sneer, he will stretch this tissue. The term "flared nostrils" is also related. As he ascends the scale, showing four to six of the upper teeth (not the lower) will also be beneficial in activating mask resonance. Stretching this tissue makes it firmer; therefore, more sensitive to the sympathetic vibrations.

Sometimes a variation of our phonation-resonation image is beneficial in activating mask resonance:

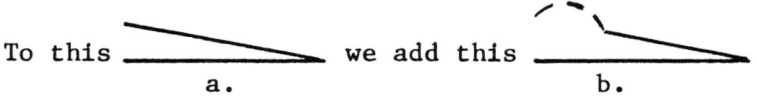

Fig. 42

---

[1] Hines, Jerome; *GREAT SINGERS ON GREAT SINGING*; Doubleday and Company, Inc.; Garden City, New York; 1982; p. 255.

RESONATION 41

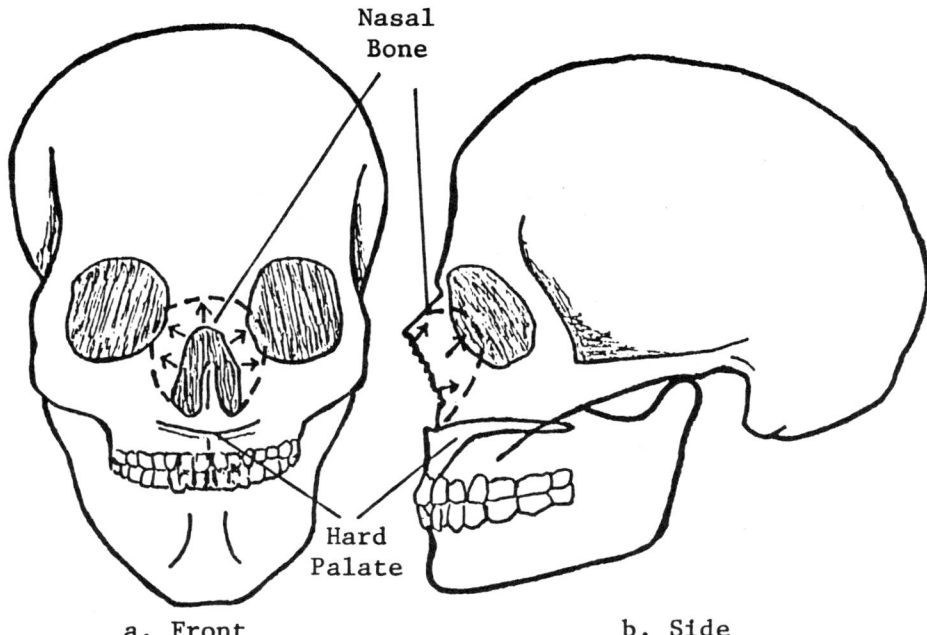

a. Front   b. Side

Fig. 43

If the singer is particularly observant, he will notice a connection of this forward, frontal stretching sensation to the soft palate, farther back, where it blends with the palatal lift, dropped jaw, and the focusing mechanism— all parts of phonation. (See Appendix VII, Imposto, p. 167.)

A device which I call the "Wee-wee-wee" exercise has been most useful in helping my students activate and remember the sensation of mask resonance. It is done in three stages, as follows:

1. Sing and sustain the word *wee* as nasally and with as much intensity as possible. The sound should be most disagreeable to the ear.
2. Repeat 1 and while sustaining the *wee*, clamp thumb and forefinger on each side of the nostrils. Although the tone will become muffled and "bottled up" behind the closed nostrils, the singer should maintain as much intensity as possible at the point of closure.
3. Repeat 1 and 2. While sustaining *wee* with closed nostrils, allow the pressure (and tone) at the point of closure to "back off," very slightly, in order to eliminate the pressure behind the thumb and forefinger. The tone will seem to rise as it backs off. The less distance the singer has to back away from the closure to eliminate the pressure, the greater will be the resultant mask resonance intensity.

WEE

a. Sing a sustained *Wee* (g above middle c)   b. Close nostrils with thumb and forefinger   c. Let compression migrate backward until nasality stops

Fig. 44

42 VOCAL DEVELOPMENT THROUGH ORGANIC IMAGERY

Anyone who has never experienced this sensation will feel a surge of ringing tonal freedom which is most exhilarating. In five minutes this exercise can be taught to voice classes and choruses with a success rate of 90% the first try. Some students have a problem of producing an intense nasal sound at first, so it is necessary to work with them until 1 and 2 of the exercise are affected. Once the class or individual has sensed the release of pressure and achieved a ringing, masky sound, they should practice applying it to changing pitches, such as the five-note scale:

Fig. 45

Two problems occur frequently with a small percent of students. (1) Some do not know how to produce a good nasal sound. Usually, this type of singer sings a "honky" kind of nasal tone that does not change in step b, when the nostrils are closed. If this should happen, the student should experiment with various nasal sounds until he finds the correct one. (2) Some students back so far away from the nasal closure in step c that they lose all the intensity and advantage of the mask resonance. Again, they should experiment until their ears and muscles agree on the proper distance the tone should "back off."

2. Head Resonance

No discussion of resonance can be complete without including *head resonance*. William Vennard calls head resonance a "...Misnomer applied to light registration with high formant resonance..." Without getting involved with acoustics and the formant theories, let us concentrate on the word, *misnomer*.

Most singers, hopefully, have a tingling sensation in all parts of the head. This sensation becomes more pronounced as the singer ascends the scale. It is a sensation well worth cultivating because it is a sign of freedom. The singer will not feel the sensation if he is tense. But this sensation is not necessarily head resonance. Again, it is an awareness of sympathetic vibration. These sympathetic vibrations tend to move from place to place in the head, depending on the pitch, vowel, and intensity. Mask resonance is a part of head resonance and should always be present in any range.

In the middle range, the singer should be aware of the tingling sensation around the cheek bones, forehead, and temples. As he goes higher, this sensation will move backward to the crown of the head. As he continues even higher, the sensation will seem to leave the skull entirely and proceed diagonally upward and backward from the crown of the head. This is the beginning of the phenomenon known as the *whistle register* (also called the *flageolet* and *bell* registers), used, for all practical purposes, only by women.

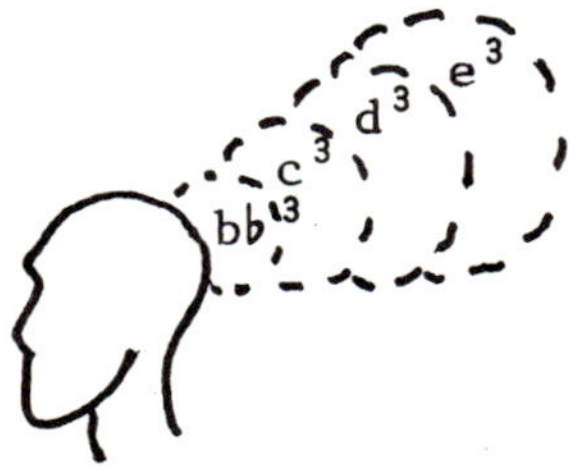

Nefertiti's Hat Resonance

Fig. 46

An exercise which works well for helping singers find the whistle register is the ascending and descending one-octave arpeggio.

Transposing upward by ½ steps on the [ɑ] vowel (refer to IPA chart in Appendix II for key to pronunciation of phonetic symbols):

[ɑ ɑ ɒ ɔ ɒ ɑ ɑ]   [ɒ ɔ ɔ ʌ* ɔ ɔ ɒ]   [ɔ ɔ ʌ æ ʌ ɔ ɔ]

*Usually [ʌ] works better for women and [ʊ] for men, but not in every case.

Fig. 47

The following is an excerpt of an article I wrote for the NATS Bulletin (used by permission), which explains the above process.

"...The note and vowel that unlock the door to the flageolet range are the B♭ (or B♮) above the staff and the [æ],* as in *cat*. Without diminishing support, the singer should strive for an increasing sensation of "light-headedness" while moving to the higher notes. For those who have acquired at least a partial ability in using head-voice, they should rely more and more on that sensation until they reach the B♭ (or B♮). At that point the singer should begin to feel a tingly sensation around the back of the scalp. As the exercise continues higher and higher, the tingly sensation will seem to move diagonally upward and backward from the back of the scalp and the light-headed sensation should become increasingly intense.

...Because of the general direction of this sensation, I call it "Nefertiti's hat" resonance. Once discovered, sopranos can usually sing up to the B♭ above high C, and a few can go even higher. This does not necessarily mean they will be able to incorporate these notes in actual songs and arias, but no one needs sing that high, anyway. The important point is the resultant freedom and flexibility, which *do* extend into their practical upper range.

For singers unused to the sensation, accompanying dizziness is not unusual. The dizziness will subside as the singer becomes more habituated to the exercise. The dizziness comes as a result of exploring "new territory" or range. It is a positive indication. It should be mentioned that another kind of dizziness, which results from severe strain— of the sort that makes the veins of the forehead stand out and the face turn purple— is a negative indication, and should be avoided at all costs! It is unlikely, however, that the singer will even reach the [first] high B♭ or B♮ using that kind of negative force..."[1]

As early as 1962 it was known that notes sung by women at c^3 (two octaves above middle C) sounded like [ɑ], no matter which vowel was being sung. John Howie and Pierre Delattre wrote about this phenomenon in an

---

[1] Leyerle, William D.; Point Counterpoint No. 17: "Certain female voices make successful use of the flageolet range,"; *The NATS Bulletin*, Vol. 41, No. 1; p. 13.

*The lips should not spread sidewise, but vertically, as the singer ascends the scale on the [æ] vowel.

article in *The NATS Bulletin*.[1] Since Howie and Delattre are both teachers of French, it is natural that they should favor the [a]. In my own experience, I find that most of the students with whom I work have more success in applying this phenomenon to the whistle register if they use the [æ] vowel. Also, I find that by lowering the pitch to B♭ or B♮, I still cannot distinguish any other vowel than [æ] and the students do not feel compelled to force their voices in order to make a distinction between the vowels. Since no distinction can be made in any case, I ask them not even to try and to take the course of least resistance.

Again, the whistle register is not only head resonance. It is also phonation. The breath and the resistor are the true factors enabling the singer to sing these notes. The tingling vibrations are only an indication that the singer is phonating properly and with a minimum of tension.

Because of this indication that the singer is phonating correctly, head resonance can be a most useful tool for both teacher and student. As many teachers base most of their methods on breathing, just as many base them on resonance. So long as their students arrive at the same goal— efficient and effective singing,— the approach *may* be negligible. A common weakness to either approach, however, is that the singer often finds himself respiring and resonating with apparent ease but without the complete voice. More about this subject will be discussed later in this same chapter on coordination of phonation and resonation.

Earlier in this chapter I stated that the oro- and laryngo-pharanges were the most important resonators of the singing mechanism; but we have devoted less actual time to a discussion of their function than to the less important ones of the mouth and nasal resonators. This is because there is not much to say about them that has not already been covered in Phonation.

If the throat is open, throat resonation is automatic. There is relatively little movement in the throat. The smallest possible amount of movement of the tongue and pharynx made by a singer, as he goes from vowel to vowel, will insure the greatest efficiency and greatest consistency of tonal production, provided that he maintain vowel integrity.

The throat should be conceived as a constantly open pipe, in one basic position. On the other hand, the size and shape of the mouth resonator are constantly changing from vowel to vowel because of the movement of the tongue. This movement should be minimized, but it can not be avoided.

C. Coordination of Phonation and Resonation

We have examined the phenomena of phonation and resonation, so far as possible, as separate entities. Occasionally, it is either difficult or impossible to separate them completely, except as abstract ideas.

---

[1]Delattre, Pierre and Howie, John; "An Experimental Study of the Effect of Pitch on the Intelligibility of Vowels;" *The NATS Bulletin*; Oct. 1958; pp. 4-7; Reprinted in *CONTRIBUTIONS OF VOICE RESEARCH TO SINGING*; Edited by Dr. John Large; College-Hill Press; Houston, Texas 77035; 1980; pp. 385-394.

Now we shall discuss phonation and resonation as a coordinated activity without concerning ourselves with their separate functions, except where it may prove advantageous or enlightening to do so.

1. Coupling

When phonation and resonation are joined together in perfect balance, they are said to be "coupled." This means that the size, shape, and texture of the resonators are in phase or in harmony with the pitch and intensity of the vibrator.

2. The Attack

The efficient attack of the first tone of a phrase is the best indication that phonation and resonation are coupled.

The test of an efficient attack is in the sound and sensation of the resultant tone. If the tone is vibrant and easily produced, it is efficient. No matter how high, low, loud, soft, dark, or bright the tone is required to be, it must *always* be vibrant and freely produced.

If the vibrator and resonator are properly balanced, the moving breath stream will do the rest. That is why so many teachers stress breath control in singing. It does, indeed, seem, at this point in the singer's development, that the breath *is* the voice. But before that happy state is reached, the prerequisites of phonation and resonation must be met.

The two extremes of an attack, both of which are incorrect, are the *aspirant* or breathy attack and the *glottal* attack. The former is too lax and the latter is too energetic— that is, energetic in the wrong places.

In the aspirant attack, too much breath gets through the vocal folds without being converted into vibration. The tone will lack intensity and not have adequate carrying power.

In the glottal attack, the breath is exploded through the vocal folds in a violent manner. There will be great intensity and carrying power, but very little grace or ease of control. Furthermore, a glottal attack can be injurious to the vocal folds. This can result in nodules (small callus-like growths on the vocal folds), which make them inflexible and incapable of even closure. (Glottal attacks are not the only cause of nodules, however.)

What the singer should strive for at all times is a balanced attack, using the best features of aspiration (smoothly flowing breath) *and* of glottalization (firmness of focus). Note that this is not a blending or mixture of the two polarities of attack, but a cooperation of the two.

In order to accomplish the above, some teachers have their students *think* an aspirant attack, but not let it be breathy. William Vennard suggests using an "imaginary *h*" as the safer approach. This activates the Bernoulli Effect, mentioned in the previous chapter. Others have their students *think* a glottal attack, but without the explosion.

This is a perfect example of solving a problem from opposite ends of the spectrum. Both methods work, but the student should be cautioned that they are both *primers* for guiding him toward an integrated attack which stems from a larger, overall concept.

46 VOCAL DEVELOPMENT THROUGH ORGANIC IMAGERY

When a tone is attacked properly, the breath will carry the tone through the rest of the phrase. The order of preparation for such an attack is:

a. correct mental conception of vowel, pitch, intensity, and timbre
b. setting the breath mechanism
c. coupling the vibrator and resonator *positions*
d. releasing the breath

Each of the steps above can be done separately; but, with practice and improvement, they can be developed so as to seem simultaneous. When this is accomplished, the singer will have the sensation of *laying* the vowel on the focal point.

Mr. Alan Case, the vocal coach/accompanist at State University College in Geneseo, gave me a most helpful image for coordinating the attack with the moving breath stream.

Rather than taking in a breath, stopping it, and then starting it again, as in Fig. 48a, the singer is advised to visualize the breath as a circular loop. Inhalation occurs on the lower part of the loop and the attack is made at the top, without stopping the breath (Fig. 48b). This has the effect of "hitching the voice to a rising star." The breath has no time to stagnate on an inflexible support system.

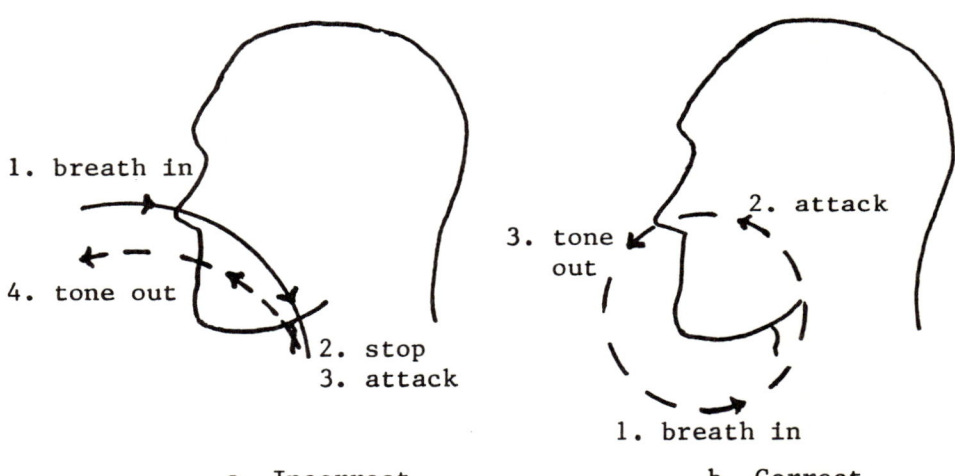

a. Incorrect   b. Correct

Fig. 48

3. Vowel Dualism

We are now in a position to discuss the *duality* of the vowel. Each vowel has two characteristics: Quality and Identity.

a. Quality Vowels

Quality vowels are more a product of phonation than of resonance, although resonance does play a role.

The quality portion of the vowel is laryngeally and pharyngeally controlled, as it is formed in a relatively fixed position, as discussed earlier. It is that part of the vowel which has color, power, and intensity.

b. Identity Vowels

Identity vowels are, principally, products of mouth resonance. They are controlled by the tongue, lips, and jaw.

The function of the identity vowel is just as the word implies: to make one vowel distinguishable from another.

All vowels should have both quality and identity at all times. Identity of the vowel becomes less discernable as the singer sings higher, however. Because of this acoustical tendency, a wise composer avoids writing music in the extreme high ranges to texts which demand understanding.

If we apply our phonation-resonation image once more, we have the following:

Identity Vowel ⟵⟶ Quality Vowel

(See Appendix IV, Vowel Focus Exercises)

Fig. 49

This brings us to Vowel Migration, or Vowel Modification. (We already had a sample of this on page 43, Fig. 47.)

4. Vowel Migration

Vowel migration is the act of altering the vowel slightly as the singer ascends or descends the scale, and as he crescendos or diminishes the tone. The purpose of this vowel alteration is twofold:

a. to maintain the integrity of the vowel (identity)
b. to prevent the tone from becoming disagreeable due to vocal strain.

In other words, in order to produce a given vowel easily and to prevent it from sounding different as the singer varies pitch or volume, he must change the vowel. If the singer does not change, the vowel *will*.

Dr. Ralph Appelman has made an extensive study of this subject, and expounds fluently upon it in his book, *THE SCIENCE OF VOCAL PEDAGOGY*.[1]

Although teachers of singing used this concept at least as early as the days of the Italian Bel Canto era, Dr. Appelman has presented an analysis of vowel migration in terms of modern scientific investigation, and sheds much light on a complex subject. We shall simplify by avoiding most of the acoustical terminology.

Before we can go more deeply into vowel migration, it will be necessary to understand the vowel triangle.

The vowel triangle was devised by speech scientists before the turn of the century when they observed that the highest forward vowel [i], the lowest central vowel [ɑ], and the highest backward vowel [u], formed by the center of gravity of the tongue, suggested a triangle (Fig. 50):

---

[1] Appelman, D. Ralph; *THE SCIENCE OF VOCAL PEDAGOGY*; Indiana University Press, Bloomington; Second printing, 1974; pp. 216-247.

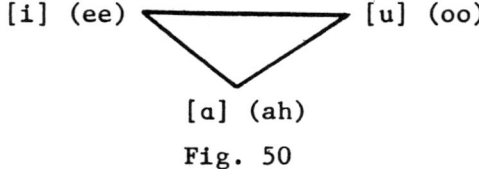

Fig. 50

This triangle was later modified to include much greater detail. It no longer resembles a triangle. It is now a quadrangle. (Consult the International Phonetic Alphabet in Appendix II for the key to proper vowel pronunciation.)

The Vowel Quadrangle

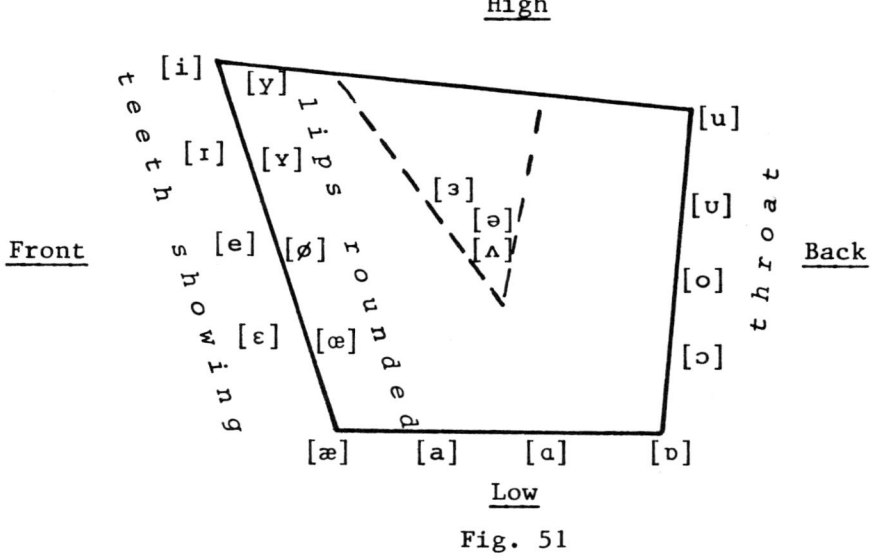

Fig. 51

From this point on, all vowels and consonants will be identified by their spelling according to the International Phonetic Alphabet (IPA).

After thirty or forty minutes of study, anyone can learn to identify most of the vowel symbols of the IPA with their corresponding sounds. The consonants take a little longer, but we will not need them until chapter VI.

Phonetic spelling is a great time saver because one can identify one given sound with one given symbol. Furthermore, through the use of phonetic symbols, singers form a more concrete idea about the precise sounds they are expected to make a part of their tonal memories. For these reasons, I do not apologize for requiring my students to learn the IPA. I do not expect them to emerge from voice classes or individual lessons knowing as much about phonetics as they would learn in a class in phonetic transcription; but any conscientious student should be willing, able, and *eager* to invest enough time and effort to identify each symbol with its exact sound.

It has been a constant revelation to me how many students cannot sing an [ɑ] when asked to do so. I am just as apt to hear an [æ] or an [ʌ]. When a singer has this problem, it may be due, in part, to some technical flaw or from having grown up in an area where a regional dialect is prevalent; but more often, it is due to pure carelessness, compounded by years of perfecting the incorrect sound.

Let us return to the vowel quadrangle.

If the singer will pronounce or sing the [i] and continue to follow the vowel quadrangle around the outer edges, counterclockwise,

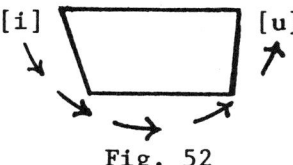

Fig. 52

he will feel the logical direction of the tongue in one fluent connected movement. He will also hear the relationship of one vowel to another in an uninterrupted continuum. He will become aware of three basic groupings:

	Direction	Position
[i] through [æ]	high to low,	frontal
[æ] through [ɒ]	front to back,	low
[ɒ] through [u]	low to high,	back

The singer will note, further, that the lips have basic movement tendencies:

- [i] through [æ]   lips spread, as in a smile
- [æ] through [ɒ]   lips open neutrally
- [ɒ] through [u]   lips rounded

These lip tendencies should not be exaggerated. Actually, they should be minimized, as any degree of concentration on them will usually detract from proper resonation or phonation positions. Occasionally, in order to make a point, a teacher might ask a student to round the lips more than necessary, in order to feel more "point" or maskiness to the voice. The singer should work in front of a mirror in order to avoid a tight, muscular appearance of the lips. The rounding inside the mouth is more important than the actual lip rounding.

If the singer sings or pronounces a slow, drawn out "why you," he will feel the reverse direction of the continuum, from [u] to [i] and back to [u], full circle. This observation has helped many of my students learn the vowel sequence faster and to retain it longer.

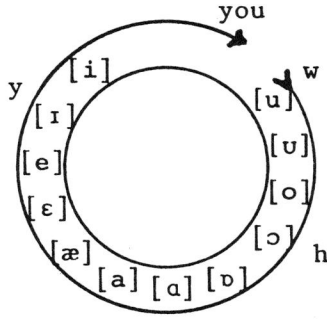

Fig. 53

If the singer will now follow the vowel quadrangle from [ɔ] to [o] to [ʊ] to [u] with the lips rounded, while the tongue rises gradually, as from [ɛ] to [i], he will be able to pronounce the German Umlauts and their French counterparts.

In other words, [y] is simply an [i] with rounded lips; [ʏ] is [e] with rounded lips, etc. To be even more precise,

[y] is an [i] with a lip-rounded [u];
[ʏ] is an [ɪ] with a lip-rounded [ʊ];
[ø] is an [e] with a lip-rounded [o];
[œ] is an [ɛ] with a lip-rounded [ɔ];

or

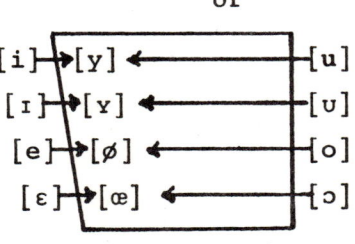

Fig. 54

The three neutral vowels [ə], [ʌ], and [ɜ] are located more in the central position of the quadrangle and, therefore, are not as easy to incorporate into the simple linear direction already suggested. A more complex pattern could be devised to include them, however.

Now we can return to vowel migration.

We have already established that, as a vocal tone ascends the scale or as it becomes louder, it must be altered. This alteration can best be accomplished by giving the tone more space in the mouth by dropping the jaw (loosely) and lowering the tongue (also, loosely).

The reader has probably already noticed that a gradual dropping of the jaw and lowering of the tongue causes the vowel to change from [i] to [ɪ] to [e] to [ɛ], etc. In other words, it follows the same pattern established by the direction of the vowel quadrangle.

Migration begins around f^1 for women and g for men. This is the *first migration* and terminates around b or c above middle c (an octave lower for men). The *second migration* begins around d^2 or e^2 for women and an octave lower for men. The order of migration for each vowel is given below, proceeding from the given vowel (what the audience should hear) through the first and second migrations:

Given Vowel:	First Migration:	Second Migration:
[i] migrates to	[ɪ] then to	[ʏ]
[ɪ] no change	[ɪ] then to	[ʏ]
[e] migrates to	[ɛ] then to	[œ]
[ɛ] no change	[ɛ] then to	[œ]
[æ] migrates to	[a] then to	[ʌ]
[a] migrates to	[ɑ] then to	[ʊ] or [ʌ]
[ɑ] migrates to	[ɔ] then to	[ʊ] or [ʌ]
[ɔ] no change	[ɔ] then to	[ʊ] or [ʌ]
[o] migrates to	[ʊ] then to	[ʌ]
[ʊ] no change	[ʊ] then to	[ʌ]
[u] migrates to	[ʊ] then to	[ʌ]
[ʌ] no change	[ʌ] no change	[ʌ]

RESONATION 51

Given Vowel:	First Migration:	Second Migration:
[ɝ] migrates to	[ʌ] no change	[ʌ]
[y] migrates to	[ʏ] then to	[ʌ]
[ø] migrates to	[œ] then to	[ʌ]
[œ] no change	[œ] then to	[ʌ]
[ɛ̃] migrates to	[ã] then to	[ʌ]
[œ̃] migrates to	[ã] then to	[ʌ]
[ã] migrates to	[ʌ] no change	[ʌ]
[õ] migrates to	[ʊ̃] then to	[ʌ]

These patterns are reversed when descending the scale or diminishing the volume, although not necessarily at the same pitch or dynamic levels of their counterparts.

The following illustration (Fig. 55) will show the migratory path of [ɑ] as it ascends the scale with its accompanying points of resonance. The singer can feel the vowel changing at these points at the different pitch levels. The vowel begins at the alveolar ridge and moves backward along the hard palate. The first migration [ɔ] begins when the palate begins to lift. When the second migration occurs [ʌ], the palate will stretch even more.

Migration of the vowel [ɑ]

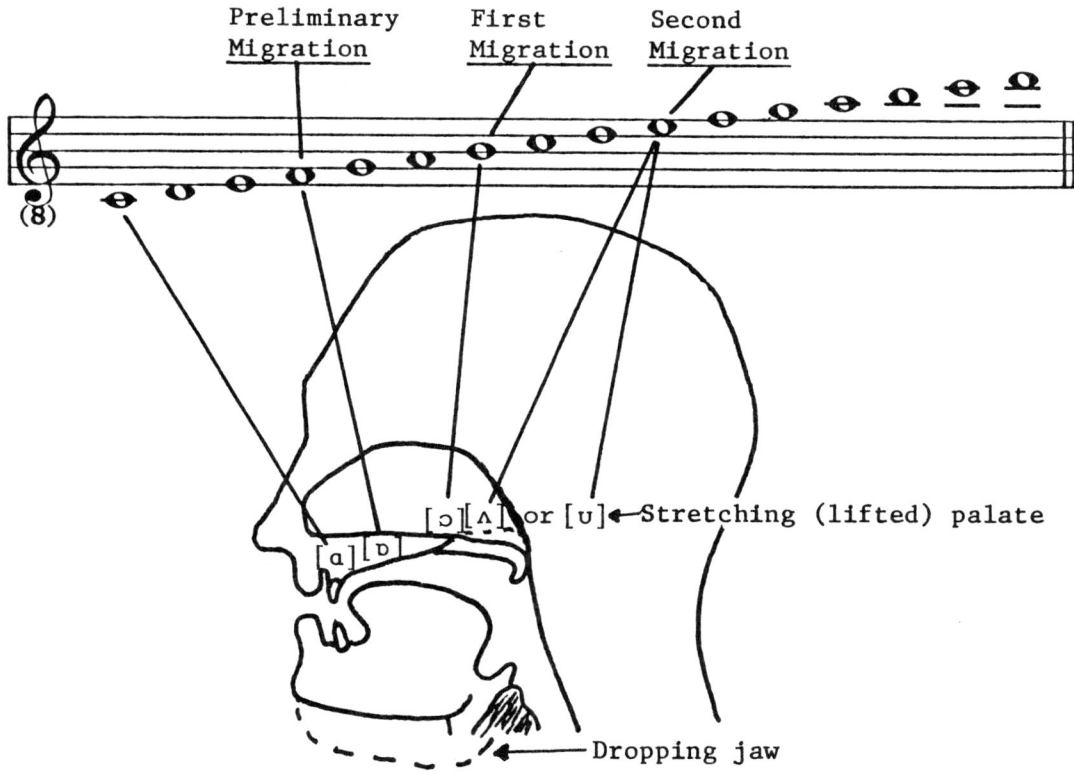

Fig. 55

The jaw drops proportionally with the lifted palate. As the singer feels the vowel migrate along the palate, *he should still be aware of mask resonance*, which remains forward at all times. Fig. 55 does not include the migration into the female whistle register, which will be illustrated later in chapter V. The [ɒ] is given here to show that the "pure" [ɑ] begins its transformation toward [ɔ] at that indicated point.

52 VOCAL DEVELOPMENT THROUGH ORGANIC IMAGERY

Actually, the degree of movement the tongue makes, when changing from an [ɑ] to an [ɔ], elicits an infinite variety of vowel changes between them. [ɑ] and [ɔ] are only parts of an outline in the over-all vowel spectrum. This may be said of the distance between any two vowels. There are literally thousands of possibilities, but our minds are trained to hear the relatively few sounds which make up that outline. For this reason, many voice teachers believe that no two singers can possibly sing the same vowels, as they are as variable as fingerprints.

There is an acceptable norm, beyond which vowels are not intelligible. Singers should not go beyond that norm. Dr. Appelman calls this undesirable sojourn "promiscuous migration,"— a delightful expression.

It should be mentioned that, while vowel migration is an important factor in maintaining vowel integrity and tonal acceptability, the concept must be treated from the proper viewpoint. A singer should not become a slave to the rules for vowel migration. This would put too much emphasis on a principle which should be spontaneous and automatic as soon as possible.

It is much the same as rules for grammar: The language existed *before* rules for grammar were established. Grammarians noted tendencies of the language and organized them as logically as possible or practical. The same is true of vowel migration. Good singers migrated long before observers analyzed and categorized. We must always remember the order of things.

A study of the rules for vowel migration is quite useful for beginning students who have no concept whatsoever about how to sing a given vowel from low to high or soft to loud, and vice versa; it is also useful for more experienced singers who find themselves having trouble with certain vowels, whereas they are not bothered by others.

On first conscious use of vowel migration, the singer may feel that altering the vowel helps him do the proper things, vocally, such as gradually lowering the tongue, dropping the jaw, etc.

As soon as possible, he should reverse the procedure. Through kinesthesis (muscle awareness) and tonal associations, the singer will learn how to coordinate these adjustments automatically. At that time, the vowel will migrate because the singer is singing correctly, not because he is *making* it happen. At this stage, he will sense *body migration* rather than vowel migration, leaving his mind free to track the *identity vowel* he wants his audience to hear. *The ear must always monitor the vowel the body feels!*

Let us examine, once more, our image for coordinated respiration, phonation, and resonation. If we visualize our basic image as having a pin through the point of the intersection,

Fig. 56

the reader will see that, when the bottom section widens, the top section widens *proportionally*. He should also note that only the *angles* of the intersecting sides widen. The point of intersection remains in the same place. A more graphic representation of the growing complexities might look like this:

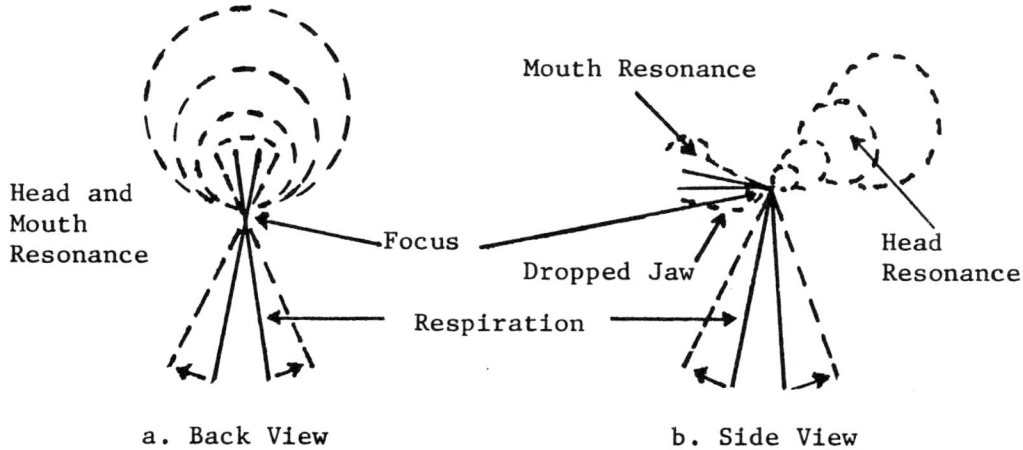

Fig. 57

As we reach the conclusion of this chapter, the reader may have noted that three significant and helpful rules can be gleaned from the foregoing commentary. *When ascending the scale or when crescendoing a tone, the singer must observe the following requirements:*

1. He must give more support.
   (Flexible belt-line support)
2. He must give more space.
   (Openness, extending to the small of the back, as well as more space in the mouth and pharynx)
3. He must migrate the vowel.
   (Always from a specific to a more neutral vowel)

When descending the scale or diminishing the amplitude of the tone, the process is reversed.

These three simple principals can be a handy rule-of-thumb for helping a singer take technical inventory of his vocalization if and when he has to solve vocal problems. He should learn them as a catechism!

CHAPTER V
REGISTRATION

Registration actually belongs, predominantly, in the domain of phonation, as it involves the adjustments of the laryngeal mechanism. Certain aspects of registration have often been confused with resonance. We hope to eliminate some of that confusion by gaining a more thorough understanding of registration in itself.

A commonly accepted definition of register, pertaining to music, is: "A particular series of tones, produced in the same way and having the same quality."

Registration, then, means: "Control of a mechanism which produces one or more particular series of tones, each series being produced in the same way and having its individual quality."

Consider the clarinet. Its lowest register (Chalumeau) has a warm, soft quality. Its middle register is brighter and "edgier." The highest register is even more brilliant and tends to be shrill without excellent technical control.

The low register is played without using the register key. The middle register utilizes the register key. The upper register is controlled mainly by overblowing the middle register. A different fingering pattern also is used. Each register has its individual sound and its particular method of producing that sound.

The greatest point of controversy on the subject of registration in singing centers around the question, "How many registers does the human voice have?" The answers, depending on the philosophy of the pedagog, range from *none* to *infinite*.

Some teachers maintain the voice has *no* registers at all and refuse to discuss the matter. On the other extreme, some maintain that each tone has its own registration. They say there are as many registers as there are varieties of pitch, intensity, and timbre.

Obviously, neither of these concepts even fits into the definition of registration, as given here. Of course, it may be argued that the holders of these philosophies did not write the definition. The reader can easily see why there is so much controversy. A definition of terms must be established before communication can begin.

A more manageable number of registers, commonly agreed upon by various factions, are: One, Two, and Three. For the present, we shall not consider two other extreme registers, which lie below (*Stroh Bass*) and above (*Whistle* or *Flageolet*) the normal vocal ranges. The specialty voice of the basso profundo will be discussed later in this chapter. The whistle register has already been discussed on pages 42-44 in the chapter on Resonation.

a. One-register theory

   The advocates of this theory maintain that one tone of a singer's range is produced like, and has the same quality of tone as, any and all other notes of his range.

b. Two-register theory

   The advocates of this theory maintain that there are two registers:

   (1) Chest   or Low   or Heavy Mechanism
   (2) Head   or High   or Light Mechanism

   Each of these two registers has characteristics different from the other. Some advocates say that these registers *blend* when one over-laps the other. Others say the registers do not *blend*— they are *coordinated*.

   In either case, unless the registers are blended or coordinated, the two registers retain specific qualities, which are quite distinct, one from the other. This is detrimental from an aesthetic standpoint.

   Could it be possible that "blend" and "coordination" are really the same thing, the former being a description of the resultant tone quality and the latter being a direction of how to achieve the former?

c. Three-register theory

All Voices	Women	Men
(1) Low	Chest	Chest
(2) Middle	Middle	Head
(3) High	Head	Falsetto

Could it be possible that the "blended" or "coordinated" part of the two-register theory is the same thing as the "middle" register of the three-register theory? If this be true, there may be less need for controversy than is thought.

Whichever theory of registration a singer adopts, he can usually make it work as it should. That is to say, if he wants to segment the voice into three parts, he can do it. If he wants to divide it into two parts, or fifty, he can do that. "Man is a rational being."

Ultimately, the voice should sound as much like one register as the singer can manage. In that light, all register theorists should strive for the *illusion* of a one-register production.

Could this *illusion* of one register by the two- and three-register advocates be the same as the *reality* of the one-register advocates? If this be true, then most of the controversy over registration would appear to be no more than a "tempest in a tea-pot."

Why should a singer wish to segment the voice into chest, head, falsetto, etc?

The proponents of the one-register theory of voice production, while denying the existence of two or more registers, often use the same exercises, images, sensations, and terminology with their students as do the multi-register proponents.

Psychologically, the one-register approach has much in its favor. Segmenting the voice may invite problems which are unnecessary. If a student can develop two and a half to three beautifully produced octaves without "taking the voice apart," why should he borrow trouble needlessly? The old saying, "Don't fix it if it ain't broke" would apply here. On the other hand, some teachers feel that certain problems can be solved more expediently by isolating one part of the voice from another.

Probably the major differences of opinion between advocates of the various registration theories stem from fear of the adverse effects of opposing philosophies.

One-register advocates maintain that it is unnecessary to segment the voice and that, in so doing, the singer may never get it back together or will be overly conscious of the points of register change. They seem to feel the slower method of the one-register concept is actually faster and more reliable in the long run.

Multi-register advocates maintain that a one-register concept is, indeed, much slower than necessary in getting to the heart of many vocal problems. Furthermore, they feel that much of the vocal potential of a singer will never be developed unless the different registers are developed individually before they are blended or coordinated.

I would like to propose the following simple formula as a possible aid for putting the matter in better perspective:

One-register system = Singer's *Objective* = Effect

Two-register system = Singer's *Method*   = Cause

The above conclusion was arrived at in two stages; the realization that:

a. The vast majority of teachers and singers agree that the polished performer ideally has one voice, evenly produced from top to bottom. Achieving this ideal uniformity is the singer's objective.

b. Teachers and singers do not utilize the multi-register concept as an end, but as a means. The qualities attributed to chest tones, or heavy mechanism, are those of power, depth, color, and stamina. The qualities attributed to head tones, or light mechanism, are those of flexibility, sweetness, lightness, and height. If, for example, a singer is proficient with his chest tones but lacks flexibility and a good upper range, it would behoove him to develop those qualities attributed to head tones.

In the case of many beginners, their two (or three) registers will be widely different, one from the other (in a particular student). Sometimes the beginner will have only one usable register. Sometimes he will have none! Whatever the situation, the student must develop each attribute required of a competent singer, then bring them all together and smooth them out into one complete voice.

Developing the flexibility attributed to head voice should not diminish the power of the chest voice when the registers are blended or coordinated. How the singer achieves this balance is his *method*.

REGISTRATION 57

If the reader agrees that all singers should have objectives and methods for achieving those objectives and if he agrees with the rationale of the above formula, he will probably conclude that there *may be* validity in all register theories, which will enable him to profit from them all.

I prefer the use of the two-register concept as a means for arriving at the one-register end.

Most two-register advocates agree that the lower register (or heavy mechanism) has a range of approximately two octaves and that the upper register (or light mechanism) also has two octaves. The lower octave of the light mechanism overlaps the upper octave of the heavy mechanism, making a total potential range of approximately three octaves.

Henceforth, the terms "blend" and "coordination" will be synonymous and without quotation marks, when we speak of bringing these overlapping octaves into balance.

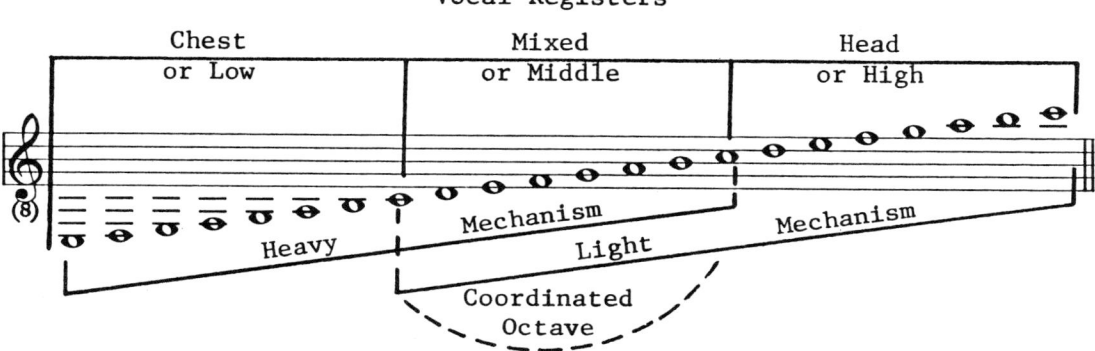

Note: *The key of C is an arbitrary selection here. A singer may have a higher or lower voice than these three octaves.*

Fig. 58

The middle or coordinated octave, which combines parts of both the light and heavy mechanisms, causes more problems in learning to sing than the other two octaves combined.

Joseph J. Klein refers to this part of the singer's range as "the bottleneck octave,"[1] an apt description for improper handling of this part of the voice. In Germany, the term "damming the voice" is used to describe the uncomfortable sensation which accompanies the bottling or stopping up of the voice.

Mr. Klein establishes the bottle-neck octave from middle C to the octave above. Other teachers place it at B♮. I prefer not to *set* it in any particular key, although the two keys given above do seem to get the lion's share of the action.

An illustration used by many voice teachers to indicate the ratio for coordinating the heavy and light mechanisms has proved to be quite effective:

[1] Klein, Joseph J.; *SINGING TECHNIQUE (How To Avoid Vocal Trouble)*; D. Van Nostrand Company, Inc.; Princeton, New Jersey, Toronto, London; 1967; p. 65.

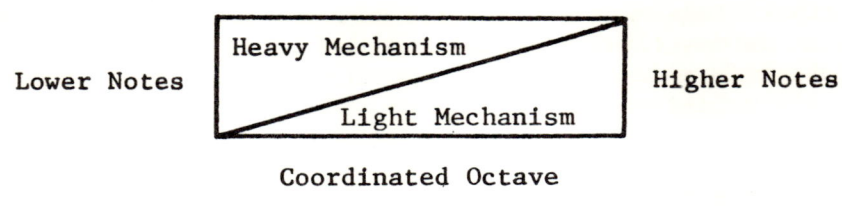

Coordinated Octave

Fig. 59

The reader will note that the heavy mechanism dominates the lower part of the octave, whereas the light mechanism dominates the upper part. The method for achieving a balanced mechanism throughout this octave is to lighten the mechanism on ascension, and to give it more weight on descension. A part of the light mechanism should remain, however, even in the lowest section of the range, and vice-versa.

Figure 59, above, represents the coordinated octave alone. Lest the reader falsely conclude that all notes below middle C are heavy mechanism tones, only, and that all notes after the octave above middle C are all light mechanism tones, we offer the following illustration:

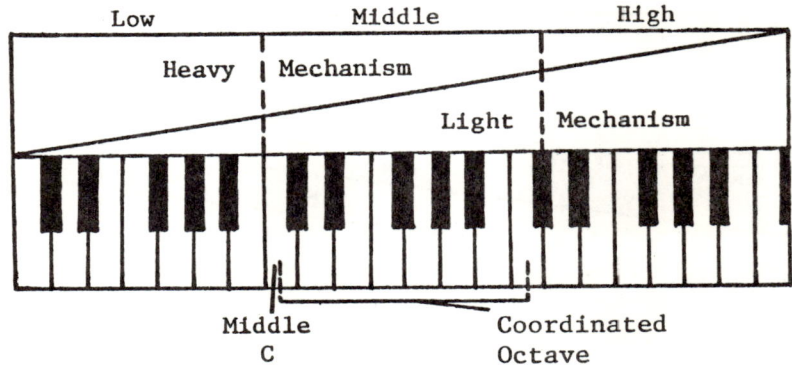

Fig. 60

Ideally speaking, a three octave range, as indicated above, should include both heavy mechanism tones and light mechanism tones throughout the entire range. Only the proportions should differ. Therefore, the singer actually coordinates the entire three octaves of his range.

Experience indicates, however, that if the middle C octave is well-coordinated, the other octaves will be "pointed in the right direction" and will "sing themselves," provided the singer follows the tendencies established in singing that C octave throughout his range. The main problem confronting the singer, then, is balancing the coordinated octave.

How does one achieve this balance?

We have already established the basic solution in our discussion of phonation: That is, *balancing focus with breath support*. Now we need only to coordinate the best resonance position with each phonated sound.

Before we can proceed with specific exercises which aid coordination of resonance and phonation, it seems appropriate to discuss the *passaggi*. The singular form of this Italian word, *passaggio*, is more common to English readers. In English, the word means *passage, transit, crossing,* or *thoroughfare*. In vocal parlance, it refers to *a point of register transition*, or, *a passage from one register to another*.

REGISTRATION 59

Two principal kinds of passaggi exist in both male and female voices: the *passaggio primo* (first passage) and the *passaggio secondo* (second passage). Important acoustical and physiological differences between the male and female voices should be noted.

Acoustically, the passaggio primo of the female is practically identical to the passaggio secondo of the male. This is the point at which both genders go from heavy mechanism to light mechanism.

Passaggio Primo

Bass   Baritone   Tenor   Contralto Mezzo-   Soprano
                                            Soprano
                                 [highest note in chest voice]

Fig. 61

Passaggio Secondo

Bass   Baritone   Tenor   Contralto Mezzo-   Soprano
                                            Soprano
[lowest note in head voice]   [highest note in middle register]

Fig. 62

Note: All the above passaggi are approximate.

However, because the passaggio primo of the female singer occurs at the lower part of the staff and the secondo of the male singer occurs at the upper part, the physical sensations peculiar to executing the passaggi differ considerably. The male passaggio, which requires more physical intensity, because of the relatively higher range, can actually be physically painful when not properly executed. Other faulty execution can be even more painful to his ego in case of *cracked tones*.

On the other hand, the female singer does not have to work so hard, physically. Her biggest problem in coping with the passaggio primo is avoiding the "two-voice syndrome" by developing the finesse required to veil two distinct qualities— head and chest— by learning to avoid either too much or not enough mix of light with heavy registration.

The distance in pitch between the passaggio primo and the passaggio secondo is called the *zona intermèdia* (middle zone). It is interesting to note that in the male voice this zone encompasses an interval of a perfect fourth; but, in the female voice, the interval is a 9th for the soprano, an 8th for the mezzo-soprano, and a diminished 8th for the contralto (all these intervals are approximate).

The intervals for the female voice were established late in the 19th century by Mathilde Marchesi,[1] who was a student of and an assistant to Manual Garcia. She taught only women— and almost exclusively— sopranos. She is one of the most successful teachers in the annals of vocal pedagogy, numbering among her students, Nellie Melba, Emma Calvé, Emma Eames, and Frances Alda. Marchesi believed, absolutely, in three registers!

---

[1] Marchesi, Mathilde; *BEL CANTO: A THEORETICAL AND PRACTICAL VOCAL METHOD*; Unabridged republication by Dover Publications, Inc., New York; 1970; p. xv.

If we equate the zona intermèdia with the middle register, we see that it is quite longer in the female than in the male voice. Because of this longer middle register of the female voice, many teachers divide it into *lower middle* and *upper middle*, constituting yet another passaggio, which Richard Miller places as follows:[1]

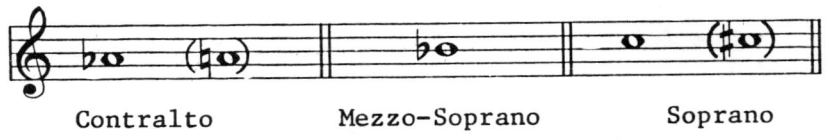

Fig. 63

Since, to my knowledge, no passaggio label has been given this particular register point, and in order to remain consistent with the other Italian terms, I call this the *passaggio intermèdio* (middle passaggio).

The reader should be aware that the pitch designations of the passaggi, as given above, are only approximate. They vary from a semi-tone to a whole-tone, depending on such factors as physical maturity, size, body structure, psychological make-up, and natural and selected timbres of the voice. In addition, when one vocal Fach (category) edges closely to its neighbor, whether higher or lower, it tends to take on characteristics quite similar to that neighboring Fach. That is, within a given Fach (say Baritone), as the voice becomes lighter, it more nearly resembles the next higher Fach (Tenor) and vice-versa. (See Appendix III, Voice Classification)

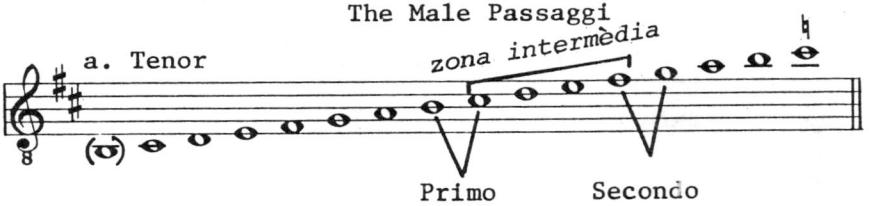

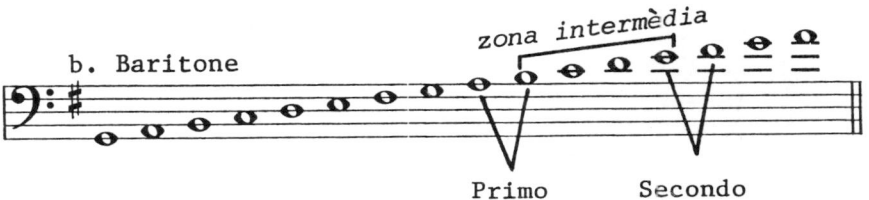

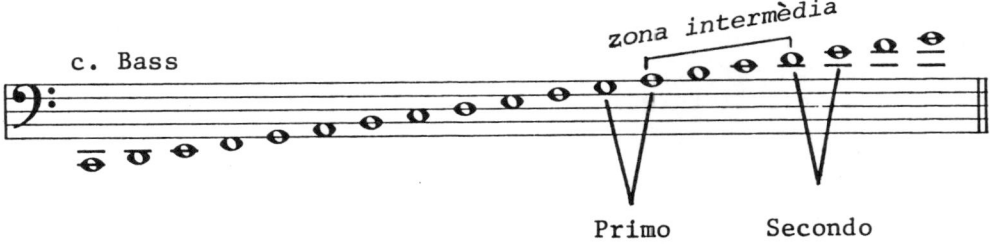

Fig. 64

[1] Miller, Richard; *ENGLISH, FRENCH, GERMAN AND ITALIAN TECHNIQUES OF SINGING: A Study in National Tonal Preferences and How They Relate to Functional Efficiency*; The Scarecrow Press, Inc.; Metuchen, New Jersey; 1977; p. 130.

The Female Passaggi

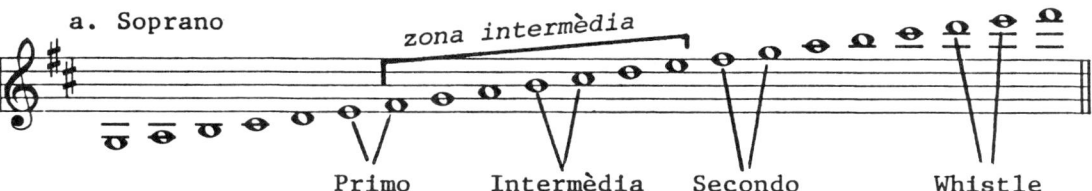

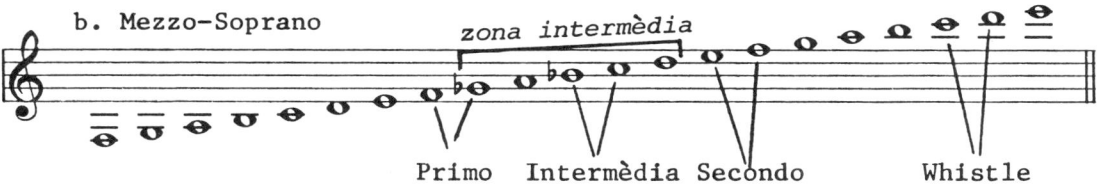

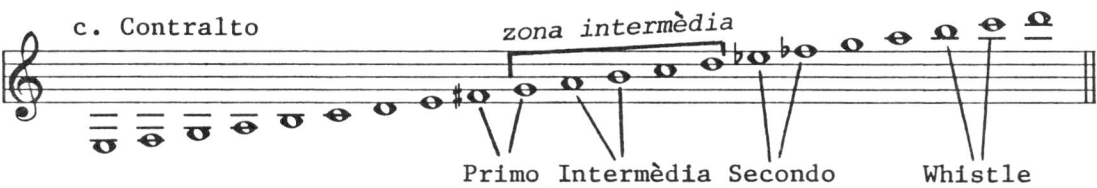

Fig. 65

The chest register is used more by men, and particularly by basses and baritones. The tenor, in order to cope with the heavy demands of a higher tessitura, must resort to a more consistent use of the head register than the lower voices. Quite frequently, as with the Verdi baritone, lower singers are required to sing in the upper extremes of their range an inordinate amount of time. The only way to sing comfortably in the upper reaches of the voice is to take off weight by lightening the registration. In the male voice, this lightening process begins at the passaggio primo and continues to the passaggio secondo. Accompanying this process are a number of other constantly changing elements such as vowel migration, resonance coupling, degrees of support, amplitude, and physical expansiveness. All these factors tend to merge and group themselves into physical sensations that can be identified, organized, and categorized by the singer. By categorizing these sensations in a logical manner, he can develop a reliable synthesis of the diverse elements of vocal production which makes the entire process easier to perform and to retain. All the sensations listed above are experienced by female singers, but not necessarily in the same parts of their range.

There is a well-known saying about a well-organized household: "A place for everything and everything in its place." The same idea is valid for singers; but the singer must discover where the "place" is before he can put it there.

Too often, vocal pedagogs are wont to quote axioms *generally* when they should be directed at *specific* events. In the former instance, the axiom can be meaningless and confusing; but, applied to the appropriate situations, they can help the singer open doors he did not even know existed. Let us examine two such axioms and see how they can aid in synthesizing some of the elements that comprise registration.

62 REGISTRATION

Axiom No.1) *Good singing is like good speech.*
Axiom No.2) *The singer should "drink" or "inhale" the tone.*

In Axiom No. 1, a number of circumstances must be clarified before the statement can be beneficial. Do we know what *good speech* is? Do we use it? Do we see a relationship of speech to our singing? Are speech and singing really the same thing?

It is my observation that a natural, ringing, unaffected mode of speech which projects easily without tiring the speaker is *good* speech. But does the speaker have the same physical sensations when moving from speech to song? Here we might reflect back to the previous statement,"a place for everything and everything in its place."

With the male voice, good speech can be equated with chest voice *up to* the pitch level of the passaggio primo. However, when he begins to take on those physical attitudes of voice lightening, something invariably happens that makes him feel more like a singer than a speaker. He activates axiom No. 2. He begins to feel as if he is *inhaling* the tone (as opposed to *exhaling* it). Therefore, within a given part of a singer's vocal register, good speech *is* like good singing. Beyond that point, however, it is different in both quality and sensation. The artistic singer must learn to blend the zona intermèdia gradually from less to more head register as he ascends the scale so the listener will not be aware of the change. When he becomes particularly adept in blending, he may even grow to be unaware of the change, himself. Not many singers are so fortunate. The zona intermèdia can now be referred to as the *middle* or *mixed* register.

After the singer has experienced physical sensations of the evolving mixed register and achieved a moderate degree of success in singing through these tones with consistency and confidence, he will be ready for the *passaggio secondo*. It has been said by a number of singers at the Metropolitan Opera, "This is what separates the men from the boys."

It is always easier for a teacher to demonstrate the passaggio secondo than to explain it. By demonstration, it *may* be easier for the student to grasp certain insights if the demonstrator exaggerates this change from mixed register to head register. In my own experience, I would advise against exaggeration as it can be uncomfortable (or even injurious) to the demonstrator and the student will get a false impression of what the well-executed passaggio secondo should sound like.

Until the passaggio primo is developed, the passaggio secondo will be a study in futility. The process of lightening the middle register paves the way to the head register by removing certain muscular constrictions which are inevitable if the vocal folds remain too thick. Some teachers and singers have described the sensation of maneuvering from the middle register into the head register as "going through the narrow portion of an hour glass."

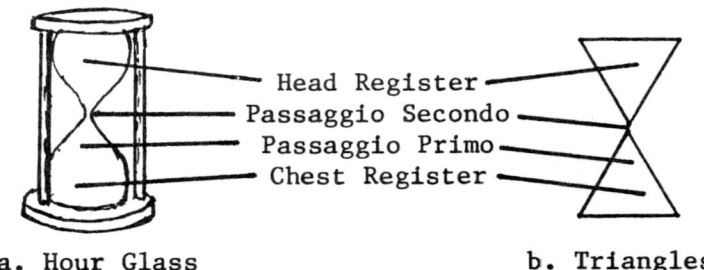

a. Hour Glass   b. Triangles

Fig. 66

Marilyn Horne suggests the hour glass as a helpful image.[1] She states, also, that two triangles, the lower like a pyramid and the upper like an inverted pyramid, is also helpful. (See Fig. 66b) This makes a lot of sense if one thinks of gradually narrowing the *weight* of the voice as he approaches the passaggio secondo. Once he is "through the little hole" he gradually puts the weight back into the voice, although that weight is felt as *more intensity of support* rather than as a *thickening of the tone!* The voice, in the upper register, must feel light and flexible but with terrific strength and intensity.

As with most analogies, the hour glass image is flawed. The sand must go up, instead of down. However, the imaginative student may, once more, snatch victory from the jaws of defeat by rejoicing in the defiance of gravity— as high-soaring resonance seems to defy gravity.

The sensation of inhaling (or drinking) the tone is not the only aid in lightening the registration. We have already mentioned the principal of vowel migration in the previous chapter. The gradual modification of the vowel will also take undue pressure off the vocal muscles while ascending the scale. These two factors, when finely coordinated, are particularly helpful in singing through the zona intermèdia.

I alluded earlier to the *Strohbass* and to the *whistle* or *flageolet* (also, *bell*) registers.

The Strohbass (*Stroh* is the German word for *straw*) is so called because the sound produced in this most extreme low register of the male voice is reminiscent of "dry rustling straw" as one walks through it. I feel a better name for this register would be helpful, but the only other reasonably descriptive terms I have heard of is *Schnarregister* (*Schnarren* in German means *to rattle* or *to rasp*, but when appended to *-bass*, it means *drone*). Richard Miller says the Schnarregister is "called the *growl* register by some English-speaking teachers."[2] To my ears, that is a more descriptive word. I would add the term "deep vocal fry" to give a bit more dimension to the previous descriptions. Authorities in phonetics use the terms, *fry, rattle,* and *scrape of the glottis* to describe the Strohbass sound.

The whistle register is the highest vocal register. It is most predominantly used by coloratura sopranos, whose repertoire frequently requires them to sing above d^3. Although the coloratura soprano is required to sing in the whistle register and the lower sopranos, mezzo-sopranos, and contraltos are not, all voices potentially possess this register— including male voices!

The phenomenon of the male whistle register can be heard on a recording entitled *VOX HUMANA*, recorded in England by Alfred Wolfsohn's group experiments in extension of human vocal range.[3] One of the singers, Thomas Faraday, sings nine octaves. Although his lowest register, which

---

[1] Hines, Jerome; *GREAT SINGERS ON GREAT SINGING*; Doubleday and Company, Garden City, New York; 1982; p. 139.
[2] Miller, Richard; *ENGLISH, FRENCH, GERMAN AND ITALIAN TECHNIQUES OF SINGING*; The Scarecrow Press, Inc.; Metuchen, New Jersey; 1977; pp.125-126.
[3] Wolfsohn, Alfred; *VOX HUMANA*; Folkways Records Album No. FPX 123; 1956; Side 1, bands 9 and 10.

64 VOCAL DEVELOPMENT THROUGH ORGANIC IMAGERY

Wolfsohn purports to go lower than the piano keyboard, is unconvincing, his middle and upper registers are real, climbing above the highest note on the piano keyboard. Although the whistle tones are real, the difficulty of preparation for producing them would preclude their usefulness in song.

Now that the passaggi of all voice categories have been defined, it is interesting to note the differences and similarities of sensation between the male and female voices as they sing their entire range. For convenience, we will use the two middle voice categories (Mezzo-Soprano and Baritone) as models. The reader should keep in mind that the higher or lower voices will vary by only a half-tone, or so, above or below the two given models.

Mezzo-Soprano: Sensations of Registration

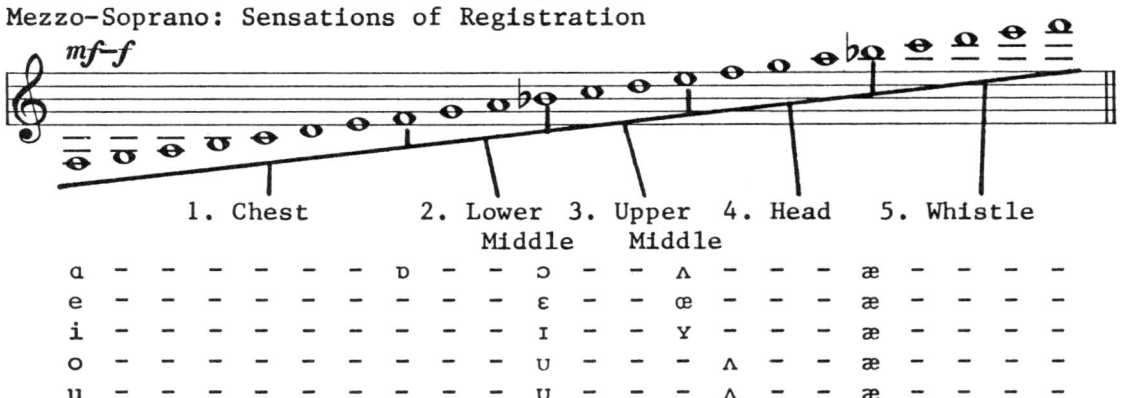

	1. Chest	2. Lower Middle	3. Upper Middle	4. Head	5. Whistle
a	ɑ — — — — — —	ɒ — —	ɔ — —	ʌ — —	æ — — — —
e	e — — — — — — — —	— —	ɛ — —	œ — —	æ — — — —
i	i — — — — — — — —	— —	ɪ — —	ʏ — —	æ — — — —
o	o — — — — — — — —	— —	ʊ — —	ʌ — —	æ — — — —
u	u — — — — — — — —	— —	ʊ — —	ʌ — —	æ — — — —

1. **Chest:** Vibrant, bright, somewhat masculine sound resembling speech production, without a yawny, orotund resonance are characteristics of this register.

2. **Lower Middle:** The beginning of yawniness, which increases slightly from f^1 to bb^2, while the resonance gradually darkens, characterizes this register.

3. **Upper Middle:** Here begins the sensation of inhaling or drinking the tone, accompanied by a sensation of firming-up the muscles at the nape of the neck (more about this later). The abdominal muscles will also begin to grow much firmer, and the breath support will seem to become more narrow and to center itself directly under the tone which is felt at the nape of the neck (focal point). The lift of the soft palate begins, accompanied by dropping the jaw. The palatal lift will seem to *draw* the tone upward, rather than the tone having to be *pushed* from below. This process *lightens* the voice, as does the sensation of drinking the tone.

4. **Head:** The muscle tension at the nape of the neck will continue becoming firmer, as will the support. However, as the drinking sensation (at 3) has lightened the registration, the added muscular energy should feel exhilarating, rather than fatiguing. The resonance will extend upward into all parts of the head, with little or no sensation below the upper teeth.

5. **Whistle:** At bb^3 the back of the head will begin to tingle and the tone will seem to be drawn diagonally upward and outward from the back of the head as the notes go even higher (Nefertiti's Hat Resonance).

Fig. 67

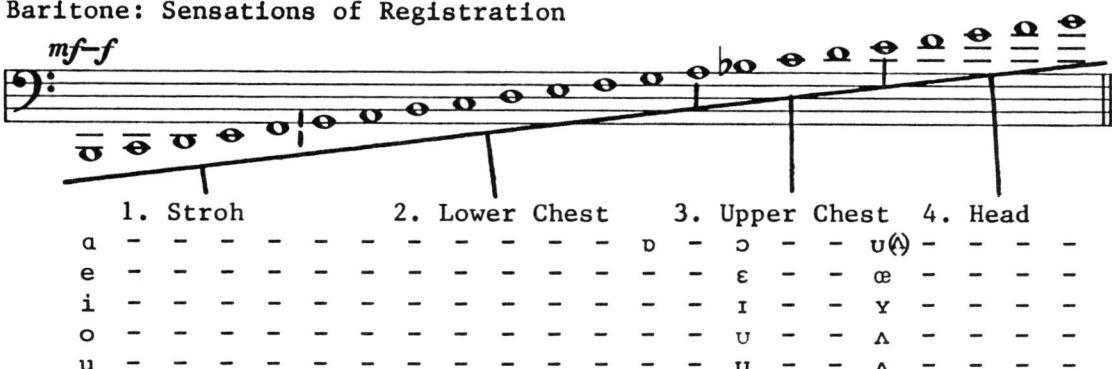

	1. Stroh	2. Lower Chest	3. Upper Chest	4. Head
a	- - - - - - - - - - -	ɒ	- ɔ - -	ʊ(ʌ) - - - -
e	- - - - - - - - - - -	ɛ	- - œ	- - - -
i	- - - - - - - - - - -	ɪ	- - ʏ	- - - -
o	- - - - - - - - - - -	ʊ	- - ʌ	- - - -
u	- - - - - - - - - - -	ʊ	- - ʌ	- - - -

1. **Stroh:** This register is tight and crackly. It is not generally a usable part of the baritone's range, but is useful for low basses; Firmness at the nape of the neck is essential.

2. **Lower Chest:** There is no major change in technique or sensation in comparison with the Stroh register, but this register is less tense. The sound resembles normal speech, without a yawny, orotund resonance.

3. **Upper Chest:** Yawniness begins, increasing slightly from a^1 to d^1. Accompanying the yawn is the sensation of inhaling or drinking the tone. Keeping the breath support centered directly under the tone during the drinking sensation is critical, but difficult to control in the beginning of development.

4. **Head:** The abdominal muscles will begin to grow much firmer and a tightening sensation at the nape of the neck will occur. The column of breath will seem to narrow as it becomes more intense. Because of the lightened mechanism (through drinking the tone), the effort of support will be greatly lessened. Registration will be equalized. e^1 is the beginning of the passaggio secondo for the baritone.

Fig. 68

In both the mezzo-soprano and baritone sensations of registration charts above, it is absolutely crucial that the column of breath support be centered directly under the tone (buzz of the voice) at all times. In the beginning, it is particularly difficult to maintain this vocal posture during the sensations of yawning and drinking the tone in the middle register; but this is one of the most important technical challenges to confront the singer and it must be met and conquered. If drinking the tone seems to make the tone shift the smallest degree, the top of the column of support must move with it, constantly tracking its slightest movement.

It may be helpful at this point to remind the reader that the column of breath support has two ends. The lower part is centered at the belt line and is supplemented by a downward movement toward the pubic bone when extra support is needed for louder and higher tones. The top part of the breath support column is felt at the nape of the neck. When the abdominal muscles at the belt line are flexed, the singer should feel an immediate reaction at the nape of the neck. The support at the top of the column should always be poised to "speak instantly." It feels as if the support column has two "platforms." One platform is at the belt line and the other is at the nape of the neck.

66 VOCAL DEVELOPMENT THROUGH ORGANIC IMAGERY

If the singer would stand ten dominoes in a straight row, spaced about one inch apart, and tip the front domino over into the adjacent domino, he would see a chain reaction, each domino falling in its turn by the previously falling one. However, there will be a slight time lag while each domino awaits its neighbor's fall.

If the singer eliminates the spaces between the ten dominoes by pushing them flush against one another, what happens when he tips the first domino? All ten respond instantly. The tenth domino moves at the same time and with the same amount of movement as the first domino. This is similar to the breath support column. There should never be any slack between the bottom and the top of the column.

I mentioned earlier that the singer should feel a tensing sensation at the nape of the neck. This tension is a muscular resistance to the top of the breath column. Although part of this tension originates at the glottis, it should be felt as far back from the glottis as possible. *Under no circumstances* should any of this tension migrate to or be sensed in the front of the neck, jaw, tongue, or lips. The latter four areas indicate negative and pernicious tension. The former is a positive and beneficial tension.

I have already discussed the sympathetic vibrations the singer feels in the cervical vertebrae (neck bone) during phonation. This is not, however, the sensation to which I now refer.

Although I have neither read nor heard about any accompanying physical sensations attributed to muscles which adduct (close) the vocal folds, it seems a reasonable deduction that the action of these muscles could account for the stretching sensation at the back of the neck.

The muscles which adduct the vocal folds are the *lateral cricoarytenoids*, the *transverse arytenoid*, and the *oblique arytenoids*. Of these three, the lateral cricoarytenoids' greater importance is their function in causing the vocal folds to be compressed medially (in the middle). The oblique arytenoids also help in this function, but to a lesser degree; but both pairs of muscles help approximate the vocal folds. The transverse arytenoid's only function is to adduct the vocal folds. These muscles, upon contraction, cause the vocal folds to adduct by rocking and/or rotating the arytenoid cartilages inwardly. The posterior ends of the vocal bands are brought into firm proximity. Only one set of muscles abducts (separates) the vocal folds— the *posterior cricoarytenoids*. This pair of muscles are direct antagonists of the lateral cricoarytenoids. See Figure 69 below.

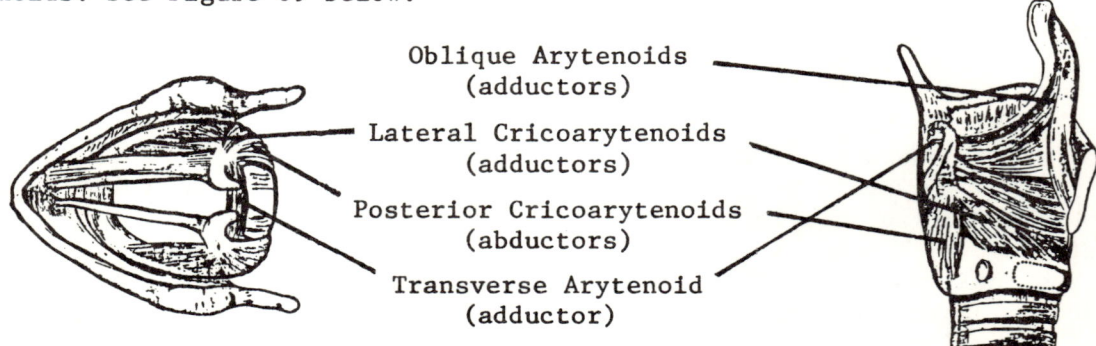

a. Interior (Seen from above)　　　　　　　　　　　　b. Side View

Muscles of the Larynx
Fig. 69

When a singer first learns to activate the sensation of maintaining closure of the glottis by feeling the grip at the nape of the neck, it will usually be more noticeable between d^2 and e^2 and at the *mf* to *f* dynamic level. However, he will soon notice that this same sensation occurs subtly while he lightens the mechanism in the upper middle register. Eventually, the singer will be able to maintain the grip throughout his entire range. It is this sensation, coupled with the upper platform of the breath support column, that is his vocal "thermostat." If he needs more intensity to withstand the increased breath pressure of a louder or higher tone, he grips more firmly. As less breath pressure is needed, the grip relaxes proportionally.

There are some who may feel that words like *tension*, *pressure*, and *grip* are too violent to be sanctioned for use by innocent young voice students. I hope it will prove sufficient in allaying those fears to say that, used in the context already described, none of the three words should result in a tight-sounding voice, reddening of the face, stiffening of joints, locking of the abdominal muscles, headaches, or a host of other problems frequently associated with those words. On the contrary, only the *correct* use of tensions will allow the singer to achieve vocal freedom! He must learn to use the muscles that are needed so he can relax those that are not.

A firm closure of the glottis at the posterior ends does not necessitate stiffening any other part of the vocal tract, although the other muscles of the larynx and throat require various degrees of tension to function as they should. Evidence of the independent action of the vocal fold adductors can be observed when a singer sings comfortably throughout a three-octave scale:

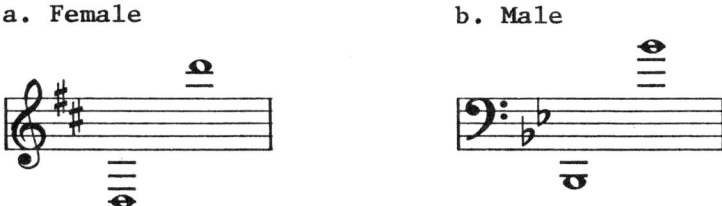

Fig. 70

This range demands activation of every register, including the Stroh register of both the male and female singer and the whistle register of the female singer. It also requires a solid closure of the glottis, throughout. That this closure can be felt throughout the three octaves, while the registration is adjusted as needed, should be adequate proof that proper adduction of the vocal folds need not interfere with the rest of the mechanism.

If, by this time, the reader has not experienced the sensation of the focal point at the nape of the neck, he might try an exercise I often use with my students: The goat (or sheep) bleat, "ma-a-a-a." Most students have already imitated this sound; so they have a reference point at which to begin. About three out of four students feel the action of the goat bleat in the front of their necks at first. I ask them to remember the sensation of the steel wire exercise and to relate the vibration of the bleat to the sensation of backward impingement. Eventually, after five or six attempts, most of my students feel a shift from the front to the back of the neck. The intermittent series of glottal strokes necessary to perform the bleat allows the student the opportunity of tracking each pulse while it moves backwards. It also has the advantage of conditioning a sense of relaxation between pulses. It is impossible to perform a good goat bleat with improper tension.

After each student senses the bleat at the nape of the neck, I ask him to firm up the beltline support so the bleat becomes a steady tone, rather than intermittent tones. When the singer firms the abdominal muscles, he usually feels the grip at the back of the neck become proportionally firmer. I am convinced that this gentle sensation at the glottal level is what Manual Garcia meant when referring to the "coup de glotte" (stroke of the glottis).

The unvoiced glottal click is yet another way of sensing where the top of the breath support column meets the resistor. The light, voiceless click is better than a voiced click, at first, to insure the student does not produce a glottal "bang." It is this harsh glottal explosion that has frightened many teachers and singers away from using, or even referring to, the glottal stroke at all, except in a derogatory way. This is unfortunate because the concept can be most useful when properly understood. William Vennard suggests this exercise is safer in the lower register and that the imaginary "h" should be favored in the upper register.[1] This is certainly good advice for *all* singers.

One other word of warning should be given here. The grip at the nape of the neck should be used only by singers whose voices have gone past the stage of puberty. Particularly young female singers who have a somewhat breathy tone production should avoid this technique if the glottal chink has not yet matured sufficiently to close normally. Developing a firmer grip for closing the vocal folds by an immature voice may force the muscles to do something for which they are not yet ready. This is one reason why many voice teachers will not work with students who are under eighteen years of age. This, too, is unfortunate, as many young singers of high school age benefit greatly from proper vocal instruction.

I will conclude this chapter with a discussion of some exercises which help synthesize the elements involving phonation and resonation. Without a doubt, the *messa di voce* is one of the most effective exercises for coordinating all registers. The literal meaning of this Italian term is "placing of the voice." Messa di voce should not be confused with another common Italian term, *mezza voce*, which means *half-voice*.

Messa di voce was used extensively during the 18th century Bel Canto era; but it has since been mis-used, abused, or ignored until comparatively recent times. It seems like a simple exercise. The singer sustains a long crescendo and diminuendo on a single pitch and vowel:

Fig. 71

---

[1] Vennard, William; *SINGING, THE MECHANISM AND THE TECHNIC*; Revised Edition, Greatly enlarged; Carl Fischer, Inc., 62 Cooper Square, New York 10003; 1967; §195, p. 48.

This exercise may be written to include several measures, if desired. In any case, the tone should be sustained for several seconds according to the individual singer's capacity. Although it *appears* to be an easy exercise, it is not. One must already know how to sing softly and loudly before he can hope to do the exercise efficiently.

As I explained earlier, a singer should not plunge immediately into soft singing because his voice will surely not be able to cope with the demands without resorting to undesirable compensatory devices. Only after he has developed both the light and heavy mechanisms of the voice to some functional degree, will he be able to coordinate them by using the messa di voce.

A perfect messa di voce is rare. Some singers do it beautifully within a limited range. Others do it passably well throughout most of their range. *Few* can execute it superbly in all parts of their voices.

Our first approach to the messa di voce, then, should be strictly as an exercise for helping our technical development. I suggest the following regimen for using the messa di voce:

a. Begin on the most easily produced pitch and vowel.
b. Begin on the softest *controllable* dynamic level. (This may only be *mp* or *mf* at first.
c. Crescendo *only* as much as possible without sacrificing tone quality or physical comfort. (Remember, you are only half way through the exercise at this point.)
d. Diminuendo to the softest possible dynamic level.
e. Repeat the exercise, entirely, striving on each repetition to maintain smooth, proportionate transition from the softest to the loudest and back to the softest tones.
f. Extend the duration of the exercise to controllable limits.
g. After security is established on this pitch and vowel, proceed one-half tone higher and/or lower. Then experiment with other vowels at the previously explored pitch levels.
h. Extend the range and vowel spectrum as far as possible, but *never* over-extend them.

(Master the easiest pitches and vowels before moving to the next in degree of difficulty.)

The above regimen cannot be done in one practice session. Depending upon the singer's aptitude for this sort of thing, excellent control may be expected in as short a time as six months. On the other extreme, excellent control may never be reached. But, even without achieving perfection, the exercise is a fine one.

The singer who has not practiced the messa di voce will usually find that it is more difficult to diminuendo than to crescendo. He may benefit from practicing the diminuendo separately from the crescendo until it is more secure. He must be *patient*.

The principal technical value of this exercise is its unique tendency to adjust the vocal mechanism indirectly, through tonal imagery, as the singer covers the entire compass of his vocal potential. Although the messa di voce is done on a single pitch, through its use the singer will learn to cope with every problem involved with registration, contrary to the opinion of many that registration has more to do with vocal range than with dynamics.

Variations of the messa di voce may be practiced to one's advantage as he progresses closer toward virtuosity. These variations include:

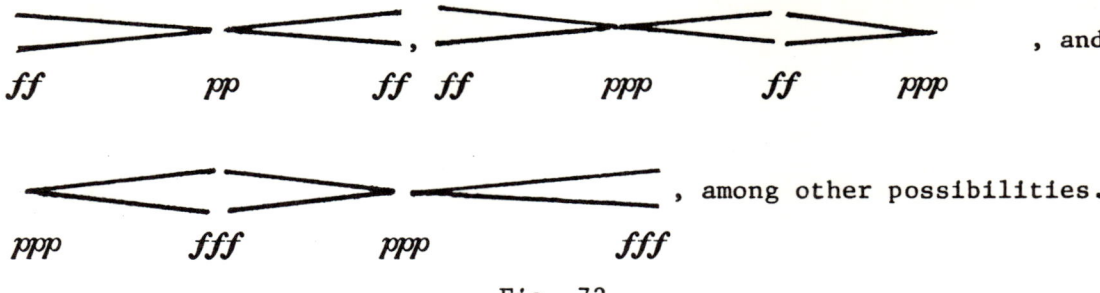

, among other possibilities.

Fig. 72

Perfection, or near perfection, of the messa di voce will contribute not only to the technical development of the singer; it will give him an artistic depth, when he uses it *sagaciously*, which is unrealized by most singers today. Indiscriminate and excessive use of the messa di voce in performance, however, will defeat its own artistic purpose and can make an audience "sea-sick" with aimless undulation.

During practice of this, or any other form of vocalization, the singer should become increasingly aware of a delicate, but firm, *pinching together* of the focal point:

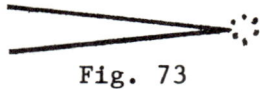

Fig. 73

Whereas the throat should feel big and open, the focal point should feel small and narrow. As long as the two sides of the image converge *at the tip*, the singer will be safe. *However*, he must avoid this:

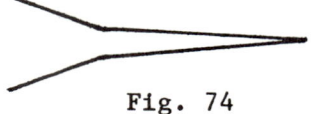

Fig. 74

This position will not allow the throat to stay open.

I often use the image of the back of my open throat as being a large motion picture screen; but, rather than have the focal point "fill up" the screen, it makes as small an image as possible on the giant screen:

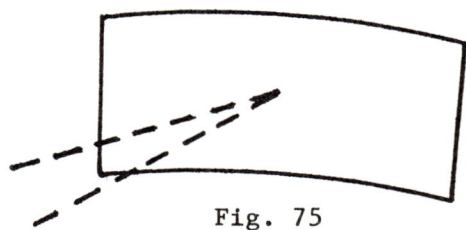

Fig. 75

The above image is particularly useful in helping the student see the relationship of an open throat and firmness at the nape of the neck. Another image is equally useful in showing the relationship of firm phonation and an "open body." The large circle represents the body as an expanded instrument. The tiny dot represents intensity of atomic energy proportions.

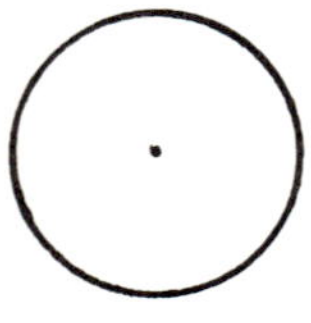

Fig. 76

The following drawing (Fig. 77) will show the events and sensations that occur as the singer traverses all registers on the [ɑ] vowel.

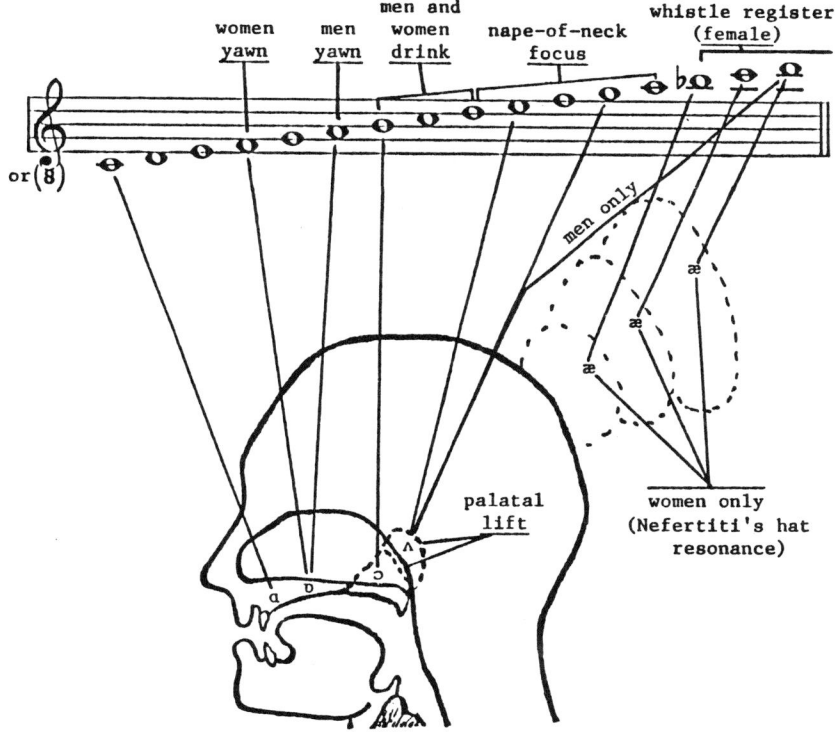

Fig. 77

I use two exercises, extensively, in coordinating phonation and resonation for balanced registration, utilizing the above system:

(All five vowels are sung on one breath. The exercise is transposed a semi-tone higher until the top of the range is reached.)

Fig. 78

(A breath is taken after each vowel. The exercise is transposed a semi-tone high- until the top of the range is reached.)

Fig. 79

I should, once more, remind the reader that the points at which the the registration events and sensations in Fig. 77 appear are subject to slight variations from singer to singer. It should also be noted that the dynamic range for the two exercises (Figs. 78 and 79) is between *mf* and *f*. Taken at louder or softer dynamic levels will necessitate even further variations by a tone or semi-tone.

Because of the complexity of illustrating Fig. 77, I omitted the vowels, [i], [e], [o], and [u]. The migratory paths of all five of the cardinal vowels on their proper scale degrees, can be seen in Fig. 66, page 64.

It should be noted, further, that the [ɒ] vowel between [ɑ] and [ɔ] indicates the tendency of a given vowel to be in a constant state of migration. If there were an IPA symbol for every possible sound, there would be a different symbol for each and every pitch. This could become tedious! The IPA was established for speech, not for singing. It is much easier to *feel* the subtle variations of a given vowel spelled with a single symbol than to *hear* it. That is why singers practice so many hours. Nevertheless, the IPA is a fantastic aid even with its limitations. We shall discuss it in much greater detail in the next chapter.

CHAPTER VI
ARTICULATION

One phonetic definition of articulation is *"The adjustments and movements of speech organs involved in pronouncing a particular sound, taken as a whole."* (Random House American Dictionary)

This definition seems as good as most for a starting point.

A. The Articulators

The Organs for Articulation

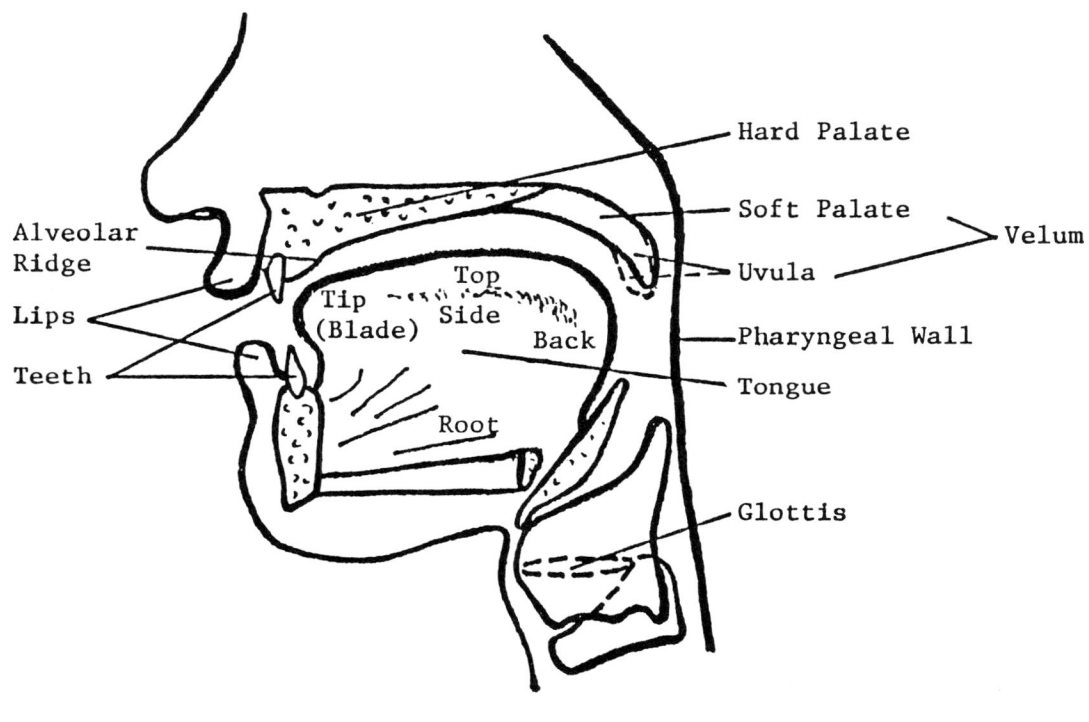

Fig. 80

1. The Tongue

There seems to be no end to the tongue's versatility. Just as it is the most important organ for articulating the vowels, it is also the most useful for articulating the consonants. At one time or another during articulation, the tongue comes into direct contact with every other articulator except the lips and the glottis. If the alphabet required it, the tongue is also perfectly capable of contacting the lips as well.

The principal parts of the tongue are:

    a. The Blade (Tip)*
    b. The Top
    c. The Back
    d. The Sides

*Some authorities designate the blade as the sides of the tongue, just before the tip.

The tip of the tongue contacts the upper teeth (Lingua-dental), as in [θ], [ð], and European pronunciations of the [t], [d], [n], and [l].

The tip also contacts the alveolar ridge (Lingua-alveolar), as in the English [t], [d], [n], [l], [ɲ], [s], and [z].

The top of the tongue and/or the sides, contact the hard palate (Lingua-palatal), as in [ʃ], [ʒ], [r], [ɚ], [ɝ], [j], [ʎ], and [ç].

The back of the tongue contacts the velum (Lingua-velar), as in [k], [g], [ŋ], [x], and [ɣ].

2. The Lips

The lips can contact each other (Bi-labial), as in [p], [b], [m], and [w].

The lower lip contacts the front upper teeth (Labio-dental), as in [f] and [v].

3. The Teeth

The teeth are stationary, except for lower jaw movement; and they depend upon the tongue and lips to complete the required action involving them.

4. The Hard Palate

The hard palate is even more stationary than the teeth and has only the tongue to complete its function in articulation. It might be argued that the upper side teeth assist the function of the hard palate and tongue on such lingua-palatal consonants as [ʃ] and [j], as the tongue's sides do actually make contact with the teeth on both sides of the mouth. Perhaps a better designation than "lingua-palatal" would be "lingua-palatal-dental."

5. The Alveolar Ridge

Actually, the alveolar ridge is a part of the hard palate. Its separate identification is useful for designating, more specifically, that portion of the hard palate which elicits the lingua-alveolar consonants.

6. The Velum

The velum (or soft palate) is the term for that section of the palate which has no bone structure, as does the hard palate. Having no bone, it is flexible.

The end of the velum— the part that hangs down in the back of the throat— is called the uvula.

It is the velum which makes the distinction between the nasal sounds and all the other sounds of the phonetic spectrum possible. When it is flexed, which stretches it backward where it contacts the pharyngeal wall, the velum closes off the nasal port, making nasality impossible. This backward stretch is what is known as "palatal lift," or "raised palate." When the velum is relaxed and lowered (or brought forward), nasality is unavoidable. (See Fig. 41, p. 39)

7. The Pharyngeal Wall

The only function of the pharyngeal wall in articulation is to form a back boundary of the throat, against which the velum can press to close off the nasal port.

8. The Glottis

The glottis is the *hole*, or *slit*, between the vocal folds. It is, principally, an organ for phonation. There are two consonants which depend entirely upon the glottis for their production. They are the [h] and [?]. Actually, [?] is not generally classified as a consonant, but as a diacritical mark; but, for this text, we shall classify it as a consonant, as its production requires the movement of a definite organ of the speech apparatus for clarifying or identifying specific sounds.

In addition to the two consonants above, all other voiced consonants depend upon the services of the glottis, of course. (See B.1. a and b, below, for information on voiced consonants.)

B. Classification of Consonants

There is a venerable adage in the vocal music world: "Sing the vowels and speak the consonants."

What we have discussed in previous chapters has concerned the vowel, primarily. We have studied *singing* more than *speaking*.

Although articulation involves vowels as well as consonants, when we think of articulation, we associate the term more with consonants. The probable reason for this is that consonants are more troublesome than vowels, once a singer has learned to phonate properly. For most practical purposes, the vowel *is the voice* and the consonant *is the interrupter of the voice*. In other words, consonants are deliberate obstacles thrown in the path of a free-flowing voice.

This is not to denigrate the function of the consonant. We need consonants. It is the skillful use of the consonant that gives meaning to the vowel, enabling the singer to accomplish his ultimate singing objective: *communication*.

1. Basic Classification of Consonants

There are two basic types of consonants:
   a. Voiceless
   b. Voiced

For many voiceless consonants, there are corresponding voiced consonants— that is, consonants which are formed, in every way, the same as the voiceless consonants, with one exception. The only difference between the two types is that the vocal folds do not vibrate for the voiceless consonants, but they do vibrate for the voiced consonants.

As an example, let us take the [s] and [z].

The [s] is voiceless, but the [z] is not. Both consonants are lingua-alveolar; that is, they are formed when the tongue makes contact with the alveolar ridge and allows a small opening at the very front tip of the tongue through which the air and sound go. Both consonants are formed in exactly the same place, but the vocal folds do not vibrate for the [s] and they do vibrate for the [z].

An easy experiment will confirm this.

Place the thumb and forefinger on each side of the larynx. Then speak a sustained [s] and, without stopping the breath stream, change to the [z]. No laryngeal vibration will be felt on the [s], but it will be strong on the [z].

The phonetic alphabet (as given in Appendix II) lists the voiceless consonants first, each being followed immediately by its corresponding voiced consonant.

2. Discriptive Classification of Consonants

Phoneticians categorize consonants, further, into four general groups, descriptive of the manner in which they are formed and by their resultant physical characteristics. These groups are:

  a. Plosives
  b. Fricatives
  c. Nasals
  d. Glides
  e. Trills

a. Plosives

Plosives are so called because their formation involves the explosion of breath through various combinations of articulatory organs. The plosive consonants are [p] and [b], [t] and [d], [k] and [g], and [ʔ].

b. Fricatives

Fricatives are so called because their formation involves a friction-like sound. The fricative consonants are [f] and [v], [θ] and [ð], [s] and [z], [ʃ] and [ʒ], [h], [ç], [x], and [ɣ].

A sub-category is often used by phoneticians, called *Affricatives*. These include the consonant couplings [tʃ] and [dʒ], [ʃt] and [ʒd], and [ks] and [gs]. Each one of these is a combination of a plosive and a fricative. Since it is possible to separate each of the couple into its individual category, this sub-category seems redundant and will not be discussed further as a separate entity.

c. Nasals

Nasal consonants are so called because their formation involves sounds which come through the nasal port, totally. (Nasal vowels come through both the nasal port and the mouth, simultaneously, as has been discussed previously.) The nasal consonants are [m], [n], [ŋ], and [ɲ].

d. Glides

Glides are so called because the tongue and/or lips make a gliding motion during the production of a sound. The glides are [w], [j], [l], [r] (English), [ə], and [ɚ].

e. Trills

I have added this category to the four above in order to accomodate those consonants which "flutter," either by use of the tongue or by the uvula. They include the [r] (European, rolled), [ɾ] (singly flapped), and [ř] (uvular, also spelled [ʀ]).

C. Coordination of Phonation, Resonation, and Articulation

Now that we have covered the anatomy and the geography of consonants, we are ready to coordinate them with the other aspects of singing.

We have mentioned that the vowel is the voice and that the consonant is the interrupter of the voice.

There is one class of sound which is neither a vowel nor a consonant, but a combination of the two, or *semi-vowel* (sometimes referred to as *semi-consonant*). To avoid semantical hairsplitting, these sounds are classified as consonants, although each has a definite vowel quality. They include the [ɹ] or [r] (American burr) and the three nasal consonants mentioned above. All the glide consonants fit into the semi-vowel class, as well.

When the breath stream is stopped, made more narrow, or diverted by the articulating organs, the sound is classified as a consonant; and the vowel it might have been is lost because of lessened efficiency of projection.

What has all this to do with coordinating phonation, resonation, and articulation?

EVERYTHING!

The singer must learn to articulate the consonants in such a manner that they never (1) stop, (2) narrow, or (3) divert the breath stream *needlessly*.

A consonant should never require more effort of production than is necessary for its identification in a word, except for rare special effects.

How does one accomplish this?

First, he must learn to use the organs of articulation fluently. Fluent articulation means flexible and effortless articulation. The singer should be able to trill an [r] without stiffening the back of the tongue or the jaw. He should be able to flip the tongue for a [t] or an [l] quickly and deftly, without changing the quality of the following vowel. He should be able to use his lips for [p] and [b] independently of all the other articulators.

In other words, he should use *only* those organs required to do the task, and he should waste no effort in doing so. His technique of articulation should be as strongly developed as his technique for phonation.

Secondly, the singer must realize that the vowel is *supreme* in singing. He must maintain his vowel position as constantly as he possibly can while singing consonants. He should develop a feeling of duality between the vowel and the consonant.

78 VOCAL DEVELOPMENT THROUGH ORGANIC IMAGERY

If a consonant ends a word, the preceding vowel should not be altered in anticipation of the consonant.

For example, in the words "fall on" [fɔl ɔn], the vowel should not wander, thusly: [fɔʌl ɔun], as so frequently happens.

If a vowel (or diphthong) succeeds a consonant, as for example, in the word "pray" [preɪ], the singer will help himself immeasurably by mentally and physically setting the position for the [e] *before* he prepares for the [pr]. If he is not used to doing this, he will be quite surprised at how different the sensation of singing the [pr] will feel than it does in his customary method. This should be a pleasant surprise because he will sense two immediate advantages:

1. Fewer muscles will be necessary for forming the [pr], making the process easier.

2. Anticipating the vowel [e] *before* the preceding consonants makes phonation more efficient.

Most of my students find it helpful to practice phonating a vowel which succeeds a consonant *before* the consonant, giving the "pre-vowel" a gentle glottal caress. Then I ask them to put the vowel closer and closer to the consonant until the two are pronounced simultaneously. With this sort of attack, the voice speaks immediately and efficiently. This works especially well for voiced consonants, which should have the previous vowels "built in" at the time they are sounded. A bit more practice is necessary to coordinate voiceless consonants with the pre-vowel sensation. Obviously, if the vowel is sounded with the voiceless consonant, it will no longer be a voiceless consonant; but the vowel should be as close to the consonant as possible for maximum efficiency.

A feeling of ventriloquization helps in coordinating the proper balance between vowel and consonant. The singer might think "Homogenize the vowels and Ventriloquize the consonants" to good advantage, as these thoughts tend to calm excessive movement of the articulators and the phonators. (See pp. 85-88, The Snerd Synthesizer, for more about this phenomenon.)

Many beginning singers utilize what I call the "wurst syndrome" of articulation. Instead of keeping the vowels open *before* their preceding consonants are activated, they open and close them in anticipation of both the attack and release of the surrounding consonants.

Take the words, "*see me go*" as an example:

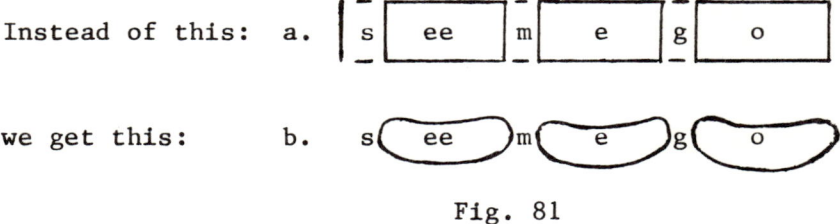

Fig. 81

The visual representation of Fig. 81b resembles link sausages; thus, the wurst syndrome. I shall avoid the obvious pun.

As I mentioned earlier, Fig. 81a will allow for much greater ease and efficiency in articulating the vowels *and* the consonants.

One other problem occurs rather consistently with many of my students. They exhibit two kinds of limitation in coordination. The first is the inability to drop the jaw while raising the tongue. This is particularly noticeable when they sing the [i] on a high or loud tone. In this instance, the [i] migrates to the [ɪ] and to [y], but the [i] should still be recognizable to the audience as an [i]. If the singer has not developed the ability to stretch the tongue farther toward the front while his jaw drops, he will usually lose too much identity of the [i] vowel (and probably the mask resonance). I suggest to my students that they practice dropping the jaw while stretching the tongue forward without singing, at first. This allows them to activate unused muscles without jeopardizing their voices.

The second weakness is the inability to close their lips while keeping the jaw dropped. Again, such a position seems foreign to them. The tendency, when the jaw drops, is to open the lips. Again, I have them practice closing the lips while dropping the jaw while they imagine singing the [u], [ʊ], [o], [ɔ], [y], [ʏ], [ø], and [œ]. After a short time, the students become accustomed to stretching the tongue and lips and can then incorporate the action in their regular technique, when appropriate.

As this is not a text on Singer's Diction, we shall not try to cover all the possible combinations of vowels and consonants in various words. All that is necessary at this point is to be aware of the broad, general principles which govern the efficient transition from word to word.

If the reader is sufficiently motivated to pursue the subject of Diction more thoroughly, as well he should be, the following texts are just a few of the excellent ones available.

THE SINGER'S MANUAL OF ENGLISH DICTION, by Madeleine Marshall; 1953
SINGER'S ITALIAN, by Evelina Colorni; 1970
SINGING IN FRENCH, by Thomas Grubb; 1979
GERMAN FOR SINGERS, by William Odom; 1981
THE SINGER'S MANUAL OF GERMAN AND FRENCH DICTION, by Richard G. Cox; 1970
THE SINGER'S MANUAL OF LATIN DICTION AND PHONETICS, by Robert S. Hines; 1970

*All these books are published by Schirmer Books, 866 Third Avenue, New York, N.Y. 10022.

TO SING IN ENGLISH, by Dorothy Uris; Boosey and Hawkes; 1971
ITALIAN DICTION FOR SINGERS, by Ralph Errolle; Pruett Press; Boulder, Colorado; 1963
A MANUAL OF FOREIGN LANGUAGE DICTIONS FOR SINGERS, by Richard F. Sheil; Tri-County Publications; Arcade, New York; 1975; Revised 1979 [Contains diction instruction for Latin, Italian, German, French, and Spanish]
ITALIAN, LATIN, FRENCH AND GERMAN, THE SOUNDS AND 81 EXERCISES FOR SINGING THEM, by John Moriarity; E.C. Schirmer; Boston; 1975
THE ART OF COACHING AND ACCOMPANYING, by Kurt Adler; Reprinted by Da Capo Press; New York; 1976 [Chapters 4-8 include Phonetics and Diction, Italian, French, Spanish, and German Phonetics and Diction]
PHONETIC READINGS OF SONGS AND ARIAS, by Berton Coffin, Pierre Delattre, Ralph Errolle, and Werner Singer; Pruett Press; Boulder, Colorado; 1964
OVERTONES OF BEL CANTO; THE PHONETIC BASIS OF ARTISTIC SINGING; by Berton Coffin; Scarecrow Press; Metuchen, New Jersey; 1981

CHAPTER VII
COLORATION

After a singer has achieved a modicum of proficiency in the basic areas of Respiration, Phonation, Resonation, and Articulation, he is ready to examine Coloration, or vocal *timbre*.

In French, *timbre* means *small bell*. In music it is synonymous with *tone quality*. In German, the word is *Klangfarbe*, or *tone color*. All these terms may be defined as *the quality or tone identity of a musical sound, as determined by the number and character of its overtones*. (More about overtones later in this chapter)

The number and character of these overtones are determined by the size, shape, density, length, and tension of the vocal folds and the size, shape, and texture of their corresponding resonators, *plus* the degree of intensity of the tone.

Even if no other factors than these were involved in determining a tone's timbre, one can readily see it can be a complicated subject— a subject that encompasses many areas of voice production.

Mathilde Marchesi distinguishes *quality* and *color* of sound as two different entities.[1] This is certainly an important distinction, of which the singer must be aware. Any tone quality has a specific color, and vice-versa. The quality is inherent in the individual's physical make-up. It is advised that the singer *not tamper with that part of his tone, directly*. Developing a fine technique through freeing the voice should allow the tone quality to flourish. Tone color is super-imposed over the singer's basic quality. Singers can and should experiment with this. However, they must learn to make this superimposition without jeopardizing the security of the *correct basic quality*.

Fortunate is the singer whose dramatic insight allows the proper color to come into his voice in a natural and spontaneous way. Some singers, for a variety of reasons, lack variety in their tonal expression. They seem to have one basic sound which has to serve them for a wide range of emotional occasions, whether or not that sound is appropriate at a given moment. This kind of singer is *monochromatic*. Three principal circumstances contribute most frequently to this inartistic state:

    a. Lack of dramatic training or experience
    b. Limited dramatic temperament
    c. Limited technical means for achieving timbral variety

Although a and b (dramatic ability) are desirable and necessary prerequisites for successful vocal performance and must eventually be incorporated, they do not belong in the purview of this chapter. We shall focus our attention on the technical aspects for achieving vocal coloration. c, above, is appropriate for this chapter.

In order to discuss tone color in a practical way, it will be necessary to review, from time to time, some of the technical ideas discussed in previous chapters. Upon these foundations, I hope to help the reader expand his concepts in terms of molding technical knowledge into useful

---

[1] Marchesi, Mathilde; *BEL CANTO: A THEORETICAL & PRACTICAL VOCAL METHOD*; Dover Publications, Inc.; New York; 1970; p. xvii.

coloration devices that can eventually be applied to Interpretation.

In order for certain terms in this chapter to make sense to those readers who have not had courses in acoustics, we must examine a few basic acoustical laws. I will keep this section as simple and brief as possible.

Musical tone, or vibration, occurs when a string or a column of air within a pipe or cavity is set into motion. The simplest example of this vibration can be illustrated by superimposing a curved line over a straight line:

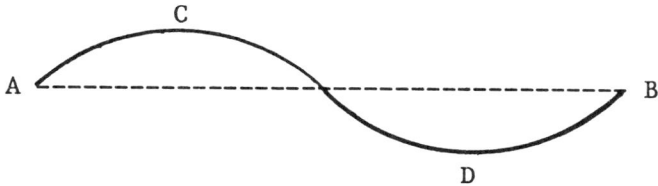

Fundamental Tone
Fig. 82

In Fig. 82, A to B represents the given pitch of a tone. The arcs, C and D, represent one complete cycle of that pitch. It would take 440 such cycles per second (cps, or more recently referred to as Hertz, abbreviated, Hz.) in order to produce the A above middle C. Also, in Fig. 82, C represents *compression* (tension) of the tone and D represents *rarifaction* (lessening of tension). In relation to the movement of the vocal folds, compression is the breath pressure that builds up immediately before exploding through the closed folds and rarifaction is the action of relaxation after the folds are pushed open.

Next, we must examine the phenomenon known as the *overtone series*.

Natural Scale	Overtone Series	Frequency
	etc.	etc.
	↑	↑
	5th Overtone	392 Hz
	4th Overtone	327 Hz
	3rd Overtone	262 Hz
	2nd Overtone	196 Hz
	1st Overtone	130 Hz
	Fundamental	65 Hz (approx.)

Fig. 83

Fig. 83 shows all the sounds inherent in the lowest tone, C (two octaves below middle C), which is the *fundamental* tone, or the actual pitch the listener hears. The ear hears all the pitches above the fundamental but has been trained to recognize only the dominant, or fundamental tone. Singers learn to *enhance* the fundamental by damping the less desirable tones— particularly those that would produce dissonance, if amplified— by intensification of the fundamental or certain of its overtones.

The overtone series of Fig. 83 represents the *natural* scale, sometimes called the "chord of nature." Fig. 84, below, shows the tempered, or equalized, scale.

82 VOCAL DEVELOPMENT THROUGH ORGANIC IMAGERY

Tempered Scale	Partial Series	Frequency
	etc. ↑	etc. ↑
	6th Partial	392 Hz
	5th Partial	330 Hz
	4th Partial	262 Hz
	3rd Partial	196 Hz
	2nd Partial	131 Hz
	Fundamental	65 Hz (approx.)

Fig. 84

In the natural scale, the intervals are not equal, or separated exactly proportionally. When we hear string players perform the natural scale, it sounds out of tune to most of us. This is because modern ears are used to the fruits of J.S. Bach's (et al) efforts, exemplified in his *WELL-TEMPERED HARPSICHORD*. In the tempered scale, each tone is numerically equal, based on the following ratio, using the C major scale as a model.[1]

$$c \quad d \quad e \quad f \quad g \quad a \quad b \quad c$$
$$1 \quad 9/8 \quad 5/4 \quad 4/3 \quad 3/2 \quad 5/3 \quad 15/8 \quad 2$$

Fig. 85

The reader should note that the C one octave above the fundamental is labeled the "1st Overtone" in the natural scale, but it is labeled the "2nd Partial" in the tempered scale. (Figs. 83 and 84)

Now, let us add only one overtone to the fundamental configuration in Fig. 82.

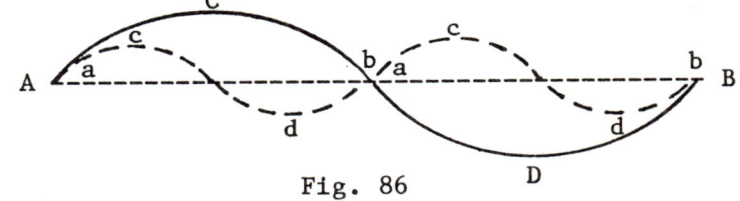

Fig. 86

The broken line (a, b, c, and d) represents only the first partial added to the fundamental (A, B, C, and D). It is easy to see what would happen if the second, third, or more partials were added. The tone becomes increasingly complex. The nature of this complexity determines the varieties of vocal color. The singer's ability to select which overtones to emphasize or to minimize determines his coloring potential, as well as his efficiency of resonation. From now on we shall refer to these overtones as *partials*.

The reader should also keep in mind that the resonators have pitch, as well as the vocal cords. In order to maintain vocal health and technical proficiency, the singer must learn how to couple these separate pitch producing organs in total harmony. The various combinations of the partials formed by laryngeal and mouth resonance frequencies are called *formants*. One such formant which vibrates at about 2800 cps is known as the "singer's formant" because its presence evokes a desirable ring or ping in the tone, no matter what the vowel or fundamental frequency may be.

---

[1] Apel, Willi; *HARVARD DICTIONARY OF MUSIC*; Harvard University Press; Cambridge, Massachusetts; 1944 (eleventh printing 1958); p. 13.

Different instruments favor certain partials more than others. With the flute, for example, the first partial is stronger than the fundamental; and the other partials are extremely weak, contributing to the "purity" of the flute's tone. With the oboe, the fourth and fifth partials are strong, the fifth being the strongest. With the French horn the strongest partials come in graduated sequence, the fundamental being the strongest, the first partial is next in strength, etc.

The human voice is the most versatile of all the instruments in terms of color because of its ability to adjust the partials while sustaining a tone by changing the ratio of frequencies of the vibrator (larynx) and resonators (pharynx and mouth) through the movement of the tongue and jaw and by changing the thickness, length, and tension of the vocal cords. *By favoring certain partials over others on a given vowel sound, the singer is able to demonstrate various vocal colors.* Vowel migration is extremely important in this respect. By changing the intensity of the tone, even more color can be added.

Now let us return to the "monochromatic" singer. We find this condition most frequently in the younger singers who have not yet found their voices, except on the most basic level. These are the singers whose larynges rise with pitch, who switch to falsetto tones in the upper middle register (for their protection) and whose general vocal profile suggests timidity.

The teacher must guide such students in becoming more healthily aggressive! Healthily, by keeping them open and, aggressive, by inducing them to trust new found vocal truths; In a sense, the teacher should convince them to throw a bit more caution to the wind— within the confines of common sense.

Florette Blank, a private voice teacher in New York City, says "I occasionally tell shy students to feel like King Kong, to feel their feet on the ground, to develop a sense of their whole body..."[1]

I refer to this image of King Kong quite frequently and ask my students to feel the transformation from *Cheeta*, the chimpanzee, to King Kong, on a sustained tone. Some timid singers rise to the occasion immediately. Not only can you see them grow physically, but you can hear equal growth of strength and confidence in their sound.

If the student is observant he will notice different vocal colors appearing during the transformation from Cheeta to King Kong. At this point, I suggest that he file them away for future reference.

In 1956 a recording was produced in England containing Alfred Wolfsohn's experiments in extension of human vocal range. I mentioned this recording earlier on pp. 63-64 in reference to the whistle register in the male voice. One of Mr. Wolfsohn's more usable exercises was related to tone color, rather than to range extension. I have modified the exercise for use in my studio and find it most beneficial in helping my students conceptualize the idea of timbre.

---

[1] Gollobin, Laurie Brooks and White, Harvey; "Voice Teachers On Voice, Part 2;" *MUSIC EDUCATORS JOURNAL*, Vol. 64, No. 6; February 1978; p. 50.

Fig. 87

Singing on one tone at the mezzo-forte dynamic level, the student is asked to imitate the qualities of the violin, viola, and cello. They are instructed not to increase the amplitude of the tone, consciously, as their instruments grow larger. Therefore, pitch and dynamics are stabilized, with the only remaining variable being timbre. This forces their imaginations into action. After a few attempts, it is easy to have the students recall the sensations of growth they felt from Cheeta to King Kong. They will also observe that the amplitude increases from the smaller to the larger instruments in spite of their efforts not to change.

The exercise also helps the student see the relationship of light to darker resonation and the connection of a younger to older (more mature) sound. Already, they have established a number of vocal colors in various degrees which they can use in interpretation. A young girl is more like a violin. An older, more authoritative character would be the cello, etc.

One of the most frequently used examples of vocal color is the Italian concept of *chiaro-oscuro (chiaro = light; oscuro = dark)*. One of my coaches at the International Opera Studio in Zurich had an interesting image for this: — = *chiaro* and | = *oscuro*. He placed these images behind the lips, thusly:

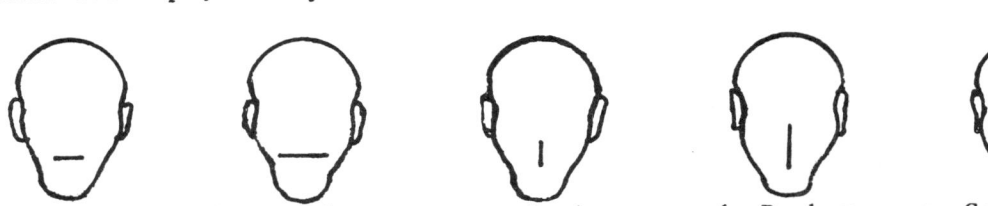

a. Bright   b. Brighter   c. Dark   d. Darker   e. Composite

Fig. 88

In other words, the length of the horizontal line determines the degree of brightness of the tone, the shorter line being less bright than the longer. Likewise, the shorter vertical line represents a tone that is less dark than the longer vertical line. These simple lines conform to the direction of movement of the mouth and jaw. For example, the bright forward [i] is produced with the lips in a more spread position in the lower range. As it migrates to the more open [ɪ] position in the upper range, it becomes less wide, more vertical, and darker. In a similar manner, the closed, rounded lip position of the [u] becomes more oval and elongated as the vowel migrates to [ʊ]. This is normal vocal technique.

Suppose the singer wants to get an unusually dark sound (*cupo*) for a special emotional effect, such as grief. He could do this by dropping the jaw, vertically, more than would ordinarily be required. For the opposite color, such as frivolity, the jaw position would be more closed (although not in every case).

Now we come to my favorite device for opening up timid singers and closed throats. I refer to it as the Snerd Synthesizer. In the first edition of this book, the Snerd Synthesizer was relegated to the appendix, possibly because I might have been intimidated by the apparent silliness of the idea. But, with each year, I have seen the concept loom into such prominance that I decided to bite the bullet and go out on a limb.

In the late 1930's, when I was in elementary school, one of my greatest joys was listening to Edgar Bergen and his companion, Charlie McCarthy, on the radio every Sunday evening. Mr. Bergen was a ventriloquist and Charlie was his dummy.

Charlie had a country cousin, another dummy, who was named Mortimer Snerd. Mortimer was far less sophisticated than Charlie, which might be another way of saying he was more natural. Just *how* natural did not occur to me until about three decades later when I began to identify with my memory of what Mortimer sounded like as I sang.

We have discussed vowel migration and ventriloquizing throughout this text. As I progressed more and more in these areas, I began to feel as if a familiar character were invading my vocal apparatus. It finally occurred to me: If I stopped singing and merely spoke while maintaining the same *vocal* posture I had used in singing, I sounded very much like Mortimer Snerd!

It is unfortunate that Mr. Bergen is no longer with us. This generation has missed a fine artist. A few of my students have had the opportunity of seeing him in television replays of movies made in the 30's and 40's. Some saw him occasionally on television talk shows before his death; but most of my students have not had the opportunity of this experience.

For this reason, I do my best to imitate Mortimer's voice for my students so they too may experience this insight into vocal wisdom. When this sound is produced, most of the concepts of good vocalization are automatically realized: The jaw is loosened; the larynx lowers (but not too low); the palate rises; the throat opens; the mask resonator is activated; contact with the breath support mechanism is facilitated, and all during the act of articulation. For these reasons, I call this empathy with Mortimer Snerd's voice the *Snerd Synthesizer*.

This concept may not be for everyone, so to be forewarned is to be forearmed.

Not long ago, when a colleague of mine suggested that Snerdian Synthesis would probably not displace current pedagogies, I had the presence of mind to reply, "Mortimer did not come to destroy the word, but to fulfill the word."

Seriously, the idea is not intended as a new "vocal method." It is only another supplemental tool, among those already discussed, which has proved, in my experience, to be most effective in generating positive results in young (and sometimes, old) singers.

Those who have heard Mortimer's dulcet tones will more easily identify with the phenomenon. For the uninitiated, the snerdian sound could be described as "woofy" and relaxed, relying heavily on a comfortable back-breath support. A demonstration would, of course, be much more effective than any written description of a particular kind of sound. In the absence of a first-hand demonstration, or even a recording or tape, the written word must suffice. If the term "woofy" does not convey enough information, perhaps "yawny speech" may help. If neither of these suggestions elicits the proper idea, the reader may wish to ask a number of acquaintances who were avid radio fans during the late 30's, the 40's, and the early 50's to give an imitation of Mortimer's voice. Also, tape cassettes of some of Edgar Bergen's early radio broadcasts are occasionally advertised for sale.

All good things can be done to excess. This is true with imitating the Snerd voice. It has been my experience, however, that most beginning students are not able to do it to excess. Instead of sounding like Mortimer when they sing, their voices invariably improve— especially in the higher range when the darkening required by the migrating vowels is so important.

There are different degrees of snerdness to the snerdian sound, ranging from *barely Snerd* to *extremely Snerd*. The former sound has hardly a trace of woofiness, whereas the latter is extremely woofy. Organic imagery can be used to activate a concept of progressiveness and continuity in developing the range of physical flux necessary to achieve effective snerdian synthesis via the *Snerdometer*. I like to think of this instrument as my little contribution to vocal science.

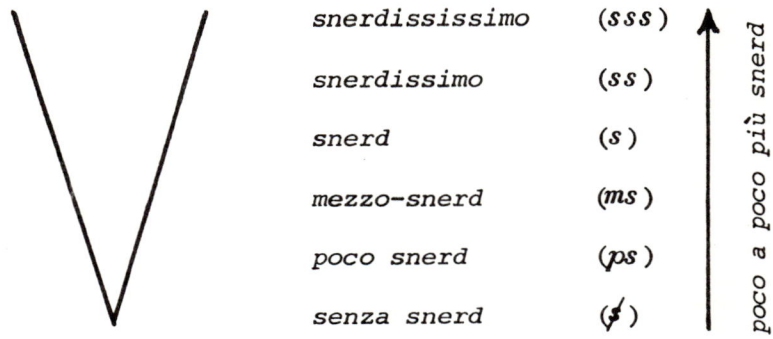

The Snerdometer

Fig. 89

The bottom of the image in Fig. 89 represents absolutely no woofiness. As the image widens toward its top, the tone grows increasingly woofy. An effective preliminary exercise, pursuant to actually singing, is to speak the vowel, [ɑ], beginning without a trace of woofiness (as in normal speech) and allowing the spoken tone to grow slowly, gradually, and inexorably more woofy, until maximum woofiness (*snerdississimo*) is reached.

Students should concentrate on maintaining a definite [ɑ] throughout the snerdian crescendo. They will, however, *not* be able to maintain the [ɑ], which will migrate to a muddy, woofy [ʌ]; but they should *think* the [ɑ] throughout the exercise.

After a student gets the "feel" of the snerdian crescendo, I ask him to say something in Snerd, such as, "Hello there, Mr. Bergen! Huh, huh, huh. How are you today?" On a scale of one to ten, I usually get a first response of about three or four. After I point this out to the student, he usually responds with a five or six. If I bully him enough, I can get him to a nine or ten in a few more attempts. Extroverts respond more quickly to this activity than introverts.

Timid singers often have difficulty going beyond mezzo-snerd in the beginning. Their egos are on the line, and they are reluctant to make fools of themselves. This exercise certainly has the capacity to make one feel foolish. It is then left to the teacher's ingenuity to help the student overcome that obstacle.

Some singers, who may or may not be timid, will lack either the imagination or the physical coordination to achieve snerdississimo. They must be handled gently at first. Gradually, with more and more success, they will grow magnificently.

After the student can produce a reasonably effective snerdian crescendo on the spoken tone, the physical sensations and changes involved should be exposed and analyzed. The singer will note that as the woofiness increases, the back-breath mechanism expands. Accompanying this back expansion will be a corresponding growth in pharyngeal resonation space, affected by the, now, unconsciously dropped jaw and stretched velum. It is one of the marvels of vocal pedagogy that proper breathing *does* motivate unconscious expansion of the resonators.

Now, having developed and applied the concept of crescendoing snerdism, the student must be told a startling revelation: In singing, the audience must *never* hear the woofiness! We see a parallel here with vowel migration. As the singer migrates the vowel, the vowel must sound the same to the audience. This parallelism is the very crux of the problem in converting the intellectualized vowel migration into the purely physical *body migration*.

When applying the Snerdometer to singing, it should be placed, approximately, in the following positions on the staff:

a. Contralto   b. Mezzo-Soprano   c. Soprano

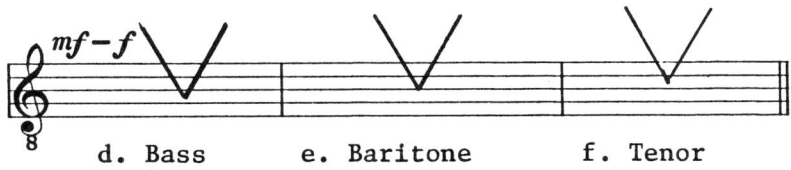

d. Bass   e. Baritone   f. Tenor

Fig. 90

The Snerdometer should be adjusted one-half tone higher for forte singing and one-half tone lower for mezzo piano and softer singing. Each singer should experiment in finding the best position for his individual voice.

Two extremes should be avoided by the singer in performing this exercise:

    (1) Too much snerdness
    (2) Too little snerdness

(1) Too much snerdness usually occurs when the singer makes the body-migrational adjustments too early for a given pitch (ascending). More patience is required for a smooth, seamless transition. This is easier to adjust than the second extreme.

(2) Not enough snerdness can result from timidity, embarrassment, weak physical coordination, weak concept, and/or, in some cases, obstinacy.

The old saying of actors about hammy acting is applicable here: "You can always slice a ham." It is easier to calm a temperament than it is to generate one, especially where none seems to exist. Of all the factors a student must consider in deciding whether or not to pursue a professional singing career, this should probably be highest on the list because one of the strongest ingredients in temperament is *imagination*, without which any would-be artist might as well call the whole thing off.

If, after several attempts, the student lacks either the desire or the imagination for achieving a good, solid snerdissimo in the upper range, the teacher should try another approach, as only frustration can result. If, on the other hand, the student indicates an affinity for the Snerdometer, both teacher and student should continue.

Snerdian synthesis works unusually well in group situations such as voice classes and choral rehearsals because of the enthusiasm one can generate in group dynamics. As an example, one of the first times I used it in a voice class with a young lady, I asked her how she thought she sounded after making the sound. She replied with "Grotesque!" The rest of the class was impressed with the fact that this was actually the very first truly acceptable tone to have emerged from this student's throat that far into the semester. I then asked her to do it again, but to make it three times as "grotesque." She did so and the tone sounded as if it came from a professional singer. The entire class reinforced my opinion; and they, more than I, were able to convince the girl that she never sounded better. One even said, "I'm jealous!" Variations of this example occur several times each semester.

I would not suggest using the Snerd synthesizer in junior high school unless the teacher controls the group with iron-fist discipline; and in *no case*, would I recommend that it be tried by public school substitute teachers.

As one experiments with the snerdian sound, he can see other timbral possibilities than those already mentioned. For example, a very snerdy sound in the middle range would be a good start for the sound of weeping. Also, by accenting the woofiness of a tone, the singer could portray a character who is not quite mentally alert as normal. And, even if snerdity should not be used at all for vocal coloration, it is still useful in maintaining a healthy vocal technique.

Figure 38 on page 38 illustrates a megaphone inside the singer's mouth, with the small end at his lips and the large end at the back of his neck. The large end represents the dropped jaw and lifted palate. The small end represents almost closed lips (but not closed teeth!).

This smaller mouth helps the singer "gather" the resonance and feel more maskiness without disturbing the openness at the back of the throat. If a singer cannot empathize with snerdian synthesis, the megaphone may be a good substitute. I often have my students think of both as they sing, the one enhancing the other.

Occasionally a student will not realize the full benefit of the megaphone image because the back-breath is not connected to the openness only partially induced by the megaphone. In such instances, it is sometimes helpful to ask the student to imagine that the megaphone bends at the back of the neck and continues down to the lowest back lobes of the lungs.

Fig. 91

This image has a similar effect of "thinking like King Kong" or "feeling like a cello (rather than a violin)." It has the combined effect of making the singer feel bigger than life and quieting excessive movement of the tongue and jaw; and it forces the singer to ventriloquize, uniting Mortimer Snerd with the other enlarging images.

Before ending this chapter, I would like to reiterate what I said on the first page of the chapter. The singer should not disturb the natural timbre of the voice, or the basic technique, in order to achieve vocal color. Richard Miller made the following observation:

> "...Vocal coloration is an important part of artistry. Artistic singing requires a palette of varied colors, lights and shadows. The essential thing, however, is to establish the *stabilized timbre* of the voice throughout all its ranges, with its full complement of spectral colors (which can be visualized through actual spectral analysis). The next essential thing is to determine how far we may momentarily depart from that *stabilized timbre* for purposes of expression and musical nuance without violating the function of the instrument. Woofy baritones, tinny tenors, strident sopranos and bovine mezzos do not substitute for healthy voices which produce timbres that sound like baritones, tenors, sopranos and mezzos because their instruments function freely."[1]

---

[1] Miller, Richard; *sotto voce:* "Woofy Baritones and Tinny Tenors"; *THE NATS BULLETIN*; Vol. 39. No. 5, May/June 1983; p. 28.

CHAPTER VIII
VOCAL PROBLEM SOLVING

In the first seven chapters of this text, we have attempted to cover the fundamental areas of voice production in an orderly and logical fashion. Vocal problems often occur in random order, however, and frequently seem illogical.

In this chapter, we shall examine some of the more frequent problems which occur in the life of the singer. Many of these problems may have already been corrected in the course of the foregoing chapters. Other problems may be correctible by re-examining information from previous chapters. Some of the problems encountered here will not have been discussed at all, previously.

We cannot cover all the problems, but hopefully this will be a good start. They will be discussed in three basic categories:

　A. Technical Problems
　B. Physical Health
　C. Psychological Health

A. Technical Problems

Most technical vocal problems seem to be physiological in nature. We shall examine them in three divisions:

　1. Tone
　2. Intensity
　3. Miscellaneous

1. Tone

The principal physical product of singing is tone. Listeners have many bases for enjoying what they hear. From a purely aesthetic standpoint, the listener hopes to hear certain qualities in a voice. Some of the qualities he would probably *not* like to hear in tone are:

　a. "Breaking" Voice
　b. Breathiness
　c. "Chesty" or "Belty" Voice
　d. Covered Tone and "Hooking"
　e. Excessive Compression
　f. Falsetto
　g. Intonation (Faulty)
　h. Nasality
　i. Stridency
　j. Tremolo
　k. Vibrato (Faulty)
　l. Wobble

a. "Breaking" Voice

The voice is said to "break" or "crack" when the singer makes a sudden shift from one vocal register to another without making a transitory adjustment. This break occurs frequently in the boy's changing voice during his period of muscular development and re-training. This is an ordinary occurrence which time will usually accommodate.

For the singer whose voice has already changed, I suggest re-examining the section on Registration (Chapter V) if he has particular need for solving the problem of the breaking voice. Also, Fig. 35a and 35b on page 34 may be helpful, as "detached focus" or "blunted focus" can very easily cause the voice to break.

Of course, if a singer believes in only *one* register, there can be no break, as there will be no shift from one register to another.

b. Breathiness

Breathiness is caused by failure of the vocal folds to close and/or vibrate evenly. This may be due to a variety of reasons:

(1) Physical immaturity can account for breathiness. When a young singer has not passed the pubescent stage, it is not uncommon for him to have a slight chink where the arytenoid cartilages adduct the cords. Adduction should not be forced on an immature singer if this should be the case. (See page 68, ¶4)

(2) Breathiness can result from organic disorders— that is— a defective laryngeal mechanism. This is not a common phenomenon among singers. Remedy, if one is possible, would require medical and/or therapeutic treatment.

(3) Uneven closure of the vocal folds may also be due to nodules, polyps, or other growths. These growths interrupt the even undulation of the vocal folds. Some growths, such as nodules, form as a protection against abuse of the vocal folds, just as calluses form on the hands of manual laborers to make them tough and resistive to abuse. Callused hands are fine for manual laborers, but not for pianists and surgeons. Nodules are terrible for singers.

Nodules should be treated by a throat specialist who knows about the singing voice. The first thing such a specialist has the patient do is to stop singing and talking for several days, weeks, or longer. After medical treatment, the singer should re-examine his vocal technique to find how he may have been abusing his voice.

(4) By far the most common cause of a breathy tone is improper vocal technique for allowing the vocal folds to close. The solution to this problem can be found on page 29, Fig. 25; also, see pp. 45-46 (The Attack).

(5) In extreme cases of persistent breathiness, I suggest that my students see a throat specialist because the methods above (4) usually work. If breathiness persists, there is a possibility of a physical disorder.

When a new student auditions for me and sings with an excessively breathy tone, I send him to a throat specialist immediately. I will not risk teaching someone who is in such a condition when I have no personal knowledge of his vocal background. If the doctor tells me this student has a healthy throat, then I will accept him for lessons.

The voice will last a life time if treated with respect.

92 VOCAL DEVELOPMENT THROUGH ORGANIC IMAGERY

c. "Chesty" or "Belty" Voice

A vocal production referred to as "chesty" or "belty" is one in which the heavy mechanism dominates. In some cases a "belter" has no trace of light mechanism in his voice. This type of singer is heard most frequently in "Broadway" musicals, where voices of good projection without the use of microphones are needed. These singers, more often than not, have fairly "natural voices" within a limited range. That is to say, belters learn to sing that way with little or no formal training. As long as they do not have to sing higher than the chest register will carry them, they can be impressive.

Too often, however, the belter does not know the limits of his powers and over-extends himself. This, of course, is bad for the listener and worse for the singer. This sort of voice does not last very long.

The solution for the belter's problem is for him to learn how to use his light mechanism, (See chapter V, pp. 54-72) and to coordinate it with his heavy mechanism.

The belter's Heavy-Light Mechanism ratio chart looks something like this:

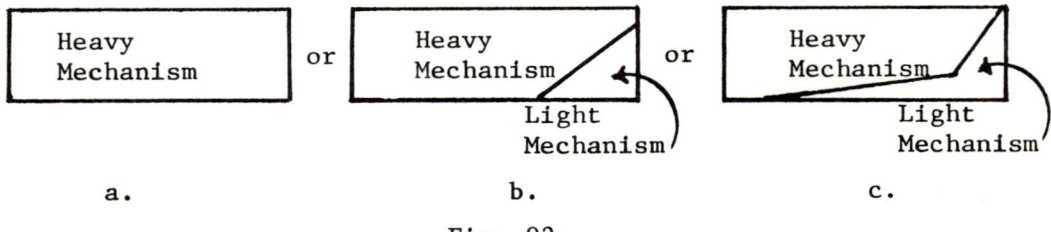

Fig. 92

All three mechanisms above are incorrect. The proper blend is illustrated in Fig. 59, p. 58.

Marilyn Horne gives an excellent analysis of how she copes with the mixed register by dividing it into eight parts (by ½ steps). "...Now my theory is... you take a ratio of fractions, so that you stop a pure chest tone on an E, say... the F is going to be seven-eighths chest and one-eighth head voice... so that by the time you get to the B you're seven eighths head voice."[1]

There is another kind of "chest" singer who has learned to use both light and heavy mechanisms, but prefers the dominant chest register. This is the more dramatic singer, such as the Wagnerian opera singer or the tenor robusto.

Even these singers must be extremely careful not to over-extend themselves, in spite of their sound techniques and healthy vocal equipment. Not infrequently does a fledgling opera singer overestimate the inherent "drama" in his vocal production with disastrous results.

d. Covered Tone and "Hooking"

The term *covering* has at least two well-known connotations:

---

[1] Hines, Jerome; *GREAT SINGERS ON GREAT SINGING*; Doubleday & Company; Garden City, New York; 1982; p. 140.

(1) Applied to Resonation: Dark vowel pronunciation, utilizing a light registration.

(2) Applied to Registration: Covered tone equals *voce coperta* (covered voice). This is an Italian term, attributed to Marchesi, which refers to the physical sensation a singer— particularly the male— has when he arrives at that point in his upper range where the light mechanism dominates the heavy mechanism, without resorting to the use of *falsetto*. (See p. 94, f. Falsetto)

These points range from 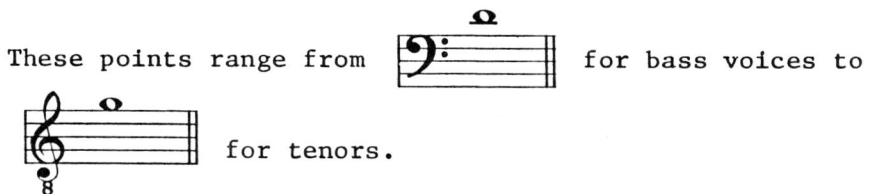 for bass voices to 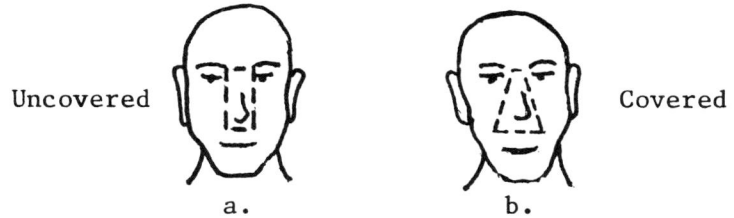 for tenors.

(1) Covered Tone - Resonation

The singer is apt to feel a bit schizophrenic when he attempts to sing with dark vowels in a light registration, especially after devoting hours of practice to singing "openly."

The covered tone (in Resonance) is a *closed* tone. This is a device for achieving a dramatic color for the voice on a soft dynamic level. Leonard Warren, Sherrill Milnes, and Carlo Bergonzi are masters of this device.

(2) Covered Tone - Registration

When a singer arrives at the "cover" point of his registration, there is a sensation of reinforcement of the mask muscles which, in many cases, suggests an inward leaning from the top sides of the nasal bone and a broadening at the base of the palate, thusly:

Fig. 93

For more specific detail about the covered tone, see pp. 58-65, particularly the section on the male passaggio secondo.

Again, I caution the reader that the above approach to singing can become too mechanical. It *must* be integrated as soon as possible with the rest of the vocal concepts, and then *forgotten* during the performance. The singer must utilize this device carefully. When it is used artistically, the audience is unaware when the singer arrives at his cover point. When it is clumsily done, the audience is painfully aware. This point of cover is referred to as a "hook" when it is clumsy and noticeable. Some misguided singers actually cultivate the sound of "hooking the voice in." This is a sign that the transition from heavy mechanism to light mechanism is erratic and uneven, or— in a word— unbalanced.

94 VOCAL DEVELOPMENT THROUGH ORGANIC IMAGERY

e. Excessive Compression

The only thing that should be excessive in singing is *FREEDOM*. Excessive compression is a certain sign that something is not free. It is out of balance.

As hyper-compression is the result of faulty breath flow, the usual cause of it can be traced either to phonation or to respiration. In the case of phonation, the valve (larynx) is not letting the air get through. If pressure is felt at the front of the throat, that is the problem.

This aspect of compression is rather complex, but, in most cases, arises when the larynx rises. Review the throat openers (pp. 22-28). One of my teachers gave me a throat-opening exercise which works wonders with large, beginning choruses and with more advanced choirs which do not sing with big, robust sounds.

He had me put my wrist in my mouth (sidewise), as if I were going to swallow it. Try it. You will find the jaw drops in the back, the palate rises, the larynx lowers. *WARNING:* Unfortunately, the tongue does not necessarily go forward. This can easily be adjusted, however. The sensation is very much like a big yawn, but with the same pitfalls. I frequently have students sing while the wrists are still in their mouths. Although the sound is garbled, this "sets" the sensation for when they take the wrists out. After the wrists are removed from their mouths, the sound burgeons forth as never before.

The chances are strong that most of the choir singers will not overdo the wrist-in-mouth position. Some of the choir *will* be over-zealous; so the director must be on guard for that possibility. This is, of course, a *gimmick* or a voice primer. It should be coordinated with respiration *as quickly as possible*.

Sometimes hyper-compression is caused when the inspiratory muscles put up too much resistance against the expiratory muscles.

The same teacher who gave me the wrist-in-mouth exercise once asked me to take a big breath and compress it. Then, without my expelling the breath, he told me to relax. Then he asked me, "Where did the compression go?"

This was a revelation to me. Until that time, I thought a singer had no breath support without that feeling of heavy compression. The singer *never* needs to "lock in" the breath. A singer who locks his abdominal muscles for support actually holds his breath and makes the entire vocal tract rigid. This causes him to sound, or be, out of breath and for the muscles around the front lower ribs to ache from fatigue. The abdominal muscles should remain flexible, ready to firm-up for the more demanding notes and relax for the easier ones.

f. Falsetto

I do not classify the falsetto register as a part of the "legitimate" voice, as so many writers have done. I agree with those who say the falsetto voice is that voice which utilizes the light mechanism, but which does not utilize the complete resources of the vocal mechanism. In other words, the falsetto has a limited pitch range and a *very* limited dynamic range. One cannot crescendo a falsetto tone, appreciably.

The falsetto exists in *all* voices, male and female. It is a useful device for helping the singer "find" and develop his light mechanism. If a singer cannot sing in falsetto, he will probably have a defective light mechanism, but not always.

In one of the NATS Bulletin Interviews, the eminent artist/teacher, Todd Duncan, in answering the interviewer's question, "What role does the falsetto timbre play in your pedagogy?" replied:

> "I use the falsetto to give the pupil a sense of nothingness in the pharynx— weightlessness and detachment. I turn to this device for voices that over-support, those that are too violent with the breath action, and for those big voices that are dark, thick, and unwieldy."[1]

This is a most sensible application of an often-time controversial medium for vocal development. The primary difference between the male falsetto and the female whistle register, in terms of function, is that the latter is a legitimate sound for singing and the former is not (unless reinforced); but the whistle register does give the female that feeling of "nothingness and weightlessness," if not "detachment."

The range of the falsetto is approximately one octave, around B above middle C to the B an octave higher. It is of special benefit for *men* to learn to sing the falsetto register fluently.

The best and easiest vowel for singing the falsetto is [u]. The octave arpeggio, ascending and descending, is useful in extending the range of the falsetto, which, by the foregoing description, eliminates the falsetto, as such.

The falsetto should be incorporated into the messa di voce exercises. When the range of the falsetto is extended well beyond one octave or when a singer can crescendo the falsetto appreciably, it is no longer falsetto, but the "light mechanism" or "head" or "high" register.

Falsetto voice, then, is a useful *tool* for developing the "full" voice, although it is limited in itself. It is frequently used, unabridged, for comic effects by both men and women, although the women might deny this.

The well-developed "full voice" should be capable of singing *all* dynamic levels throughout the entire range. The falsetto voice will not project effectively in even the smallest theatre.

g. Intonation

Intonation is the process of singing on pitch. Our concern at this time is with those singers who do not, or cannot, sing on pitch. There are several reasons why singers do not sing on pitch. The principal ones are:

   (1) Organic tonal perception disorder (rare with singers)
   (2) Improper audio-kinaesthetic balance
   (3) Insufficient technique
   (4) Carelessness

---

[1] Duncan, Todd; "The NATS Bulletin Interviews"; *The NATS Bulletin*, Vol. 37, No. 5, May/June 1981; p. 6.

(5) Sloth
(6) Musical ignorance

(1) Organic tonal perception disorder

Some singers or students of singing have a legitimate reason for singing off pitch. This is the inability to hear tones correctly or to reproduce them because of a faulty hearing mechanism. This is an unusual situation, and especially so in the case of singing, as those people who are so afflicted rarely pursue the subject with much enthusiasm. As this problem is not in our area, we shall dismiss it.

(2) Improper audio-kinaesthetic balance

This problem is usually due to inexperience on the part of the singer. After a reasonably short period of time, voice students should learn to balance what they hear with what they feel. Their hearing should become coordinated with their muscles.

This inbalance is predominant with young children who are just learning to sing. Many times these youngsters learn songs in a group and may not be able to hear themselves. It is not unusual for them to sing out with great zest, but not great accuracy. A lot of this sort of practice sets the habit firmly in some singers. Psychological problems may complicate the situation when, much later, the song leader suggests to the singer, "Johnny, you have a tin ear!"

Students with this sort of background *can* learn to sing on pitch, but this is remedial work and should be treated on an individual basis or in homogeneous grouping.

(3) Insufficient technique

There are many technical reasons why a singer may sing off-pitch. His breath support, focus, resonators, articulators, or posture may be used incorrectly. There are so many possibilities that a general solution cannot possibly cover the subject. I hardly ever worry about the singer who does not sing on pitch for purely technical reasons because the problem is so easy to solve through the methods described in chapters I through VII.

(4) Carelessness

There is one solution to carelessness in any circumstance: Attentiveness. The singer should work on his ability to concentrate.

(5) Sloth

Slovenliness in an aesthetic undertaking seems to me to be a contradiction of terms. It is inexcusable. If this is not apparent to the singer, there is little hope for him in any other phase of vocal development.

(6) Musical ignorance

Frequently a singer will sing off-pitch because he does not know which note he is supposed to sing. The solution to this problem is easy: Learn the music! This is, actually, not an intonation problem.

h. Nasality

We know the causes of nasality (See pp. 39-40), so we know the solution lies in control of the velum. Some singers seem to have inordinate problems with this kind of control.

A good exercise for training the velum and for becoming aware of when the nasal port is open or closed is the "hung ah."

When the singer sings or speaks a sustained "hung," the nasal port is open. He will feel the back of the tongue pressing against the lowered velum. When the singer changes from "hung" to "ah," without stopping the tone between words, he will feel the tongue lower and the velum spring up and back against the pharyngeal wall. The nasal port is then closed.

Doing this exercise a few minutes each day will accustom the singer to the sensations of the open and closed nasal port. If he does not want nasality in his tone, he must keep the nasal port closed.

There is an old saying about resonance and nasality: "Keep the tone in the nose; not the nose in the tone."

i. Stridency

The strident tone is another indication that the vocal mechanism is out of balance.

This time the culprits are probably the tongue and jaw. The strident tone is shrill and harsh. These qualities reflect pain and anguish, which is often what the singer feels as he performs such tones. Certainly, a strident tone is not pleasurable to an audience, rock and roll music notwithstanding.

If the strident tone is caused by compressed tongue and tight jaw, the solution is obvious: (1) relax the tongue and (2) loosen the jaw.

This solution will be easier for some than for others. Many individuals go through their daily routines and are unaware that they are tense. Tension attacks vision, the respiratory system, the circulatory system, and every other bodily function. Some people resort to Yoga exercises to find release from these tensions (an excellent idea for singers) by gaining control over their involuntary muscles. Other relaxation techniques are gaining popularity. Most prominent among these is the Alexander Technique. Specialists in this technique give frequent classes in various centers around the world. Spin-off techniques of the Alexander method are also beginning to make the rounds.

Fortunately, the tongue and jaw are controllable by the voluntary muscles. We have already discussed the tongue in sufficient detail. If the singer cannot tame his tongue to relax in one or two attempts, he should not give up. This difficulty has been compounded by years of tightening. He must have patience.

The jaw is usually easier to train than the tongue, as it has fewer movable parts. A tense tongue and tight jaw frequently go together.

It is quite helpful for the singer to practice relaxing both the tongue and jaw simultaneously. This promotes faster and more efficient coordination of the two. (See p. 79, ¶ 1 and 2)

j. Tremolo

This term is applied to both instrumental and vocal music, but to each in a different sense.

In instrumental music, tremolo is an acceptable device, similar to the vibrato. Instrumental tremolo is different from instrumental vibrato in that it calls more attention to itself. It provokes excitement. The instrumentalist deliberately manufactures the tremolo to be noticed, whereas he uses vibrato more subliminally, only to produce a more beautiful tone.

In vocal music, tremolo is unacceptable.

Many writers call vocal tremolo, simply, a bad vibrato. Instrumental tremolo indicates "excitement"; but vocal tremolo indicates "panic"— or at best— a singer who is out of control of his pitch mechanism.

It is probably safe to say that, if a singer develops a good vibrato, he will have no more tremolo. In that respect, tremolo *is* a bad vibrato. (See k. Vibrato, for the solution to vocal tremolo)

k. Vibrato

Vibrato is the fluctuation in pitch, intensity, and timbre of a given tone. It is desirable in singing, both aesthetically and technically.

From an aesthetic standpoint, a correctly produced vibrato is pleasant to the ear and adds warmth to the tone. By "correctly produced" (the technical aspect), I mean a tone which fluctuates smoothly and proportionally in the three areas of pitch, intensity, and timbre.

Fluctuation is a back and forth, or up and down movement. In the case of pitch, a good vibrato should go approximately one quarter-step above and one quarter-step below the center of pitch at a proportionate time rate of about six to seven times per second. The intensity should fluctuate with pitch: as the pitch rises, the intensity increases; as the pitch falls, the intensity decreases. The timbre becomes more vivid with more intensity and less vivid with less intensity. The fluctuation of the pitch, intensity and timbre illustrates perfectly the phenomenon of tension and release; but the tension must build smoothly and wane smoothly.

A singer with a good vibrato has a healthy tone production. If a singer has *no* vibrato or has a faulty vibrato, his tone production will probably be faulty— especially with amateurs. Some professional singers learn how to sing vibratoless tones, without injury or undue fatigue, for special musical or stylistic effects.

Vibrato can be acquired, or it can be corrected. Sometimes the process may be arduous, but the acquisition of a good vibrato is a worthwhile endeavor.

If a singer has no vibrato, one way to approach its development is by mechanical means, as follows.

The singer should:

(1) select the easiest note in his range (let us say middle C).
(2) sing the [ɑ] vowel on the above pitch, changing to one-half step higher and then one-half step lower at the rate of one quarter note per second:

Fig. 94

(3) increase the rate of pitch change gradually and deliberately, and with absolutely *no* tension.

At this point, he will probably be aware that the pitch changes are felt in the front of the neck.

(4) move the work from the front of the neck to the back and belt-line muscles.

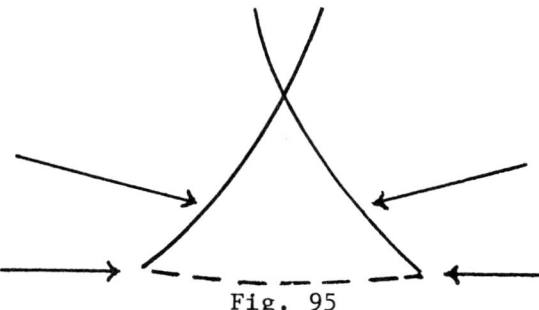

Fig. 95

and let *them* change the pitch— still gradually and deliberately.

(5) feel the deliberate pulsation and rhythm of the back muscles and try to let them do the work automatically. Several attempts may be necessary and, possibly, over a period of several days or weeks. The object is to maintain the consistency of the deliberate pulsations *after* conversion to the automatic pulsations.

This transfer is similar to the drum roll. In the beginning, the drummer controls two beats in the right hand, and then alternates to two beats with the left hand and continues this alternation at a slow tempo. After he develops strength and evenness, he gradually goes at a faster tempo. At a certain tempo, he will no longer be able to control each beat individually but will control the right stick for one stroke and let it bounce one time; then he will control the left stick for one stroke and let it bounce one time, and so on, alternating faster and faster as his strength and timing develop more securely.

After a certain amount of time and through the kind of consistent practice suggested above, both the vibrato and the drum roll will feel like "spontaneous combustion" has taken place. It just happens.

Many teachers disagree with the method above for developing the vibrato. They maintain that the vibrato will come without cultivation if all the other factors of correct vocalization are adhered to.

I like to give it a little nudge on the premise that perhaps some of these other "factors" of correct vocalization are *not being adhered to*; otherwise, the singer would already *have* a vibrato. In learning the vibrato, some singers can correct those other factors.

The method given here for developing vibrato may also be used for correcting both tremolo and wobble. Other factors may need attention in various instances; but most problems of vibrato, tremolo, and wobble can be handled in the above manner.

1. Wobble

Wobble is a slow, sometimes irregular, vibrato; whereas *tremolo* is a fast and frantic vibrato. Neither wobble nor tremolo is a desirable vocal quality. The solution for controlling wobble can be found on the section, above, under Vibrato.

2. Intensity

In Latin, *intensus* means *tightened*; *facere* means *to make*. *Intensify*, therefore, means *to make tighter*.

In vocal music, this is precisely what intensity does. It tightens the vocal folds or focus, allowing firmer resistance against the increased breath stream.

In a broader, acoustical sense, intensity means *relative energy of a sound wave*. This energy is the result of focus resisting breath.

When one discusses intensity, other terms which are closely related inevitably follow. I believe it is important for the singer to understand the differences and similarities of these terms:

    a. Volume
    b. Amplitude
    c. Projection

a. Volume

Volume is the relative *loudness* or *softness* of a tone. If a singer gives more volume, he sings more loudly; if he gives less volume, he sings more softly. Oftentimes, when a person hears the word *volume*, he thinks of it only in terms of loudness, not softness.

Whereas *intensity* is an acoustical (objective) term, *loudness* (or volume) is a psychological (subjective) term.

It is not unusual for the intensity of a given sound to register higher or lower on a measuring device than on a person's subjective impression of that sound. This has a direct application to singing if one considers the *even scale*.

The ideal vocal scale seems to ascend and descend evenly and at the same dynamic level from bottom to top. This is a subjective evaluation, however. Scientific tests show that, with the even scale, intensity increases in proportion to pitch— that is, higher pitch.

VOCAL PROBLEM SOLVING 101

Our ears and minds are accustomed to hearing this crescendo as a constant volume. Subjectively, then, the tone does not become louder. The tone must get more intense as it ascends because much more energy is needed.

If a singer wants the *subjective* effect of becoming louder as he ascends the scale, he must give even more focus and support than usual. Conversely, if the singer needs more sound in the lower range, he must do the same things that help produce a crescendo, namely, give more support, more space, and more vowel migration.

Pursuant to this, the same week I was revising this chapter, one of my students brought an aria to her lesson. It was Donna Anna's vengeance aria, "Orsai chi l'onore" from *DON GIOVANNI*, by Mozart. The first two phrases of the aria presented a problem.

Fig. 96

Although this soprano was successfully handling the high notes, she could not project the low F♯, G, and A, on the words, "*l'onore* and *me volse*. I challenged her choice of vowels (Fig. 94a). She quickly defended her choice by saying "but I migrated the vowels." I agreed, partially, suggesting that she did not migrate the lower ones. Being a very bright young lady, she countered with, "I didn't think I had to migrate the low notes." Then I asked her if she remembered an earlier discussion when she discovered that higher notes project, by nature, more loudly than the low notes. She remembered, and blushed. She quickly revised her vowels (Fig. 94b) and the low notes balanced the top notes beautifully.

b. Amplitude

Amplitude, in Latin, means *largeness*. Amplitude, as an acoustical term, means *a tone's extension in space, especially in breadth and range*.

Amplitude is the spatial counterpart of intensity. Whereas intensity may be equated with phonation alone, amplitude must be equated with both phonation and resonation combined.

c. Projection

The Latin word, *projicere*, means *to fling forth* (pro = forth; jacere = to cast).

Acoustically, projection means *an extension of a tone in space*. Vocally, a projected tone is one that can be heard from a distance. The particular distance is relative to, and dependent upon, the quality of that tone's projection. Projection is the end product of vocal production. After that, the tone is a matter for *reception*. The singer has done all he can and the rest is up to the listener.

The quality and quantity of a singer's projection, then, is the object of everything we have discussed about voice production. Its importance is obvious.

The principal question which is of concern to the singer in regard to projection is "Can my beautiful voice be heard in any reasonable acoustical environment?"

(1) The "small voice"

For many years I have heard it said, "There are singers with large voices and singers with small voices, and training will not make a small voice large."

After thirty-four years of teaching students of all ages and grade levels, and forty-two years of my own singing, I have yet to see a singer whose voice cannot be trained to project *well* in any reasonable situation. This observation has been made by numerous teachers the world over; but the idea persists in many circles that the singer with the small voice must learn to reconcile himself to that limitation.

Some fine artists prefer *not* to develop a large voice, for various reasons. A case in point is the very lyric soprano, Kathleen Battle, who specialized in soubrette roles and garners the lion's share of praise in every performance. As Bernard Holland stated, "It is a sound, however, that actually challenges the definition of 'small.' There is a shimmer, a gleam, above all, a heart, which together convey the elusive 'ping'— that confluence of timbral focus, pure intonation and sheer musical caring."[1]

Mr. Holland stated further that Miss Battle was not bothered by the 3800-seat Metropolitan Opera House or the huge Richard Strauss orchestra (Der Rosenkavalier) in her efforts to communicate.

Miss Battle refuses to accept roles not suited to her voice. She also refuses to "push" her voice in the roles she does sing, in order to carry over a heavy orchestra. She says of her steadfastness in this respect, "I know I'm pushing when I no longer have control over dynamics, when I lose control of expression, when I can't sing below a mezzo-forte in any part of my voice, when I can't play with a phrase— when singing becomes hard."[2] Smart lady!

If a singer has an open throat and intensity in his voice, the voice will project. A singer with a small voice (although the term *small* is now debatable) lacks either one or both of these qualities, thus there is no "ping" to allow the voice to carry.

The solution, therefore, is to open the throat and focus the tone. It is as simple as that. The required resonance will come, automatically, with the open throat and proper pronunciation.

---

[1] Holland, Bernard; "A Very Special Soprano"; *THE NEW YORK TIMES MAGAZINE*, Section 6; November 17, 1985; p. 82.
[2] Op. cit.; p. 85.

I use a "voice primer" with singers who seem timid or who have never experienced the feeling of robust singing. I ask them if they have ever cheered for their team at ball games. Usually they have. I then ask them for a demonstration of the kind of enthusiasm they might show for their home team with "Fifteen rahs."

Nine times out of ten the "mouse will roar." Suddenly the small, colorless voice will assume volume, intensity, and personality. It is as different as night from day.

The purpose of this priming device is only to show the singer (and members of a voice class) that there is unused potential in the voice, which is immediately findable.

A frequent reaction I get from students who do this for the first time is, "But that isn't singing."

Fifteen rahs is not singing, of course; but, if the student will isolate just one good "rah" and sustain it, he cannot help being aware of the difference and improvement in that tone above any he sang previously. From that tone, he has established the basis for building a solid technical vocal production. He should *take his best tone and clone*.

Someone once told me that "Singing is educated yelling." I am inclined to agree with that statement, but I also recall another comment which dims its effect somewhat: "Any ass can bray."

Balance, balance, balance!

(2) The "large voice" that does not project

Frequently a singer has what is called a large voice; but, for some reason, he can neither be heard nor understood clearly in various parts of a theatre or auditorium.

Presuming that this unintelligibility of text is due to projection, rather than diction or room acoustics (and there is a difference), then this singer is probably over-opening his throat and/or not focusing the tone. This sort of tone is said to be *throaty* or *swallowed*; and he is probably pushing the voice.

The singer who over-opens usually feels as if he has a powerful voice. The opposite is true. If it does not project, it is not powerful. The singer is only "spinning his wheels," not his voice. A singer should never sound more "important" than his technique will allow. This sort of posturing will impress no one but close friends and relatives.

As I said earlier, an overly-opened throat is as pernicious as a closed throat. It is worthless for both singer and audience.

It is possible for a singer to have a *properly* opened throat, but without adequate focus. He will be healthier than the singer who over-opens, but his voice will not project as well as it should. His solution is to focus more clearly and firmly.

3. Miscellaneous

There are technical problems which do not fall conveniently into the category of either *Tone* or *Intensity*. Because of their diverse nature, we shall file them under *Miscellaneous*. They are:

   a. Breath Flow
   b. Breath Control
   c. Humming
   d. Position
   e. Range
   f. Timing
   g. Trills

a. Breath Flow

The importance of breath flow has already been stressed in previous chapters, but perhaps not emphatically enough.

If the larynx is viewed as a valve through which sound flows, one will readily see that the free-flowing sound (or breath) is an adjunct of phonation and not of resonance.

It may be interesting to note that, although phonation is a cause and resonation an effect of voice production, the singer may very well treat the effect as a cause to great advantage. This should only be done *after* he has established balanced phonation with respiration, however. In other words, it may be helpful for a singer to think of breath flow as being synonymous with mask resonance.

It should also be mentioned that the stretching of the tissue around the nasal bone (see Fig. 43 on page 41) is a priming device for initiating the sensation of mask resonance. After the singer has achieved this, he may discover that the sensation works better for him if the arch is moved backward a few centimeters, immediately above the juncture of the hard and soft palates. This will help him avoid the pitfall of closing the throat while chasing the forward placement (mask resonance). He will still feel the forwardness of the tone without sacrificing the prerequisites. Many singers say they feel the resonance arch move even farther back as they ascend the scale. I cannot argue with that point, as I also experience the sensation.

The important thing to glean from all this is: Once the singer has established the tone, *it must flow*.

The sensation of mask resonance facilitates this flow. The singer should feel that the tone is being "lifted" from the nasal arch, rather than being "blown up" from beneath the glottis. This feeling of suspension will eliminate that bane of many singers— short-windedness. In most such cases, too little breath is not the problem. Getting rid of the breath is. Let it flow! This is a fundamental link in coordinating respiration, phonation, and resonation.

b. Breath Control

We have discussed Breath Support and Breath Control in chapters II and III. The reader will recall that control of breath results from the balanced actions of the muscles of inhalation (principally, the diaphragm) and of exhalation (the abdominals); also, Breath Flow, or the measured release of the breath during phonation is important in breath control. Some singers and teachers find it useful to study the function of the *epigastrium* as a means for maintaining breath control.

The epigastrium is the upper section of the abdominal muscles. It starts just beneath the sternum and continues downward to just above the navel. When the muscles for respiration are well developed, the epigastrium is capable of bulging outwardly with great strength and, frequently, great size.

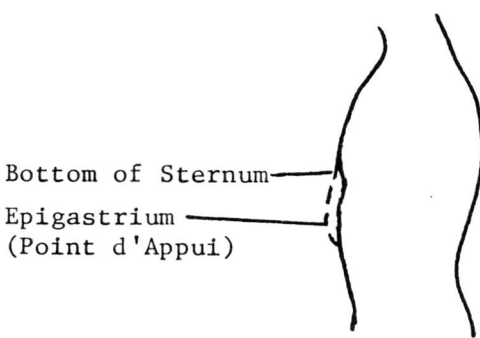

Fig. 97

When the top section of the rectus abdominis tightens for expiration, the diaphragm will also become firmer to resist exhalation. This causes the rectus abdominal bulge, or epigastrium. Thus, the study of this bulge has given many fine teachers and singers something to ponder in relation to breath control. Not the least of these teachers was Giovanni Sbriglia (1832-1916).

Dr. Berton Coffin wrote of Sbriglia's methods in his *Vocal Pedagogy Classics*.[1] Although Sbriglia never wrote about his methods, Margaret Chapman Byers wrote an article for *THE ETUDE* (1942), entitled "Sbriglia's Method of Singing," which provided Dr. Coffin with most of his technical information.

Sbriglia believed the center of support was the epigastrium, which he called the *point d'epui* [probably more accurate would be *point d'appui*, from the French, *appuyer* = *to support*]. *S'appuyer* means *to lean on* or *to rest against*, which is identical to the Italian term for support, *appoggiare (appoggiarsi)*.

Leaning on this point d'appui controls the amount of breath emitted from the lungs. According to Sbriglia, if this area were properly supported from below (incorporating the rest of the abdominal muscles), there would be absolutely no effort or tension above that point. Since Sbriglia also advocated a high chest (without tension), well-developed abdominal and lower back muscles, and a straight spine, with neck and shoulders free and loose, I find his methods difficult to fault. That his students included the likes of Jean and Edoard de Reszke, Pol Plançon, Lillian Nordica, Sybil Sanderson, and Ruth Miller Chamlee would make any hint of criticism from me foolhardy, indeed.

---

[1] Coffin, Berton; Vocal Pedagogy Classics; "Sbriglia's Singing Method"; Margaret Chapman Byers; *THE NATS BULLETIN*; Vol. 40, No. 3, Jan./Feb. 1984; p. 38.

Ruth Miller Chamlee was the wife of one of my teachers— Mario Chamlee. I am sorry to say that, during the brief time I had the opportunity to study with Mr. Chamlee, I did not know of his wife's connection with Sbriglia. What a golden opportunity missed!

If the singer takes a full-sized back breath, and couples it with Sbriglia's concepts, above, he will feel something like this:

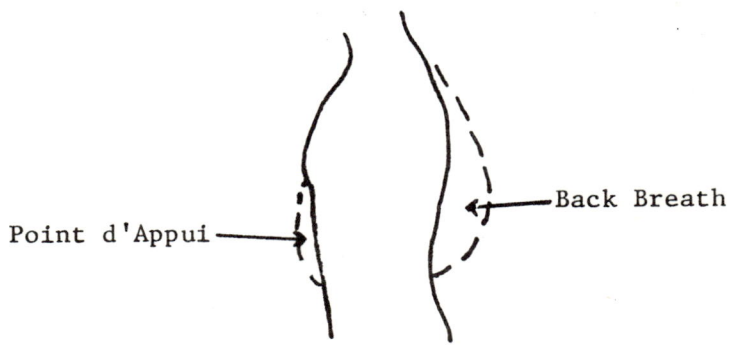

Fig. 98

What a potential powerhouse for breath control the singer has at his disposal. I suggest only that focus on the point d'appui must produce positive results for the singer. If efforts to apply this concept causes tensions, discomfort, and/or stiff vocalization, he should stop. He is doing it incorrectly. One reason I did not discuss the epigastrium in the earlier edition of this book is because it is easy to misunderstand, especially from a book. However, I have been using it more and more with my voice classes with good results, but only after going through the first seven chapters. Once more, the reader should handle the point d'appui with caution and common sense— and in the presence of a teacher who understands it.

c. Humming

The usefulness of humming is another one of those debatable subjects. Giovanni Battista Lamperti, the son of another illustrious voice teacher, Francesco Lamperti, made some rather confusing statements about humming which seem self-contradictory:

"If you cannot sing with your mouth open, you can not with it closed."[1]

and

"The 'hum' in the voice is the unifying principal."[2]

and

"It is the rainbow bridge connecting voice and breath."[3]

After all this, he admonished, "Don't hum!"

---

[1] Lamperti, Giovanni Battista; *VOCAL WISDOM*; Transcribed by William Earl Brown; Taplinger Publishing Company, New York; 1931; p. 104.
[2] Op. cit.; p. 105.
[3] Op. cit.; p. 105.

Giovanni Battista's father was more adamant about not humming. He wrote, "The pupil is also warned to avoid humming, as, wanting in the support of the chest, there is nothing which more fatigues the throat, or renders more uncertain the intonation."[1]

The danger of humming, in the elder Lamperti's terms, stems from lack of proper support of the chest. Therefore, maintaining this support of the chest (epigastrium) while humming would remove the danger. I would also suggest that the hum be "connected" to the back-breathing mechanism. Otherwise, there is a danger of disengaging the hum from proper focus.

One of the most common abuses of the hum is the propensity for students to sound a pitch before singing a phrase. Most hum the pitch with a high larynx, then try to sing the phrase with a proper low laryngeal position. They have already confused their kinaesthetic memories. Ironically, it is not necessary for them to sound the pitch in the first place because they can only hum the correct pitch if they already know what it is.

Another common abuse of humming is its use while learning new repertoire. Again, this is usually done with a high larynx, further building in muscular confusion. If the singer utilizes a sound vocal technique while humming, humming will not work to his disadvantage. But what are the advantages of humming, now that we need not fear the disadvantages?

  (1) Humming can be useful as a guide for developing nasal resonance.
  (2) Humming promotes relaxation of the throat, when properly performed.
  (3) A comfortable hum is an excellent means of "marking" while studying repertoire. (See Appendix VI, footnote)
  (4) Correct humming is an excellent way to "warm up" the voice when a practice room or other facilities are not available.

d. Position

Position is usually distinguished from Posture. As discussed in chapter I, posture concerns the general bodily stance, dependent upon the skeletal frame. Position is a sub-division of posture. It relates to more detailed aspects of posture, such as the shape of the lips, jaw, tongue, palate, epiglottis, ribs, diaphragm, etc.

We have already given considerable attention to all of the above except for the lips.

Again, there are several schools of thought about lip positions, but they fall into two basic groups:

  (1) Smiling Position
  (2) Non-smiling Position

Ideally, the lips should only reflect proper voice production. Lip position should be an effect. If lip positions are conceived as cause, there will be an *inevitable faulty adjustment* of more important parts of the vocal mechanism.

---

[1]Lamperti, Francesco; *THE ART OF SINGING*, revised edition (with translation by J.C. Griffith); G. Schirmer, Inc., New York; p. 19.

When the lips are controlled directly, they take on a muscular look. This is not only a sign of strain; it is also unattractive.

The problem of either concept— to smile or not to smile— is one of extremes. The smiling position aids many singers in keeping the vocal folds approximated, but it frequently puts too much "edge" to the voice. Such a singer would fare better if he allowed the lips to form a less pronounced smile and found a better way to keep his vocal folds together.

Singers who prefer not to smile feel they would lose the integration of the open throat with mask resonance if they assumed a smiling position.

The natural positions are best.

In the lower and lower-middle parts of the singer's range the [i] and [e] are formed in a smiling position, but the corners of the mouth should not be held tightly. The [o] and [u] are formed with rounded lips. The [ɑ] is somewhere between the [e] and the [o].

As the singer ascends the scale, toward the upper middle and high part of his range, the lip opening elongates vertically. Many singers feel their lips as an oval. Others feel them as an inverted triangle with two to four of the upper teeth showing. How these singers feel must be reconciled with how they look by checking themselves in a mirror.

In the lower parts of the singing range, a singer can smile more easily. As he ascends the scale, the smile should diminish. If he wishes to convey a smiling attitude in the upper range, he must learn to "smile with the eyes." Some teachers suggest smiling with the cheek bones. Once that is accomplished, he may find that is also the best way to smile in the lower range as well.

e. Range

Most well-developed voices have a range of approximately three octaves— two of which are under complete control. Some singers have more than three *usable* octaves, but that is exceptional. Some excellent singers do not have three octaves. That is not so unusual, especially for tenors. Tenors are fortunate to have two really good octaves from C below middle C to the C an octave above.

Range is one means of determining voice classification, but it is not the best way. The *tessitura* is generally conceded to be the best determiner of the category for which a singer is best suited.

Tessitura means the most frequently used part of a singer's range. A baritone or bass can sing notes in the tenor's upper range, but not for long! It is "all right for a visit, but they wouldn't want to live there." Endurance has to be a factor in determining a singer's tessitura. Color of a singer's voice is also of extreme importance, especially for those who are prone to "type cast" operatic roles.

Naturally, range has to be a consideration in voice classification. If a soprano is required to sing an E♭ above high C and does not have that note, she will not be able to sing many coloratura roles.

If an alto does not have an impressive A below middle C, she will not be an impressive alto. A bass without a good low F above low C has either not learned to sing or is not a bass. For more on this subject, read Appendix III, Voice Classification.

f. Timing

Rhythm and Tempo excluded, the importance of timing in singing technique should be obvious.

Breathing must be timed as accurately as the rhythmic configuration of the notes and rests.

Breath support must be gauged in relation to the pitch of a given note, or it could be too strong or too weak for its purpose. Gauging involves timing.

In articulation, if a singer is to anticipate the vowel position *before* its preceding consonant, timing must be perfect.

The act of coordinating any of the elements of vocalization must happen at that point in time which is most advantageous for achieving the desired result. "Timing is of the essence." One can easily see that a profound awareness of the music is an absolute necessity in terms of realizing proper timing from a purely technical standpoint. Not only is music a *temporal art*; it is a *temporal science*.

g. Trills

The trill is a musical ornamentation which involves a rapid oscillation of pitch between a composed tone and its neighboring tone of a given tonality; also, in phonetics, the trill is a rapid vibration of one organ of speech against another. For vocal music, the latter is used almost exclusively for the [r] of foreign languages.

The *ornamental* trill originated in the 16th century; and, for approximately three centuries, it evolved by following certain harmonic dictates prevalent in each period of musical history. The trill varies, then, in different musical periods.

THE HARVARD DICTIONARY OF MUSIC, by Willi Apel,[1] gives a concise, four-part historical development of the trill. As our interest here must be limited to the technical aspects of the trill, the reader should keep in mind that additional study will be necessary in order to learn its correct musical application. The early Baroque trill required a rapid repetition of notes on a given pitch. Our attention will be devoted to the trill which involves a rapid alternation of two pitches.

The interval of the trill is usually limited to a minor or major second, although some of our modern music extends the interval size to minor and major thirds and, in rare cases, to even wider distances. Once the technique for minor and major seconds is set, however, the larger intervals will fall in place through an extension of the same principles.

---

[1]Apel, Willi; *THE HARVARD DICTIONARY OF MUSIC*; Harvard University Press; eleventh printing 1958; Cambridge, Massachusetts; pp. 760-762.

When trills first began (16th century), the practice was to start one scale degree above the given note and to proceed downward to that given note (See Fig. 99a). The modern trill (19th century) starts on the given note and trills upward. (See Fig. 99b.)

Manual Garcia calls the given note the *Principal* and the note above (or below) the *Auxiliary*. Henceforth, I shall use his terminology.[1]

Principal Note

Trill

a. b.

Fig. 99

The use of the trill has diminished greatly in modern times. Although composers have indicated trills in their compositions for all voice categories, the soprano seems to have almost exclusive rights to the ornament. I think this is unfortunate. There are occasions in any singer's music when a *well-performed* trill is a valuable means for evoking certain moods. Perhaps it is the indiscreet use of the trill which has contributed to its decline; or perhaps singers have not applied themselves to developing the trill adequately to warrant its continuation.

I believe all singers should develop a trill whether they intend to use it in performance or not. We should not throw away our "tools of the trade" and let them disappear forever through abuse or disuse. Every time a student opts to make life easier for himself by avoiding certain areas of knowledge, he sells himself short. Not only does this approach to life limit the broad area of a person's art; it activates adverse psychological forces within him which tend to undermine his confidence in every other thing he does thereafter.

Our object here will be to develop the trill on intervals of minor and major seconds.

To begin the development of a good trill, a singer must be able to do two things:

(1) Hear two notes simultaneously (the principal and the auxiliary notes)
(2) Assume and maintain the physical position for singing these two notes simultaneously

Until he can do this, the singer's progress will be unrewarding.

One approach to developing the trill is to sing the first note (let us begin with the auxiliary note) as a grace note and sing downward to the principal note. This should be done slowly and deliberately at first. As security is gained, acceleration will be possible, thusly:

---

[1]Garcia, Manual, translated by Beata Garcia; *HINTS ON SINGING*; Publisher, E. Ascherberg and Co.; London, 1894; p. 42.

[These pitches are optional. Lower pitches may work better; however, head voice tones are more flexible.]

Fig. 100

As the singer progresses through the above exercise, he should begin to feel that the grace note and the principal note become *equalized*. By that, I mean the accent should gradually disappear and the two notes should take on the same time value.

Consequently, the musical configuration will look and feel more like this:

Fig. 101

It is important for the singer to feel a rapid vertical *beating* (or oscillation) in the neck,

Fig. 102

but with absolutely *no neck tension!* The energy of this oscillation must be controlled by the breath support mechanism. A possible organic image of this act could be:

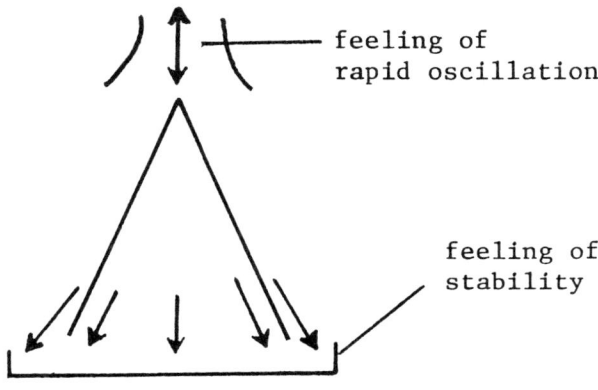

Fig. 103

The singer must develop the facility of "letting go" at the neck, yet maintain an awareness of oscillation. He must also *not* feel as if the support mechanism oscillates. It must stay firm and flexible. Through consistent and patient practice, the singer will become increasingly aware of the necessary proportions of effort for achieving balance between supporter and oscillator.

The *phonetic* trill is frequently difficult for both the beginning and the advanced singer. The principal problem is a stiff or lazy tongue. Before a singer can develop a sustained trill, he usually has to develop a *flipped* (or *flapped*) [ɾ]. A common method for doing this is to imitate the British pronunciation of the word "very." They pronounce the word "veddy." The student should practice this word, thinking an [r] but saying a [d], until he becomes quite fluent and relaxed. Then he should note the flapping tongue's movement and begin getting two or more flaps on one breath stroke. This should point him in the right direction for developing a sustained, buzzy trill.

B. Health Problems

Physical and mental health are subjects which the non-singer does not usually associate with singing. In fact, a large number of would-be singers are unaware that there is a *vitally* important relationship between singing and good health. We shall examine health problems under two categories:

1. Physical Health
2. Psychological Health

1. Physical Health

It is often said that singers are vocal athletes. I agree with that idea whole-heartedly. How many football or basketball coaches would allow members of their teams to be careless about physical *or* mental health? Not many *successful* ones, one can be sure.

A successful coach will have specific requirements for his athletes in regard to the following:

  a. Rest
  b. Diet
  c. Physical Training
  d. Morality (undegenerative thoughts and actions)
  e. Maladies and Afflictions

The same should should apply equally to vocal athletes.

  a. Rest

  A singer should never perform, practice, or study from a position of weakness. Fatigue is weakness. Whether fatigue results from over-work, dissipation, or a physical predisposition for it, the singer should avoid singing when he is in that condition. If his stamina is low, he should work toward building it through proper study, practice, and living. How one achieves this is an individual problem. What works for one may not work for another. The guide-line is simply: When tired, do not sing; but strive to keep singing.

  b. Diet

  I will not presume to tell anyone what he should eat or drink. There are signs which should be all too apparent to the singer himself that his diet needs change. Any time a singer's diet contributes to a deficiency in his energy or function, it should be obvious that a change is in order. What that change should be is probably best decided by the singer's doctor.

Another aspect of diet concerns food or drink which may be *temporarily* advantageous or detrimental to a singer's performance. For example:

>Should he drink milk before a performance?
>Should he eat chocolate?
>Should he drink stimulants, such as tea, coffee, cola, or alcoholic beverages?

The only answer to any of these and similar questions is: *NO*, if it affects the singer's energy or function adversely, and *YES*, if it does not.

It is my personal opinion that alcohol serves no useful physical or psychological purpose in regard to singing. Certain tests have been made which indicate that the vocal folds swell almost immediately after alcohol is taken internally. If this be true, alcohol is definitely bad for singing and the serious singer should avoid it.

Coffee, tea, and cola may, or may not, be detrimental to certain individuals. The chances are greater that they are more detrimental than beneficial, however, as caffeine, in my experience, tends to make more people nervous than calm.

Some singers refuse to sing without having drunk milk or eaten chocolate shortly before a performance. Others avoid either of these for hours or days before a performance.

Amounts of food and timing of food are also subjects which con- concern singers.

Some performers are so nervous before a performance they are incapable of eating within five or six hours, or longer, before they have to sing. Others are impervious to this sort of problem and eat immediately before the performance and during intermissions. It seems to be very much an individual problem; however, a tight stomach will not allow the singer as much breathing space, which could cause problems with singing.

The question, "What should a singer drink before and during a performance to combat thirst?" is appropriate. Again, there is no best answer. "One man's meat is another man's poison!" applies here. Could you suck a lemon? Many singers do. Could you eat an apple or orange? This is even more popular. Water is also popular, as are many exotic mixtures, too numerous to list here. Some singers chew gum, or just *pretend* to chew, in order to activate the salivary glands.

The best suggestion I can offer is *Experiment*; but experiment at those times where a bad decision will not be so costly. I would not recommend experimenting on the day of an important recital or public performance. It would be much better to test out any new concoction before a daily practice session.

c. Physical Training

A singer's physical training is handled in two ways:

(1) Training the vocal mechanism
(2) Training the body for general good health

(1) **Training the vocal mechanism**

We have discussed this subject sufficiently in the previous chapters.

(2) **Training the body for general good health**

No matter how well a singer has developed his vocal mechanism, his singing will be better if the rest of his physique is in equally good condition.

A strong, healthily conditioned body contributes more than the physical vitality and dexterity reflected in the quality of a person's singing. There is the additional psychological advantage of *knowing* he is physically fit and responsive to all contingencies. Every singer can benefit from a regular, sane, and balanced regimen of physical exercise.

d. **Morality (undegenerative thoughts and actions)**

As this is not a text for theologians, I shall broach only those moral subjects which are directly related to vocal health.

Degenerative thoughts are those thoughts which undermine productive vocalization. They may be as innocuous as thoughts which disturb concentration when concentration is needed for vocal pursuits; or they may be as insidious as the worst obsessions. This aspect of morality best belongs with psychological problems.

Degenerative actions are those actions which work at cross-purposes with healthy vocalization. These actions include taking of drugs for reasons other than medicinal; excessive use of intoxicants or other stimulants not considered as dietary; physical over-taxation of an immoral or intemperate nature. I shall leave it to the fertile imagination of the reader to decide if and how these excesses apply to him.

e. **Maladies and Afflictions**

Thus far, our discussion of health has covered only the *preventive medicine* aspects, as applied to singing. Not being a physician, I could not attempt to discuss neurological or organic disorders, except to say that a singer must be in *adequate* physical health when he undertakes the rigorous task of singing. Whenever there may be doubt, a student should contact his physician for advice. If a student should have a heart condition, for example, only his doctor would dare say if his nerves or the physical demands of singing would make this a dangerous activity for him.

In many cases singing has proved to be therapeutic for those who have various physical disorders.

Two of my former students suffered from severe cases of asthmatic allergies. They would often come for voice lessons and appear to be very much indisposed. Before the lessons were over, lethargy and sniffles generally changed to enthusiasm and apparent good health. Their doctors condoned this activity.

Frequent indispositions of this sort would tend to make consideration of a singing career highly impractical. However, there are many singers in the world who have no desire to be professional. They just enjoy singing.

Upper respiratory disorders are the most common illnesses which afflict singers. Of these, the cold is the most frequent culprit. A singer should be able to perform with a head cold at no loss of comfort or vocal quality. But a cold which involves chest congestion and/or a sore throat is a legitimate problem. If a singer performs in that condition, it could easily progress to worse problems, such as tracheitis, bronchitis, pharyngitis, or laryngitis. Therefore, he should not sing with a severe cold.

Colds strike everyone, but they most assuredly strike those who allow themselves to be physically run-down.

Tests within the past few years indicate that the taking of aspirin before a performance is not a good idea. Van Lawrence writes that taking aspirin "...increases the fragility of capillaries."[1] This, he says, contributes to greater incidence of hemorrhage in the vocal folds. A singer could activate such a hemorrhage trying for a high note with excessive sub-glottal pressure, which could put him out of business for two or more weeks.

Phlegm (catarrh) is usual when a singer has a cold. With a head cold, presuming he has a good technique, he can sing *through* or *over* the phlegm. If he does *not* have a cold and has an excessive amount of phlegm, Mother Nature might be trying to tell him he is misusing his voice. Phlegm is nature's cushion against excessive grating of the vocal folds. A throat specialist should advise anyone in this predicament.

The throat loves moisture. Singers should train themselves to breathe through their noses when not singing, as this does not dry the throat as mouth-breathing does. Frequently a singer will breathe through his mouth while sleeping. This is one of the quickest ways of getting a sore throat. Sometimes the singer may be able to train himself for nose-breathing while sleeping, but it is not an easy task. Another means of fighting dryness is by drinking enough liquids to minimize body water loss. Dr. Van Lawrence tells us "...throats which have wet, watery coatings don't produce awareness in us. The larynx which is moist and well-lubricated won't make us feel the need to cough and clear and grind. The larynx whose vocal folds are vibrating against each other 125 times per second, covered with a thin profuse lubricant won't produce the sense of glue, the dry buzz, the fuzz in the voice."[2]

2. Psychological Health

A singer's psyche has an immeasurable influence upon his musical success. It is fraught with both positive and negative forces. Some of the more common of these are:

    a. Confidence

---

[1] Lawrence, Van, M.D.; Laryngoscope: "When All Else Fails Read The Instructions;" *THE NATS BULLETIN*, Vol. 39, No. 3; Jan./Feb. 1983; p. 16.
[2] Lawrence, Van, M.D.; Laryngoscope: "Post-Nasal Drip"; *THE NATS BULLETIN*, Vol. 39, No. 1; Sept./Oct. 1982; p. 28.

b. Ego (Self-Image)
   c. Excitement
   d. Lethargy
   e. Motivation (Enthusiasm)
   f. Nervousness (Fear, Stage-Fright, etc.)

a. Confidence

"Nothing succeeds like success." A singer must build a growing repository of *little successes* in his development from student to virtuoso. The surest way to achieve this is to start with a positive attitude and then learn, thoroughly, those *prerequisites* for achieving his goal. Knowledge insures confidence. Applied knowledge gives it *double indemnity*.

Ethel Merman once said "Why should I be nervous? I *know* my lines." When a singer is *that* sure of himself, he has confidence.

My high school civics teacher once quoted a philosopher (whose name I never knew) as saying, "Act as you'd like to be, and soon you'll be the way you act." This is good advice. If a singer acts in a confident manner, he will soon achieve confidence. Of course, this is like *Freedom*. You have to fight for it to keep it. But it is worth it.

b. Ego (Self-Image)

The singer should not let the old proverb, "Pride goeth before the fall!" deter him professionally. He must know his worth. Every singer should have a *touch* of Narcissism if he hopes to project a strong theatrical image. Certainly, he must keep this trait under control, or he will alienate those he needs as allies— his audience and his colleagues. A singer can possess a well-defined ego without being obnoxious, but he must tread carefully.

c. Excitement

Many singers associate excitement with panic or stage-fright. A more positive approach is to consider excitement as *elation*. Through this concept, a singer can divert *all* excitement, including stage-fright, into productive channels. (See pp. 16-17)

d. Lethargy

Lethargy is *a state of inaction or indifference*. Although lethargy feels *physical*, it is definitely a *psychological* problem. The only way to fight lethargy is to recognize it for what it is and *demand* of oneself a positive substitute— *ENTHUSIASM*. Enthusiasm is the most positive force in positive thinking.

Remember: *ACT enthusiastic and soon you will BE enthusiastic.*

e. Motivation

If a person is properly motivated, achievement is assured. Strong motivation is enthusiasm, personified. If a singer is not enthusiastic about developing his art, he should forget it! He will be both miserable and unsuccessful.

f. Nervousness

Nervousness results from being unprepared and *knowing* it, or from the *suspicion* of being unprepared.

In the former instance, nervousness is justified. The singer *deserves* the anguish that comes with nervousness. The solution here is over-preparation, which allows the singer a margin for error in judgement.

In the latter instance, the singer may be immaculately prepared and only *think* he is not ready for performance. Some artists of international repute never combat this problem satisfactorily. Lily Pons was reported as having to regurgitate before many of her performances; but this did not diminish her excellence; only her comfort.

Sometimes singers set unrealistic standards for themselves and are never able to meet them. This is the same, for them, as being unprepared. Others are afraid of falling below standards they have already met.

Another instance of nervousness occurs when a performer is reasonably confident that he is well-prepared, but fears the consequences of bad luck or accidents not necessarily due to his own efforts. This, of course, is negative thinking and can best be countered by positive thinking.

The following advice is not always possible for everyone, but everyone should try it: *Enjoy the performance!*

If it is too painful, perhaps it is the wrong business.

CHAPTER IX
THE WHOLE ELEPHANT

I would like to introduce this chapter with my adaptation of John Godfrey Saxe's well-known poem, "The Blind Men And The Elephant," based on an old Hindoo fable and written sometime before 1887. (Mr. Saxe's poem is included in Appendix IX, as a reference for those who may not be acquainted with it.)

THE DEAF MEN AND THE DIVA

Six worthy men of Academe
  Whom study never tired,
While listening to a diva
  (Though all were deaf) aspired
To learn by close analysis
  What was to be admired.

The *First* proposed a postulate
  His insight did advance,
Observing how erect she was,
  Her figure to enhance:
"My goodness, but her artistry
  Stems from her noble stance!"

The *Second*, noting how she could
  Her torso so disport,
Was moved to chance an estimate
  And loudly did report,
"It's clear to me what makes her great:
  Abdominal support!"

The *Third* responded eagerly,
  The first two to negate.
"I feel it, most distinctly,
  Upon my very pate;
Induced reverberation.
  My word, she can phonate!"

The *Fourth* spoke out, forthrightly
  The others to confound;
"See, when the lips purse gently,
  The jaw drops toward the ground?
It's clear, the upper partials
  Do make her voice resound."

The *Fifth* replied astutely,
  The secret to unlatch.
"Look how her mouth so deftly
  Her tongue and teeth do match?
With fine articulation
  The words she can dispatch!"

The *Sixth* would give no quarter;
  With ardor he averred,
"Her obvious expression,
  Above all else preferred,
Proves her supreme involvement
  With each and every word."

And so these men of Academe
  Did argue hard and strong,
Each firm in his conclusion
  What makes a well-sung song,
While each was partly in the right,
  And all were in the wrong!

MORAL

So oft in theoretic jousts
  The combatants, quite absurd,
Fight on and are oblivious
  To one another's word,
And bicker o'er a diva
  Not one of them has heard!

For a number of years, I have been impressed with the ironic wit and potential applicability of Mr. Saxe's poem to the area of vocal pedagogy. Although the general tenor of both "The Blind Men And The Elephant," and the adaptation, above, may seem somewhat negative, I always like to look for that silver lining behind the clouds.

Everyone has, at least, a *piece* of the elephant. Few are so complacent as to think they own the entire beast; otherwise, there would be no need for further exploration in the quest for vocal excellence. This chapter, then, is directed toward those who are still continuing that search; those who still feel a need to gather their resources; those who look to capitalize on becoming conversant with *all* the parts of the elephant in a way that will synthesize them into a complete entity. Certainly, not all the answers will be found in this chapter or in this book; but, for some, it could be a beginning. It is the ongoing effort that is important, even if we never get it all together.

In his editorial column, *sotto voce*, "Have You Read The Literature?," Richard Miller makes a telling point for those vocal pedagogs who have long closed their minds to any and all modern investigation into the subject.

> "...It is improbable that the particular technique chance and circumstance have dictated to a singer is the *only* or even the *most*, efficient approach to vocalism. 'After all, if it works for me, why should I look elsewhere?' is no more applicable to the teaching of singing than to other disciplines..."[1]

In this chapter we shall be concerned with approaches to learning vocal technique more from philosophical and utilitarian standpoints than from a technical one. The areas we shall cover are:

A. Balanced Directions
B. Metaphysical Concepts
C. Characterization
D. Mirrors, Tape and Video Recorders, and Recordings
E. Imagination

A. Balanced Directions

A perplexing situation frequently occurs with a singer who is extremely conscientious: Instead of progressing, he regresses. The harder he works, the farther he falls behind. This seems like gross injustice to him, and it probably is. Presuming this is not a psychological problem, such as a hidden desire to fail, then the solution may lie in his approach.

Throughout this book I have stressed the importance of balance as applied to vocal technique. If a zealous singer attempts to improve his voice by tackling Resonation, for example, he will have problems in a short time with Phonation or something else. Why?

Assuming this individual had his voice under reasonable control before he tried to improve his resonance, the act of isolating one parameter of the vocal mechanism in such a manner will throw the other factors out of balance. The singer may not realize what is happening until he is out of control.

I like to use what I call the *spiral* approach to vocal improvement. Rather than jumping from one factor to another, as follows,

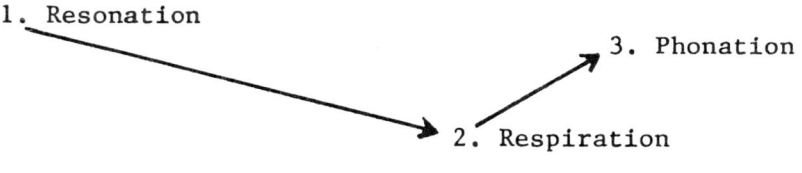

Fig. 104

---

[1] Miller, Richard; *sotto voce*: "Have You Read The Literature?"; THE NATS JOURNAL, Vol, 42, No. 2; November/December 1985; p. 36.

120 VOCAL DEVELOPMENT THROUGH ORGANIC IMAGERY

which is somewhat helter-skelter, I visualize a spiral continuum:

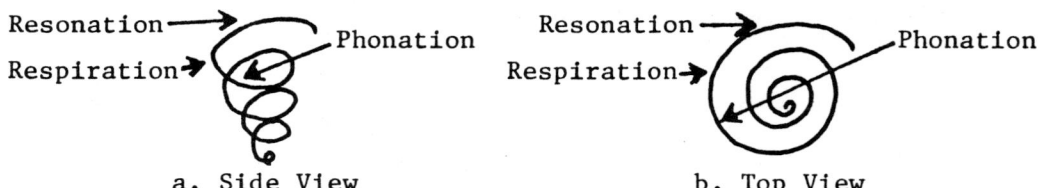

a. Side View   b. Top View

Fig. 105

The advantage of this approach is that not so much distance is put between one factor and another by isolation. There is an everwidening expansion. If one factor grows, all the others grow proportionally (almost). Balance is maintained.

B. Metaphysical Concepts

The concept that "The whole is equal to more than the sum of its parts" is one which might well have been written for the vocal arts. No matter how much we study the process, an inspired vocal performance defies complete analysis.

Since an attempt to comprehend the incomprehensible is probably futile, this part of the text will seem especially Quixotic to the reader. Nevertheless, Don Quixote was not deterred, nor shall I be. It is a noble quest.

After about one year's study, I require my students to read Richard Bach's short, inspired story, *JONATHAN LIVINGSTON SEAGULL*.[1]

It has been my observation that any significant undertaking in life might be considered as a microcosm of life. I firmly believe that singing belongs in this category. Mr. Bach obviously feels that way about aviation because the philosophy comes shining through with Jonathan, from the gull's initial insight to his final (as far as the story takes us) achievement.

I apply one concept, which the Elder Chiang taught Jonathan, to an exercise I call the *J.L.S. vocalise*. That concept is: "Perfect speed is *being* there."

By paraphrasing this in vocal terms, we have: "In perfect vocalization, all the notes are already sung." With this philosophy, the work is done *before* the performance. It is easy to see the advantage of such an arrangement. The vocal exercise, to which I have referred, is in chapter XI (Fig. 119, p. 140). I shall repeat it here, for the sake of convenience:

J.L.S. Vocalise

[Sing this exercise on any vowel]

Fig. 106

---

[1] Bach, Richard; *JONATHAN LIVINGSTON SEAGULL*; The Macmillan Company, pub., 866 Third Avenue, New York, N.Y. 10022; 1970; p. 65.

For several years I thought I had originated the above exercise. It is an humbling experience to find it has been done more than two centuries earlier.

The value of this exercise is in the graduated intervals. The singer always returns to middle C, so that note is the stabilizer. Many singers get nervous and/or lose control, the wider these intervals become. With the J.L.S. concept, this fear is unnecessary, as he has already sung the notes before he starts. The singer should *enjoy the flight*.

One consistent problem a number of my students have in learning to do this exercise is finding *do* (the tonic) after singing the higher notes. The descending scale seems especially more troublesome in this respect. They seem unwilling to *let go* of their support and do not drop low enough. Another benefit of this exercise is the relaxation (or a feeling of *neutrality*) effect of dropping into *do* on pitch and without locking the support muscles.

Before leaving the subject of Jonathan Livingston Seagull, let me mention just three of the many gems of truth to be gleaned from this little masterpiece:

"The gull sees farthest who flies highest."[1] [Ambition]

"Break the chains of your thought and you break the chains of your body, too..."[2] [Freedom]

"...You don't need me any longer. You need to keep finding yourself, a little more each day..."[3] [Independence]

I am hesitant to introduce the next metaphysical aspect of singing because I have mentioned previously (p. 29, ¶ 1) that the singer cannot control the intrinsic muscles of the larynx directly. There are those who take exception with that statement, although most voice teachers have accepted the idea that the laryngeal muscles cannot be controlled directly.

For beginning voice students, I believe that theory should be advocated. More advanced students, however, may want to challenge the premise. Those who have become involved with yoga and transcendental meditation believe that an individual can actually isolate any part of his body from the rest and train it— inherent musculature and all— to do his bidding. I would like to think that is possible, but I still hold some reservations. The importance of yoga and transcendental meditation is not whether the proponent actually controls the larynx (or any other part of the vocal apparatus) directly or indirectly, or if he only *thinks* he is doing so. What is important is that the mechanism be controlled in *some* way. If the singer really believes in direct control and gets the desired results, more power to him. He may be right.

Frederick Husler and Yvonne Rodd-Marling wrote, more than twenty years ago, about different experiments conducted by the Bell Telephone Company, by the University Clinic of the Sorbonne in Paris, by Kurt Goerttler

---

[1] Bach, Richard; *JONATHAN LIVINGSTON SEAGULL*; The Macmillan Company, pub., 866 Third Avenue, New York, N.Y. 10022; 1970; p. 86.
[2] Op. cit.; p. 104.
[3] Op. cit.; p. 115.

(Leipzig), and by R. Husson, regarding "Self-Vibration of the vocal folds." In essence, their findings indicated that it is possible for the vocal folds to vibrate without breath! The brain alone can make them vibrate.

Of course, not much sound was produced without breath because, as Husler and Rodd-Marling stated, "...breath is simply the element that carries and forms the sound."[1] These writers state that the evidence has not gone unchallenged and is still unsubstantiated.

In an interview with Cornelius Reid, Deborah Seabury quoted him as saying, "We have to breathe to live,... but I am increasingly convinced that breath has almost nothing to do with singing at all."[2] After explaining that the average lungs have a vital capacity of 2,200 to 5,000 cc. (cubic centimeters) Reid continued, "Singing well, one uses about 36 cc of breath per second, so it is obviously unrelated to vital capacity."[3] On this point, Reid concluded by explaining that the inexpert singer wastes breath, using about 280 cc per second.

What the voice student may glean from the foregoing (and this is implied by Husler and Rodd-Marling) is this: Even if self-vibration of the vocal folds should not be substantiated, experiments to attempt self-vibration could contribute greatly to the ease of vocal production. In order to come even close to achieving this phenomenon, all muscles of the throat must be absolutely relaxed (or, at least, comfortably tensed). In such a state, a minimum of breath would be far more efficient than otherwise. The breath would have little more to do than carry the sound. This, apparently, is what inspired Mr. Reid to make his observations.

C. Characterization

All interpretation involves characterization. Characterization should be *laid over* phonation— not mixed with it.

Technically, characterization is determined by articulation (both vowels and consonants), vowel color, timing, intensity, and body usage. These qualities must *never* interfere with healthy phonation or any aspect of vocal production.

I once had a student who, in order to sing a musical comedy role calling for a "Brooklyn" accent, began by mutilating his throat in order to get the effect. Through diligent study, he learned how to get the accent by timing, articulation and vowel substitution, rather than by using a "croaky" vocal production.

Another common mistake with many performers is getting too subjectively involved with their characterization. Some feel it is marvelous to cry real tears in a performance. I once saw a performance of Shakespeare's play, *OTELLO*, in which the title character was so caught up in the emotion of this magnificent drama that his voice became garbled and the diction completely unintelligible for a large portion of the play. Crying real tears in a vocal performance is not artistry; it is self-indulgence!

[1] Husler, Frederick and Rodd-Marling, Yvonne; *SINGING: THE PHYSICAL NATURE OF THE VOCAL ORGAN*; October House Inc.; New York; 1965; pp. 54-56.
[2] Seabury, Deborah; Voice Teachers II: "The Singer's World" (The second of a two-part article); *OPERA NEWS*, Vol. 43, No. 8; December 16, 1978; p. 16.
[3] Ibid. p. 16.

D. Mirrors, Tape and Video Recorders, and Recordings

We never see and hear ourselves as others do. Practice in front of a mirror is of inestimable value for singers. The mirror will not only indicate good or bad posture and stage presence; it will tell the singer when he is straining or violating good vocal practices. One frequent problem I have encountered with a number of my students is their hesitance to look at themselves while they sing. Although they may be facing the mirror, they seem to be looking *through*, rather than *at* themselves. I ask them, "Is what you see so horrible that you can't bear looking?" This should be an instant tip-off that something is wrong. The mirror does not lie (except to present left as right and vice versa). The student can make a quantum leap forward by learning to accept what he sees and then adjust it as needed.

The same may be said of a tape recorder. The student is invariably shocked when he hears his voice for the first time. This is because his image of his voice differs from reality. Through proper use of a tape or cassette recorder, a singer can develop a more objective ear for his own voice. All my voice majors bring cassette tapes to their lessons.

Seeing oneself on video-tape replays is even more revealing. With the increasing availability of video cameras, video taping of performances is growing rapidly.

Singers should also listen to as many recordings and live performances of first-rate artists as they can. Without imitating these singers, they will form higher standards of tonal imagery for themselves. One can see the importance of this when he remembers that tonal concept is the very first thing a singer must have before he utters his first sound in performance. (See 2. The Attack, p. 46; ¶1)

E. Imagination - The bottom line

It would be remiss of me to discuss everything that has gone before in terms of *balance* and *coordination* without mentioning *Imagination*. Without a well-developed imagination, any pursuit in life can only be drudgery. A *drudge* can never hope to sing or to do anything else in life which demands *flair*.

The measure of an artist's success is directly proportional to the quality of his imagination and his determination to succeed. These qualities promote *enthusiasm*, without which it is inconceivable that one would commit himself to the rigorous demands of singing.

I believe that imagination can be cultivated just as any other discipline. All learning involves sensing, analyzing, organizing, relating, and concluding. This is exactly what happens in the process of imagination.

1. The singer must be aware of his environment; he must sense.

2. The singer must understand what he senses; he must analyze.

3. The singer must sift and juxtapose what he analyzes; he must organize.

4. The singer must understand how one organ, organism, or organization affects another; he must relate.

5. The singer must recognize the form resulting from his efforts; he must conclude.

Man has at least five senses: sight, hearing, smell, taste, and touch. His ability to intensify each of these will make his life more vivid; hence, flexible in terms of developing a better imagination. A gourmet is one who has developed his gustatory and olfactory senses to the point of virtuosity.

Suppose an actor who has only reached the "meat and potatoes" stage of appreciation for food were called upon to portray a gourmet in a sophisticated play. Would his portrayal— everything else being equal— be as convincing as one given by a true gourmet? The reader can use his imagination to see how this heightened awareness of sensory perception will apply to the other senses and to the quality of his own imagination.

Of course, a gourmet did not get that way on fundamental sensory perception alone. He had to go through the other four stages in order to develop a high degree of discernment about food.

Similarly, a music critic (a really fine one) develops a very *good ear* for what he hears. But he too must analyze, organize, relate, and conclude before he can really "hear." So we come full circle. Perception is necessary for knowledge and knowledge heightens perception. Both are the life-blood of imagination.

I have noted that those of my students who seem to have well-developed imaginations are not only capable of giving more artistic performances, generally; they are also quicker to respond to suggestions of a purely technical nature. Consequently, their vocal progress is greater.

Oftentimes a student seems to have the potential for developing a strong imagination but cannot quite get it started. In most such cases the enemy is *prejudice*. Prejudice will stymie imagination more completely than ignorance. One of the sad facts about prejudice is that the perpetrator is unaware of it. More time is spent by voice teachers in *unlocking* prejudices of students with one to four years of previous incorrect training than it would take to develop a rank and file beginner.

Before such a singer can free his voice, he must free his mind. A mind set free is an imaginative mind. This is the reason the concept of organic imagery works so well with beginning voice students. If it accomplishes nothing else, it forces the student to use his power of mental imagery. The more vividly this is developed, the more efficient is his progress.

William Bates, the noted ophthalmologist and author of *BETTER EYESIGHT WITHOUT GLASSES*,[1] maintained that, if a person who has vision problems would close his eyes and imagine a small black dot on a light background, his vision would improve. The problem with this is the difficulty of imagining a *perfectly* black dot. Most of us see a haze around the dot, or streaks running through it, or a lack of sharpness in delineation of it.

Dr. Bates and his advocates cured or improved many visual problems by helping their patients develop better mental images of the black dot and other forms through *relaxation*. A person's ability to imagine is

---

[1] Bates, William H., M.D.; *BETTER EYESIGHT WITHOUT GLASSES*; Holt, Rinehart and Winston; 1940 and 1943; Pyramid Books (Paper Back), 919 Third Ave., New York, N.Y. 10022, eighth printing; 1975; p. 72.

impeded if he is tense. Does that sound familiar? Dr. Bates advocated relaxation as an aid for improving the *memory*, as well as vision.

Another famous doctor once stated, "The only disease is congestion; the only cure is circulation."[1] Think about that.

One of the best exercises I have seen for helping a performer expand his imagination was used at the International Opera Studio in Zurich, Switzerland. Lotfi Mansouri was the principal stage director there at that time. He had each singer sit in front of the rest of the studio members and, with no time limit, begin to smile. The smile grew to a snicker and slowly crescendoed into a loud guffaw.

After the singer reached his particular climax of laughter, he started to diminish the laughter again, very slowly, until he was not even smiling. Then he went slowly toward the other extremity, beginning with a whimper and moving to extreme anguish and back again, finally to a completely neutral state— neither of joy nor sadness.

Some of the singers were more successful at laughing than crying; for others, the reverse was true. In discussing the exercise afterward, the comments of each singer about himself and how he felt as he progressed from one emotional degree to another was most revealing. Some thought of very unhappy events in their lives to help evoke tears. Some did not think at all. They "just felt." One neither thought nor felt— he only went through the motions. Needless to say, the latter performance was unconvincing.

The reader should remember that the above exercise is *only* an exercise. If it should induce real tears or real laughter, the student must be aware that it is a priming device for triggering a better understanding of the emotions of despair or joy, and parts in between. As an artist, he must then bring them under *objective control*.

Obviously, one key ingredient for imagination is *experience*. The more assiduously a performer collects and organizes his experiences, the greater will be his arsenal of ideas.

Singing and acting are interpretive arts. A limited imagination will beget a narrow interpretation. It will be *congested*. Circulation is the cure. Let your senses circulate; let your breath circulate; let your voice *move*.

A three-fold guideline can assist the singer in finding this cure: (1) If it hurts, it is definitely wrong. (2) If it is neutral, something is missing. (3) If there is physical, emotional and spiritual ecstasy, it is definitely right! You are on the track of *the whole elephant*.

The imagination has no walls if you turn it loose. It is boundless.

---

[1] Corbett, Margaret Darst, (quoting Dr. S. Weir Mitchell); *HELP YOURSELF TO BETTER SIGHT*; Prentice-Hall, Inc.; Englewood Cliffs, New Jersey; 1949; Wilshire Book Company (Paper Back edition), 12015 Sherman Road, No. Hollywood, California 91605; 1974; p. 23.

CHAPTER X
USING THE IPA

The IPA (International Phonetic Alphabet) was devised by the International Phonetic Association (also abbreviated, IPA) or, as it was originally known, *Association Phonétique Internationale*. This organization was founded in 1886 by a group of prominent phoneticians from France, Germany, Britain, and Denmark.

Phoneticians have always had an interest in how words are pronounced; but, only toward the end of the nineteenth century, did they begin to feel a real need for methods of showing how the tongue articulated speech sounds. During the remainder of the nineteenth century research in the field abounded, although the quality of that research was limited by crude scientific instruments and embryonic methods; but it was a start. Today, with the logarithmic growth of technology, the machinery for this type of investigation has become quite sophisticated, culminating, thus far, in most acceptable synthesized speech.

The ingenuity of the earlier investigators should be respected, in spite of their limited yield. For example, as early as 1780, Baron Wolfgang von Kempelen devised the first speaking machine of any significance. After two unsuccessful attempts, he emerged with an instrument comprised of a bellows, a tuning pipe, and several resonance cavities. This machine could produce vowels (with artistic help from the operator) and the following consonants: [l, m, n, r, p, b, t, d, k, g, f, v, s, z, ʃ, h, w, j][1]

Much earlier than von Kempelen, Leonardo da Vinci made several contributions to phonetics and voice science. Many may not be aware that he was the first person to:

1. Make drawings of phonetic and phoniatric subjects;
2. Recognize the part played by the ventricles in phonation;
3. Realize the importance of the larynx as the primary voice-producing organ;
4. Express some notion of subglottal pressure;
5. Write of whispering;
6. Demonstrate clearly the production of the voice by means of the lungs, larynx, and trachea (using the corpse of a goose);
7. Discover the maxillary sinuses; and
8. Draw pictures of anomalies of lips, jaw, and teeth.

In addition to the above, da Vinci could explain the cooperation of the larynx in phonation and the nature of sound waves. This man did much more than paint pretty pictures, sculpt statues, and design buildings.

Jean Badouin de Courtenay, who distinguished between the *phone* (a speech sound) and the *phoneme* (a class of speech sounds) is probably the first linguistician to establish a phonemic theory. He was a Polish philologist who founded a school of linguistics in Russia. Through his students, he became known in Western Europe. One of these students, Kruszewski, actually made the distinction between phone and phoneme, but De Courtnay formulated the theory.

---

[1]Moses, Elbert R. Jr.; *PHONETICS - HISTORY AND INTERPRETATION*; Prentice-Hall, Inc.; Englewood Cliffs, N.J.; 1964; pp. 173-174.

USING THE IPA 127

The eminent British phonetician, Daniel Jones, used the phoneme [k] to explain how the one consonant is used slightly differently in the three words, [kiːp] (keep), [koːl]* (call), and [kuːl] (cool) for orthographic, grammatical, and/or semantical purposes; "...the three different k's... are classed together as belonging to the same phoneme, because the variety of k used in kiːp is never used in English before oː or uː, and the k of kuːl is never used before iː or oː, and so on."[1]

At about the same time de Courtenay was formulating his theory (in the 1780's), Henry Sweet, an Englishman, was doing similar, but independent, work. Sweet did not use the terms "phone" and "phoneme," but referred to "broad" and "narrow" types of phonetic transcription.

Broad transcription is much less detailed than narrow transcription, using a minimal number of diacritical marks. This is more common in the various examples we encounter in the standard foreign language diction and English diction texts and in those vocal technique books that use the IPA.

Narrow transcription is more complex, appearing in highly specialized texts demanding the closest possible scrutiny of phonemic groupings, as in comparison of dialects, study of non-European languages, etc. Two common diacritical marks used in narrow transcription, for example, are [̥] and [̪].

The [̥] makes a usually voiced sound voiceless. Peter Ladefoged[2] gives the words "ply" and "try," [pl̥aɪ] and [tr̥aɪ], to illustrate how the little circle takes the *voice* out of the *l* and *r*. The positions are set for these consonants, but the vocal cords do not vibrate until the subsequent vowels are pronounced.

The [̪] beneath a consonant indicates that the sound is formed as a *dental*, rather than as an *alveolar*. These consonants are so pronounced when the gravity of their neighboring consonants forces them into it, as in the words, "heighth" [haɪt̪θ], "health" [hɛəl̪θ], and "width" [wɪd̪θ]. The "th" sound [θ] tends to force the preceding consonants into the dental position; whereas, in such words as "heighten" [haɪtn̩], "held" [hɛəld], and "widely" [waɪdlɪ], the corresponding consonants are produced alveolarly. (Notice that the word, "heighten [haɪtn̩] used still another diacritical mark— the syllabic *n* [n̩].)

As phonemic theory advanced, other distinctions arose. By 1916, de Courtenay and his followers determined that the phoneme should be considered in two ways: psychologically and physically.

Psychologically, the *phoneme* is a more general sound that one envisions in his mind. Physically, the *phone* is a more stable sound, or more concrete. It is the sound one actually hears, not imagines.

This development resulted in two kinds of phonetics: *psychophonetics* (envisioned sounds) and *physiophonetics* (concrete sounds). Corresponding to these two types were two types of phonetic transcription: the *psychophonic*, which represented only phonemes (now called *phonemic* or *linguis-*

---
*British English pronunciation of [kuəl].
[1] Jones, Daniel; *THE PHONEME - ITS NATURE AND USE*; W. Heffer & Sons, LTD.; Cambridge, England; 1950; p. 11.
[2] Ladefoged, Peter; *A COURSE IN PHONETICS*; Harcourt Brace Jovanovich, Inc.; New York - Chicago - San Francisco - Atlanta; 1975; p. 37.

128 VOCAL DEVELOPMENT THROUGH ORGANIC IMAGERY

tically broad transcription) and *physiophonic* (now called *allophonic* or *linguistically narrow* transcription).[1]

At this point we shall adopt the phonemic (broad) transcription for simplification, whenever possible.

The IPA is presented in three ways in this text. In Appendix I, the official alphabet of the International Phonetic Association is given (by permission of that organization). On this chart are many symbols and diacritical marks that are not frequently used in transcription of the conventional art songs. For those who may find them useful or interesting, they are available herein. These readers may also be interested in a small booklet entitled "*PRINCIPLES OF THE INTERNATIONAL PHONETIC ASSOCIATION*," which can be obtained from the Phonetics Department, University College, London, England.

Appendix II presents the IPA in a different form, comparing English, Italian, German, French, and Spanish words. Only four diacritical marks are necessary here.

Within this chapter, the IPA will be presented in still another way, giving a more detailed examination of all the more frequently used symbols and suggestions on how to pronounce them.

In 1964, Berton Coffin, Ralph Errolle, Werner Singer, and Pierre Delattre produced *PHONETIC READINGS OF SONGS AND ARIAS*.[2] This was the first serious collection of song lyrics from the standard repertoire to be spelled with the IPA. The volume included art songs and arias from the leading anthologies and collections available, gleaned from an earlier four-volume set by Dr. Coffin, *THE SINGER'S REPERTOIRE*.

PHONETIC READINGS OF SONGS AND ARIAS contains 115 texts in Italian, 195 in German, and 103 in French, for a total of 413. This book is an excellent source for phonetic spelling in repertoire for beginning, as well as advanced, students. It is surprising that additional volumes of this sort have not yet been published (twenty-one years later), as 413 songs and arias only scratch the surface of the available repertoire.

In 1977, Leyerle Publications produced the first song anthology to include phonetic spelling (as well as word-for-word translations) of the foreign language songs. This was *SONG ANTHOLOGY ONE*, edited by my wife, Anne, and me. It was used originally as a song supplement to this text, but it now seems to have developed "a life of its own." Since its publication, we have produced two more volumes, *SONG ANTHOLOGY TWO* and *FRENCH DICTION SONGS*; and we have, still more recently, published a volume of Italian songs, edited by Professor John Glenn Paton, entitled *L'ARIA BAROCCA*. All these volumes include IPA spelling and word-for-word translations.

That all the above books have been very well received by teachers, students, and singers— both professional and amateur— indicates a growing interest in the use of the IPA. Although there is still a con-

---

[1] Moses, Elbert R. Jr.; *PHONETICS - HISTORY AND INTERPRETATION*; Prentice-Hall, Inc.; Englewood Cliffs, N.J.; 1964; p. 35.
[2] Coffin, Berton; Errolle, Ralph; Delattre, Pierre; and Singer, Werner; *PHONETIC READINGS OF SONGS AND ARIAS*; Pruett Publishing Company; Boulder, Colorado; 1964.

siderable number of "hold outs," the number is diminishing. I have difficulty in understanding why not *all* teachers and singers have not yet enthusiastically adopted the IPA. It is one of the most potent aids in our profession.

Without a thorough knowledge of, at least, the vowels, spelled with the IPA, it would be impossible to read Berton Coffin's magnificent book, *OVERTONES OF BEL CANTO*.[1] Dr. Coffin not only had to resort to all the available vowels in the IPA, but to compose one of his own in order to complete his Chromatic Vowel Chart. The principal purpose for this volume is not for diction, but for technique! Again, I am struck by the question why any voice teacher or singer would deny himself the opportunity of reading this book because he has not *invested* the time (45 minutes) to learn the vowel symbols. Once the vowels are learned, the consonants come quite easily. Most are already familiar, since we use them in our regular alphabet. Others can be learned quickly if the student or teacher has experience in foreign languages. The German umlauts, French nasals, and other sounds we do not use in the English language will already be familiar as sounds. Learning to make these sounds agree with the phonetic symbols is also quite easy. This leaves only a few tricky sounds such as *gli* [ʎi], *ich* [iç], and *ach* [ɑx].

The format for this section of the IPA is based on three columns. The first vertical column lists each IPA symbol. The second vertical column gives the equivalent familiar sound from an English word, or, when necessary, from a foreign word that has no easy English equivalent. Then that English or foreign word is given, spelled in italics. If any additional information is necessary after that, more detail on pronunciation is given.

The first column, containing the IPA symbols, will occasionally have two symbols. In such cases, these symbols are interchangeable, as they are pronounced the same way. I will give the more standard (in America) symbol first. The IPA symbols will always be enclosed in brackets, [ ], in order to distinguish them from the regular English and foreign language spelling and symbols.

IPA   Pronounced as
Symbols: the:

[i]   e   in the English word *eat*. Front, close,[2] unrounded.
[ɪ] [ɩ]   i   in the English word *it*. Front, quarter-close, unrounded.
[e]   e   in the German word *gehen* or the French word *été*. Front, quarter-close, unrounded. The tongue is slightly higher and more forward than for the [e], making it brighter.
[e]   a   in the English word *date* (but without the [ɪ] off-glide,[3] [deɪt], when used in European languages). Front, half-close, unrounded.

---

[1] Coffin, Berton; *OVERTONES TO BEL CANTO - Phonetic Basis of Artistic Singing*; The Scarecrow Press; Metuchen, N.J. and London, England; 1980.
[2] A vowel is termed *close* or *closed* when the tongue is higher than for its corresponding *open*, *half-open*, or *quarter-open* vowel. *Close* has the highest tongue position; *Open* has the lowest, etc.
[3] *Glides* are so called because the tongue and/or lips make a gliding motion during the production of the sound. A similar motion is made in moving from one accented vowel to an adjacent unaccented vowel (including diphthongs). The unaccented vowel is the *off-glide*.

IPA Symbols:	Pronounced as the:	
[ɛ]	e	in the English word *set*. Front, half-open,[1] unrounded.
[æ]	a	in the English word *rat*. Front, three-quarter open, unrounded.
[a]	a	in the British-English word *lamb*. Front, open, unrounded. It sounds half-way between the [ɑ] and [æ].
[ɒ]	o	in the British-English word *hot*. Back, open, rounded. It sounds half-way between the [ɑ] and [ɔ].
[ɚ]	er	in the English word *after*. Unaccented.
[ɝ]	ur	in the English word *hurt*. Accented.
[ɑ]	a	in the English word *father*. Back, open, unrounded.
[u]	oo	in the English word *food*. Back, close, rounded.
[ɯ]	oo	in the English word *food*, (Southwest USA dialect). Back, close, unrounded. It sounds half-way between the [u] and [ʊ].
[ʊ] [ɷ]	oo	in the English word *book*. Back, quarter-close, rounded.
[o]	o	in the English word *boat* (but without the [ʊ] off-glide, [boʊt], when used in European languages). Back, half-close, rounded.
[ɤ]	o	in the English word *jovial*. Back, half-close, unrounded. It sounds half-way between [o] and [ɔ].
[∪]	o	in the English word *joy*. Back, three-quarter open, unrounded. Bright. It sounds somewhere between [ɑ] and [ɔ]. This is a symbol Berton Coffin created for his book, *OVERTONES OF BEL CANTO*.
[ɔ]	a	in the English word *ball*. Back, half-open, rounded. Dark.
[ə]	u	in the English word *upon*. Central, unrounded. Unaccented. When used in European languages, the lips should be gently pursed. (Known as the *schwa*.)
[ʌ]	u	in the English word *up*. Back, half-open, unrounded. Accented.
[ɐ]	a	in the English word *sofa* or in Lisbon Portuguese *para* (second *a*). Low central, three-quarter open, unrounded. Also, sometimes used to denote the quality of long [ɜː] in narrow transcriptions of Southern English.
[y]	ü	in the German word *fühlen* and
	u	in the French word *une*. Front, close, rounded. It is formed by saying [i] while rounding the lips for [u]. It is easier for some singers to form the lip position *before* sounding the vowel. No English equivalent, except in Scotch and Irish dialect.
[ʏ]	ü	in the German word *hütte*. Front, quarter-closed, rounded. It is formed by saying [ɪ] while rounding the lips for [ʊ]. No English equivalent.
[ɥ] [y̆]	u	in the French word *depuis*. Front, close, rounded. This is classified as a consonant, but it is very much like the [y]. Some call it a semi-consonant. It is formed by saying [w] and [y] simultaneously. No English equivalent.
[ø]	oe	in the German word *Goethe* and
	oeu	in the French word *boeufs*. Front, half-close, rounded. It is formed by saying [e] while rounding the lips for an [o]. No English equivalent.
[œ]	ö	in the German word *öffnen* and
	eu	in the French word *seul*. Front, half-open, rounded. It is

---

[1]A vowel is termed *open* when the tongue is lower than for its corresponding *close* vowel. See footnote [2] on previous page.

IPA Symbols:	Pronounced as the:	
		formed by saying [ɛ] while rounding the lips for [ɔ]. No English equivalent.
[õ][1]	o	in the French word *don*. Back, half-close, rounded. Nasal. Form by speaking the first part of the English word *don't*, not completing the *n*. Another way is to speak the [o] while letting air escape from the nose, as well as from the mouth, simultaneously. No English equivalent. See footnote[1].
[ã][1]	am	in the French word *camp*. Back, half-open, rounded. Nasal. Form by speaking the first part of the English word *dawn*, not completing the *n*. Another way is to speak the [ɔ] while letting air escape from the nose, as well as from the mouth, simultaneously. No English equivalent. See footnote[1] in order to avoid confusion about the [õ] and [ã] vowels.
[ɛ̃]	aim	in the French word *faim*. Front, half-open, unrounded. Nasal. Form by speaking the first part of the proper name *Anne*, not completing the *nne*. Another way is to speak the [ɛ] while letting air escape from the nose, as well as from the mouth, simultaneously. No English equivalent.
[œ̃]	un	in the French word *un*. Front, half-open, rounded. Nasal. This is the most difficult of the French nasal vowels to teach. Since we already know we make [œ] by saying [ɛ] while rounding the lips for [ɔ], by adding nasality (letting air escape from the nose and mouth, simultaneously) the singer should achieve the desired result. If that does not work, try a nasal grunt. No English equivalent.
[aʊ]	ow	in the English word *now*.
[oʊ]	o	in the English word *no*.
[eɪ]	ay	in the English word *day*.
[ɔɪ]	oy	in the English word *boy*.
[aɪ]	ie	in the English word *lie*.
[w]	w	in the English word *witch*. [w] is actually the vowel sound, [ʊ], with a lip glide. (See footnote on page 129.)
[ʍ] [hw]	wh	in the English word *which*.
[j]	y	in the English word *you*.
[ʎ]	gl	in the Italian word *gli*. Form by placing the tongue in the forward, European [l] position while speaking the [j]. The English name *William* may be helpful in activating this concept. By isolating the *li*, one gets a close approximation of the correct sound. No English equivalent.
[l]	l	in the English word *let*. The English [l] is preceded by an [ə] with the tongue in the [l] position (alveolar). This differs from the Italian [l], which is pronounced on the tip of the tongue, without the preceding [ə] (dental).
[l̩]	l	as above, but sustained with the [ə] simultaneously. Syllabic.
[ɫ]	л	in the Russian word голубой. This variety of Russian *l* sounds like the American dark *l*, as in the English word *law*. Form by sounding the [l] and [ʌ], simultaneously.
[r] [ɹ]	r	in the English word *raw*. The English [r], or [ɹ], is preceded by an [ə], thus, [ər] or [ɚ]. In European languages

[1] The original phonetic spelling of these two vowels was an unfortunate one, as [õ] is really pronounced [o] with nasality and [ã] is really pronounced [ɔ] with nasality. Changing the spellings would be traumatic to so many that we have not done it, although many diction texts have made the changes.

IPA Symbols:	Pronounced as the:	
		the [r] is trilled and is *not* preceded by an [ə]. For convenience, we shall use the [r], and not the [ɹ] (burred), for both English and foreign languages. (See [ɾ], below.)
[ɾ]	r	in the Italian word *amore*. The [ɾ] is singly flapped, as contrasted with the European [r], which is rolled (trilled). Form by pronouncing the word *very* as *veddy* (British English), with a slightly exaggerated thrust of air toward the tip of the tongue. A few minutes of this kind of practice is usually enough to assure success for most singers. The easily flapped tongue is also the beginning of a successful trill, and the basis for learning the trilled [r].
[h]	h	in the English word *hop*. Aspirant.
[ʔ]	–	glottal click preceding a vowel, as in "Uh, oh!" Often used between two words when the second word begins with a vowel and a separation of the words is required. Formed by gently closing the glottis[1] and allowing a burst of air through the glottis when initiating the vowel.
[p]	p	in the English word *pat*. Voiceless.[2]
[b]	b	in the English word *bit*. Voiced.[3]
[t]	t	in the English word *two*. Voiceless.[2]
[t̪]	t	in the English word *heighth*. Dentalized. Voiceless.[2]
[t̬]	т	in the Russian word опять. Another way of transcribing the symbol is [tj], which makes it sound almost like [tʃ], but not quite so severe. This "soft" Russian [t] is always followed by the Russian symbol, ь, which has no sound of itself, but only signifies that the preceding consonant is softened, or palatalized. The ь's counterpart is the ъ, which hardens the preceding consonant.
[d]	d	in the English word *did*. Voiced.[3]
[k]	k	in the English word *kiss*. Voiceless.[2]
[g]	g	in the English word *glass*. Voiced.[3]
[ç]	ch	in the German word *ich*. Voiceless.[2] Form by saying a voiceless [i] while blowing air between the soft palate and the raised tongue, which is in a high forward position. No English equivalent, except when English singers want more thrust for an [h], in which case they substitute the [ç]. Example: *hue* [çju].
[x]	ch	in the German word *ach*. Voiceless.[2] Form by saying a voiceless [ɑ] while blowing air between the soft palate and the raised tongue, which is in a high, backed position. No English equivalent.
[ř] [ʀ]	r	in the French word *beret*. Uvular trill. Pronounce by forming a [g], but instead of getting a "hard" explosion, let the uvula undulate freely. This kind of r is appropriate only for cabaret singing in French. Classical French singers should avoid it.
[ɣ]	g	in the Spanish word *rogar* or
	r	in the German word *waren*. Similar to, but usually less intense than, the uvular [ř]. This voiced velar fricative should not be confused with [ɤ], the back, half-close, unrounded vowel given on page 130. The velar fricative

[1] The glottis is the opening (or slit) between the vocal folds (cords).
[2] A consonant which does not cause the vocal cords to vibrate.
[3] A consonant which causes the vocal cords to vibrate.

IPA Symbols:	Pronounced as the:	
		extends below the line of writing, whereas the vowel does not. I will give them here together, to show greater contrast: [ɣʏ].
[f]	f	in the English word *for*. Voiceless.[2]
[v]	v	in the English word *very*. Voiced.[3]
[β]	b	in the Spanish word *hablar*. Voiced.[3] Form by speaking a [b] and [f] simultaneously. No English equivalent.
[θ]	th	in the English word *bath*. Voiceless.[2]
[ð]	th	in the English word *bathe*. Voiced.[3]
[s]	s	in the English word *sue*. Voiceless.[2]
[z]	z	in the English word *zoo*. Voiced.[3]
[ʃ]	ss	in the English word *mission*. Voiceless.[2]
[ӽ]	s	in the English word *shawl* (as contrasted with the English word *sheet*, which uses the [ʃ], but not so far back as the [x], therefore, [ӽ] is a combination of [ʃ] and [x]. The symbol was created by Mrs. Maya Rybalka, who translated some Basque songs for Leyerle Publications which appeared in *SONG ANTHOLOGY TWO*. Voiceless.[2]
[ʒ]	s	in the English word *vision*. Voiced.[3]
[tʃ]	ch	in the English word *church*. Voiceless.[2] Affricative.
[dʒ]	dg	in the English word *nudge*. Voiced.[3] Affricative.
[ʃt]	shed	in the English word *rushed*. Voiceless.[2] Affricative.
[ʒd]	ged	in the English word *rouged*. Voiced.[3] Affricative.
[m]	m	in the English word *mow*. Nasal.
[n]	n	in the English word *no*. Nasal.
[n̩]	n	in the English idiomatic phrase *ham n' eggs*. Syllabic consonant. Nasal.
[ŋ]	ng	in the English word *sing*. Nasal.
[ɲ]	ni	in the English word *onion*. Nasal.

DIACRITICAL MARKS

~ over a vowel makes the vowel nasal.
ː lengthens the previous vowel.
ˈ placed at the upper left side of a syllable means that syllable should be accented.
ʔ placed before a vowel indicates the vowel should have a slight glottal stroke.
. under a symbol indicates a raised (higher tongue) variety, e.g. [ẹ]
▭ placed under a consonant indicates that it is dentalized.
ˬ placed under a consonant indicates that it is palatalized, or softened.

As I mentioned previously, many other diacritical marks are given in the IPA chart in Appendix I which are more esoteric than we need to be concerned with, generally.

Although the IPA is the best means we have for notating words as sounds, it is not infallible. Even the symbols themselves are altered from language to language, and some phoneticians disagree even how words

---

[1] See footnote[1], previous page.
[2] See footnote[2], previous page.
[3] See footnote[3], previous page.

should be spelled phonetically. Many authorities have developed their own systems, which are at slight variance with the official IPA alphabet.

I have already shown that the French nasal vowels [ɔ̃] and [ã] are really misspelled, logically and that some authors of diction texts have made the changes. In his book, *SINGING IN FRENCH*, Thomas Grubb makes the distinction between [œ]* and [ə]*; preferring in most cases to use the [œ]. However, none of the French dictionaries with which I am familiar make the distinction. They spell everything with the Schwa [ə]. Since I encourage my students to use the dictionaries, I spell in accordance with the dictionaries; but I tell them to sing [œ] instead of [ə], except when it occurs on such a weak syllable or rapid note that it is not necessary.

For many years there has been a trend for several authors to rewrite the spelling of German diphthongs. For example:

1. *mein* used to be spelled [maɪn] instead of [maen];
2. *Maus* used to be spelled [maʊs] instead of [maos];
3. *heute* used to be spelled [hɔɪtə] instead of [hɔøtə].

In our song anthologies, we have accepted the change in example 1 and agree that example 2 is probably accurate, although we have retained the old phonetic spelling. But we are not yet convinced that example 3 does not create more problems than it solves, causing undue exaggeration of the unaccented [ø] by zealous students. Since this is not a text on foreign language diction, I think it best to leave it to a linguistic specialist to do the "fine tuning." For the beginning student, the IPA is "close enough for jazz;" but he should be prepared to avail himself of the services of a knowledgeable diction coach or teacher.

The student should be aware of one other important consideration when using the IPA with his repertoire, technically. Whether he sings in English or in a foreign language, he should know the difference in the pronunciation in *speech* and in *singing*. When he migrates to a higher pitch or a louder dynamic range, the diction will not seem "right" to him at first; so he will have to become accustomed to that fact. Foreign languages will seem the strangest because most students have enough trouble just learning the correct pronunciation of that language in speech.

With experience, the vowel migrations become habituated and, in turn, become "body migration." This should free the mind to think the pure vowel as it should be in speech, but cannot always be in singing. While the body does all those technical things that allow the vowels to migrate, the mind *purifies* the vowels.

Many of the phonetic devices for learning correct diction and vowel migration only scratch the surface of possibilities. For example, the common way to teach the umlaut [y] is to have the student form an [u] mouth and say [i]. This works exceedingly well; but with experience and muscular development, that student can sing a pure [i] (rather than [y]) even with rounded lips. The professional singer eventually feels that he really is singing the pure vowels because migration happens so spontaneously. Putting this "cart before the horse" approach for beginning singers, however, can greatly retard their progress.

*That is, the *short* or *unstressed* [œ], for which the [ə] is frequently and indiscriminately substituted.

CHAPTER XI
VOCALIZATION

Vocalises serve a useful purpose, but many singers have taken their use to extremes, singing vocalise after vocalise, hour after hour. This, in itself, would not bear condemnation; but what frequently accompanies that sort of practice is a lack of thought. Five minutes of thoughtful, concentrated vocalising is far more productive than five hours of simply "going through the motions."

All vocal practice should be purposeful!

Each singer should select those vocalises that are best for his needs at the moment. Then he should incorporate them into some sort of systematic regimen of practice. Various kinds of vocalises and exercises can help the singer accomplish specific goals. They include exercises designed for:

A. Warming up the body
B. Warming up the voice
C. Extending the range
D. Extending breath control
E. Developing flexibility
F. Developing dynamic control
G. Developing articulation
H. Developing chromaticism
I. Developing a "floating" tone

Some of the above examples overlap in function. What may warm up the body may also warm up the voice simultaneously; developing flexibility might also extend breath control (it usually does!), etc. The point is, the singer should be certain that the exercise he selects *does* aid him in his immediate objective, even if it may extend to other functions.

A. Warming up the body

Before a singer dares enter a performance situation, he usually has to be physically "loose." This is true of any activity which demands physical dexterity in performance. Athletes never go into a game without some sort of preliminary exercise of a relatively undemanding nature. They start *slowly!* Dancers warm up religiously before a performance or rehearsal, again, gently at first, working gradually to the most inhuman contortions. The dancer's lot is probably the most difficult of any performer in this respect.

Some physical warm up exercises are less productive than others, and some can even be detrimental. Swimming, for example, is one of the best activities for physical development, but it bothers the sinuses—especially in chlorinated pools. This may not be good for many singers. Jogging might "jar something loose" if the jogger does not wear the right shoes and run on safe surfaces. Weight-lifting can cause the lifter to lock his throat muscles, which could result in vocal strain without singing a note. However, having said that, some limited research in the areas of jogging and weight-lifting indicate these activities, when carefully controlled, are beneficial to the singer in terms of power, control, endurance, and agility.[1] This same ex-

---

[1] Large, John and Patton, Robert; "The Effects Of Weight Training And Aerobic Exercise On Singers;" *JOURNAL OF RESEARCH IN SINGING*; Vol. IV, No. 2, 1981; pp. 23-32.

periment indicated no negative effects on the singers. Because the experiment had no control group with which to contrast the results, it was not possible to ascertain if the singers' improvement was the result of the exercise or from vocal practice.

Swimming, jogging, and weight-lifting may be construed more as a "lifestyle" than as warm-up exercises. One may wish to consider something more "compact," such as sit ups and leg lifts (for abdominal exercise), bend-overs, exercycling, bicycling, and walking (for general body exercise), dog panting (a popular exercise for warming up the breathing muscles and coordinating support), isometric exercises (when one has limited space and/or no access to the out-doors). There is no law that says exercises cannot have overlaid advantages. Barry Morrel, a Metropolitan Opera tenor of the 1960's, used to chop wood before performances.

Whatever physical warm-up a singer chooses, it should start gently and not undermine the very thing he is trying to accomplish— to loosen up.

B. Warming up the voice

After the body is moving freely, the singer is ready to loosen the voice. One of the best exercises for this is one which William Vennard coined as the "yawn-sigh." The singer yawns and sighs on a pitch-of-no-resistance and allows the tone to glissando downward. After he gets the feel of this exercise, he extends the pitch slightly higher, never straining or laboring heavily. This exercise has the advantage of activating most of the singing muscles without invoking the discipline of thinking or of producing a specific pitch, rhythm, or dynamic level.

After this, the singer is ready to commit himself to specific tones, but not strenuously. Simple scales of a third, ascending and descending, and vice-versa, progressing up and down by half-steps, are good:

Moderato mf-f

    a. Ascending-descending   b. Descending-ascending

[Sing on all vowels]

Fig. 107

Some teachers believe the singer should always begin vocalizing on a descending passage. Their thinking is that it is safer to bring the head voice down than to take the chest voice up. Those who opt for that approach should start on Fig. 107b. It must be remembered, however, that "everything that comes down must eventually go up." Be prepared!

Another excellent vocalise for warming up the breath and coordinating it with vocalization is:

Moderato mf-f Sing with vigor and an imaginary *h* before each [ɑ].

[ɑ ɑ ɑ ɑ ɑ ɑ ɑ ɑ ɑ ɑ ɑ ɑ]

Fig. 108

After the voice is pliable and moves easily, scales to intervals of a fourth, fifth, and sixth are logical progressions:

a. Fourth   b. Fifth

Sing on the vowels [ɑ], [e], [i], [o], and [u].

Fig. 109

Then, arpeggios of a fifth, progressing by half-steps work well:

Sing on the vowels [ɑ], [e], [i], [o], and [u].

Fig. 110

Once the voice functions well in the easier exercises, the singer is probably warmed up enough to progress to those more advanced, for specific work on technique.

C. Extending the range

I like to use the octave arpeggio, first, as a range-extending exercise:

Sing on all vowels.

Fig. 111

This exercise is easy to learn, and, taken at a brisk tempo, helps prevent the student's locking the abdominal muscles. It is easier to sing high notes quickly than to sustain them. The student has less time to worry about the higher notes if he can make a hasty exit. However, he must eventually be able to sustain them as his technique matures. The tones do not really belong to a singer who cannot sustain them.

After working with the octave arpeggios, I like to do florid scales:

Sing on all vowels.

Fig. 112

Then, ascending scales with descending broken chords:

Sing on all vowels.

Fig. 113

Notice that I have limited these vocalises to a liniar direction for the sake of simplicity, as their function at this stage is intended principally for range extension. They could easily be used as flexibility exercises if the singer's intention is to concentrate on flexibility.

After singing the exercise in Fig. 113, I like to do what I call the "radar vocalise." The first stage of this exercise involves singing a one-octave glissando on each of the vowels, [ɑ], [e], [i], [o], and [u]. (Some people call this a "siren" exercise.) Then I extend the range to two octaves, and, much later, to three octaves:

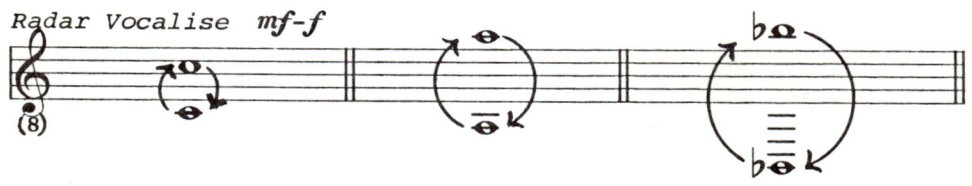

    a. Beginner   b. Intermediate   c. Advanced

Fig. 114

I like the glissando because there are no intervals. It is a *sliding scale* which can be started at the top, bottom, or middle pitches (or any point between) and is the most chromatic of scales. I envision the glissando progression in a clockwise direction, in the form of a circle. This gives the glissando a consistent form, therefore, a kind of rhythm. I call it the *radar vocalise* because it is easy to imagine a constantly sweeping arm from its center, following each pitch.

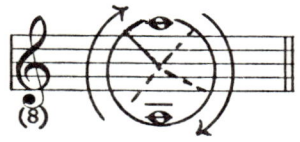

Fig. 115

If registration is not smooth, the radar detects the "blip" and I can pinpoint the problem pitch. Beginners should start with the one-octave exercise first, singing the five vowels, [i], [e], [ɑ], [o], and [u], not necessarily in that order, and progressing upward by half-steps. As soon as they develop a repertoire of more than two octaves, they can then move to the two-octave glissando, treating it in similar fashion. Students should not be impatient to do the three-octave glissando. The object here is to complete the exercise with the legitimate voice only. Men should not resort to singing in falsetto just to cover the three-octave range (although this might be helpful in discovering how to gain more control over the falsetto— but that would be another objective).

As the singer's pitches are constantly changing on the radar vocalise, he will probably want to sing it with no vibrato (If vibrato creeps in, the glissando has stopped moving, except when sung at a very slow tempo). This eliminates another variable so more attention can be given to coordination of support, phonation, and resonation.

D. Extending breath control

In addition to extending range, the radar vocalise might aid in improving extension of breath. The singer can time himself with a stopwatch, or second hand of a regular watch, to see how many seconds he can keep the circle moving in a consistent swing. The two-octave exercise is probably best for this purpose. If the student logs his accomplishments in the practice room, he will be able to keep track of his progress. If he can extend the exercise over an eight second period the first day (or week), he can try for nine or ten seconds the next, etc.

In addition to solving the problem of practical necessity— having enough breath to get through reasonably long phrases— the ability to sustain long phrases is an indication that the singer is probably singing well. Efficient singing usually results in the capacity to sustain long phrases of the sort frequently encountered in the songs and arias of Bach, Handel, Mozart, and other Baroque and Classical composers. Therefore, working on achieving longer breaths is another way of developing one's technique. The only way a singer can really know if he is making progress in this area is to time himself, whether it be on the radar vocalise or any other exercise in which its length can be extended as needed.

I should mention that there is a good reason why music of the Baroque and Classical eras demand the capacity for singing longer phrases, generally, than music of the later periods. The voices did not have to be so big as they are from the middle Romantic era on. They did not have to fight to project over large orchestras in huge theatres; therefore, they could sing with a lighter mechanism, which allowed the singer to negotiate longer phrases. As style is usually the handmaiden of technology, when a singer performs Baroque music stylistically, he should use a lighter mechanism than for Verdi; and it would be totally inappropriate for a Wagnerian sound to interpret Handel's "Lusinghe più care."

If the singer does not have the technical facility for adjusting his voice to stylistic differences, he should sing only those things he can perform adequately (and keep studying). Most singers eventually make a decision to specialize in one or two genres of vocal music. Few are so versatile as to handle all musical eras expertly.

E. Developing flexibility

Flexibility without lightness is as plausible as the "bull in the china shop." In developing the light mechanism for breath extension (D., above) the singer has laid the foundation for flexibility exercises.

Flexibility and velocity often go hand in hand, but not always. The arpeggio exercise (Fig. 111) and the combined scale and arpeggio exercise (Fig. 112), taken at a brisk tempo, can be used to develop flexibility. But more complex vocalises are also in order, such as:

140 VOCAL DEVELOPMENT THROUGH ORGANIC IMAGERY

Rapid skips of a third:

Sing on all vowels.

Fig. 116

Descending triplets of a second (sing the triplets evenly):

Sing on all vowels.

Fig. 117

and

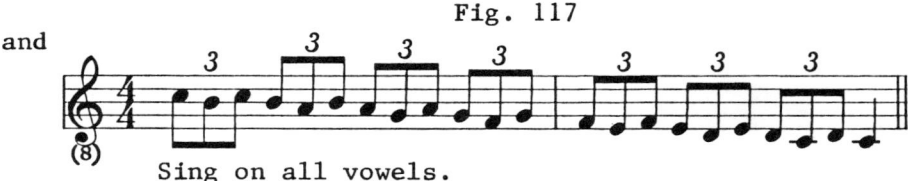

Sing on all vowels.

Fig. 118

Progressively larger intervals:

[Jonathan Livingston Seagull Vocalise (See p. 120 for its metaphysical possibilities)]

Sing on all vowels.

Fig. 119

This exercise (Fig. 119) should be extended upward and downward to the limit of the singer's range. Two advanced variations of the exercise are:

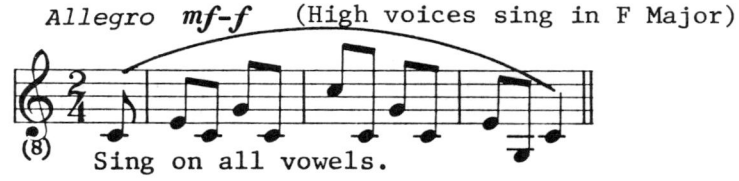

Sing on all vowels.

Fig. 120

and

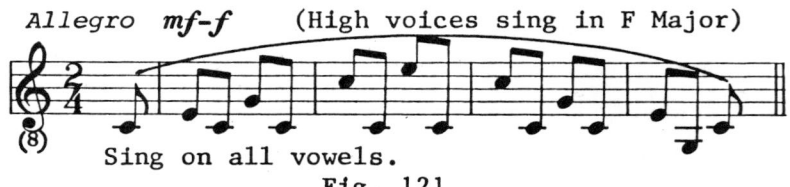

Sing on all vowels.

Fig. 121

Another advanced vocalise for developing floridity is:

Fig. 122

Two flexibility exercises not involving velocity are:

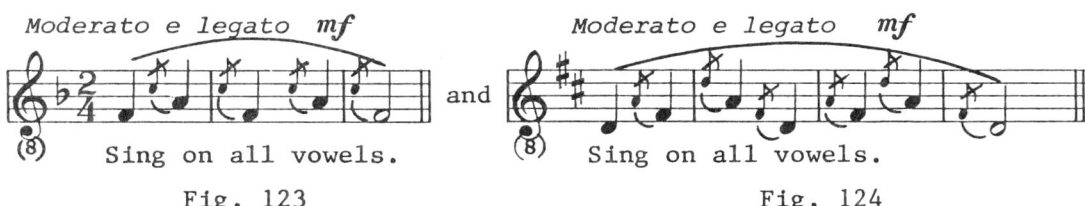

Fig. 123 and Fig. 124

In the above two exercises, the grace notes should be sung more lightly than their corresponding principal notes and the phrases should not be detached.

A vocalise that works as well for breath extension as for flexibility is a combination of three previous exercises:

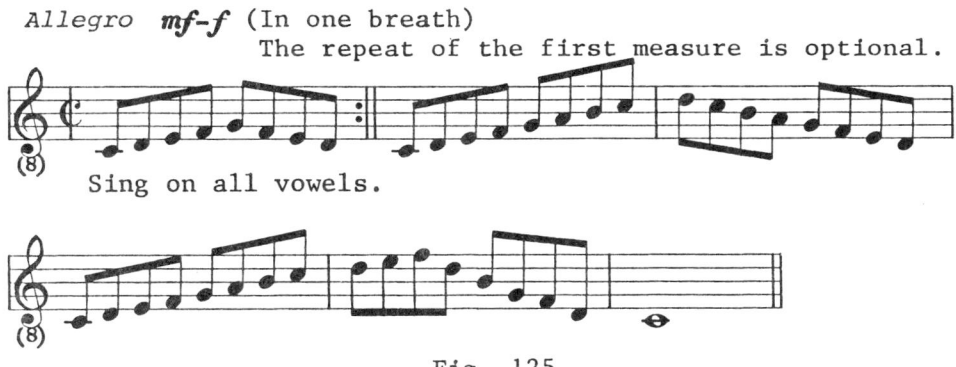

Fig. 125

Another exercise for developing flexibility is the *pulsation drill*, a term coined by Dr. Ralph Appelman. He suggests using five- and nine-note patterns on a single pitch, singing the neutral vowel, [ʌ]:

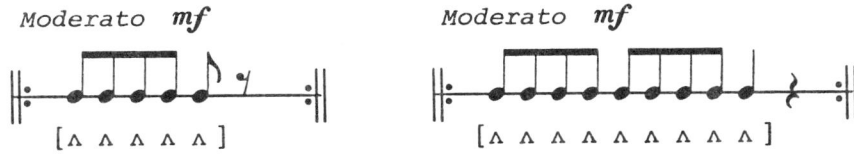

a. Five-note pattern   b. Nine-note pattern

Fig. 126

In performing this exercise, there must be no throat tension. All effort should be concentrated at the belt line and the dynamic level should not be so high as to cause violent pulsations. The tempo should be relatively slow at first. As coordination improves, the tempo can accelerate. I suggest to my students that they imagine the beat of an American Indian's tom-tom to establish the feeling of rhythm and pulse. A *pulse* is a rapid surge and release of tension. It is extremely important that the singer distinguish the *release* of tension. The inability to do this is the principal problem singers have in learning the Jonathan Livingston Seagull exercise (Fig. 119).

After he has coordinated the pulsation exercise on a single pitch, the singer can perform it on a five-tone scale, and then, to more complex vocalises. He should procede with patience! Ultimately, this pulsation will prove to be the key to velocity singing, providing strength and lightness.

I use the pulsation drill on fast octave skips for beginning students who have mastered the easier pulsation drills. Then they move on to intervals of a 10th, 12th, and 16th. My advanced singers— usually only women with well developed whistle registers— can do three octave pulsation drills, but beginners should avoid it unless they have a *natural* affinity for it.

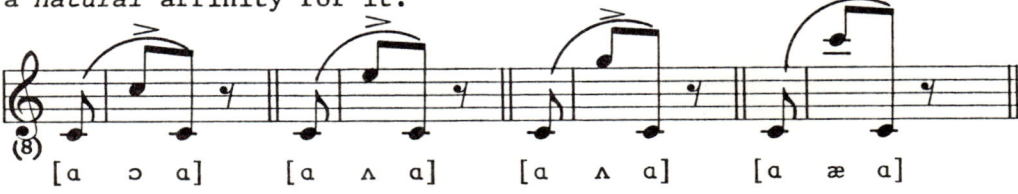

Fig. 127

The exercises in Fig. 127 can be extended to include more than three notes:

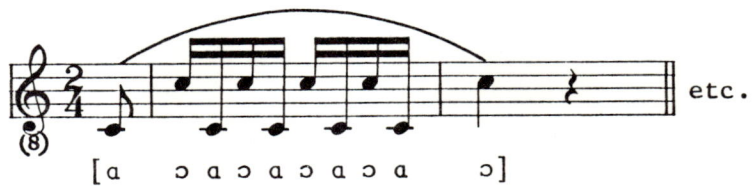

Fig. 128

I suggest to my students that the sound and sensation of doing this exercise reminds one of trying to start an old T-Model Ford.

Not all voice students will be able to perform the pulsation exercises fluently. Dr. Appelman notes that, out of a group of twenty students, half are able to do the preliminary exercise well when it is first introduced; five have trouble, but eventually overcome the problem; and three to five have so many problems of coordination they are frustrated and never really master the exercise.[1]

Although I have never made an organized experiment with my own students regarding the ratio of their success with pulsation exercises, my instincts are in agreement with Dr. Appelman's estimate. As he

---

[1] Appelman, Dr. D. Ralph; *THE SCIENCE OF VOCAL PEDAGOGY*; Indiana University Press; Bloomington and London; 1967 (second printing 1974); pp. 19-23.

points out, the students who cannot master pulsation will always have difficulty singing a certain substantial amount of repertoire, although they may be able to perform well in areas not requiring that particular skill.

F. Extending dynamic control

The best vocalise for extending dynamic range (and all other facets of breath control) is the messa di voce exercise and variations of it (discussed on pp. 68-70). If the singer has more trouble diminuendoing than crescendoing, he should concentrate on the weaker aspect of the messa di voce. He should practice on all vowels and controlable notes of his range, remembering, that if and when vocal quality begins to deteriorate, he has over-extended the exercise and should take a new breath— and, perhaps, a brief rest.

After the singer has developed a high degree of consistency in producing the messa di voce on one tone, he can begin applying it to the other vocalises and to his repertoire (when appropriate). He will probably discover that this will be more difficult than staying on one tone because of the added complications of changing pitch, rhythm, and diction.

G. Developing articulation

There are so many possibilities for articulation combinations that each singer should probably best compose his own, suitable for any particular kind of challenge that may have presented itself.

For a beginning exercise, I would suggest something simple, to which more complex variations can be added, such as:

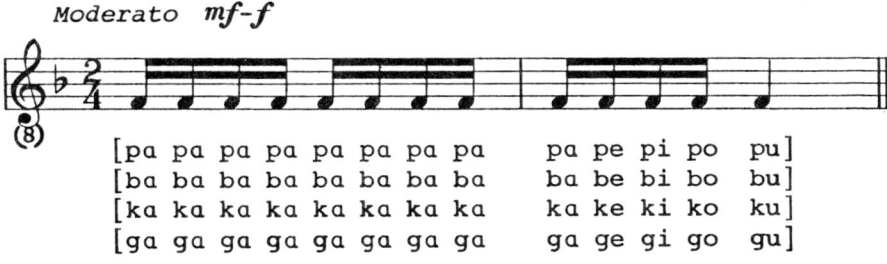

[pa pa pa pa pa pa pa pa   pa pe pi po pu]
[ba ba ba ba ba ba ba ba   ba be bi bo bu]
[ka ka ka ka ka ka ka ka   ka ke ki ko ku]
[ga ga ga ga ga ga ga ga   ga ge gi go gu]

Fig. 129

Then, more complex:

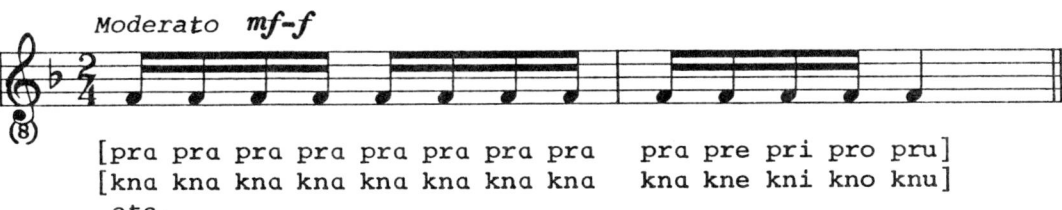

[pra pra pra pra pra pra pra pra   pra pre pri pro pru]
[kna kna kna kna kna kna kna kna   kna kne kni kno knu]
  etc.

Fig. 130

In addition, other previously given exercises can be used for various combinations of consonants and vowels. For example, even the complex vocalise on page 141 (Fig. 125) could be used effectively by such combinations as [tu ki tu ki], [ti ki te ki], [tra gi da gi], [bli gi bli gi], etc.

A singer who has just learned to trill his r's may devise an exercise which presents only a slight challenge in using the trill. Inventing a vocalise which is too difficult to handle can be discouraging. He should add gradually to his daily successes on a consistent basis. That is the key to the big successes.

I would reiterate one guideline that can help facilitate articulation: *Ventriloquize the consonants*. This helps free the tongue, lips, and jaw to shape for the proper vowels and their migration.

I frequently use an image with my students which helps conceptualize the ventriloquizing posture. I call it the *Umlaut Cone*. It is based, once more, on the reversed megaphone.

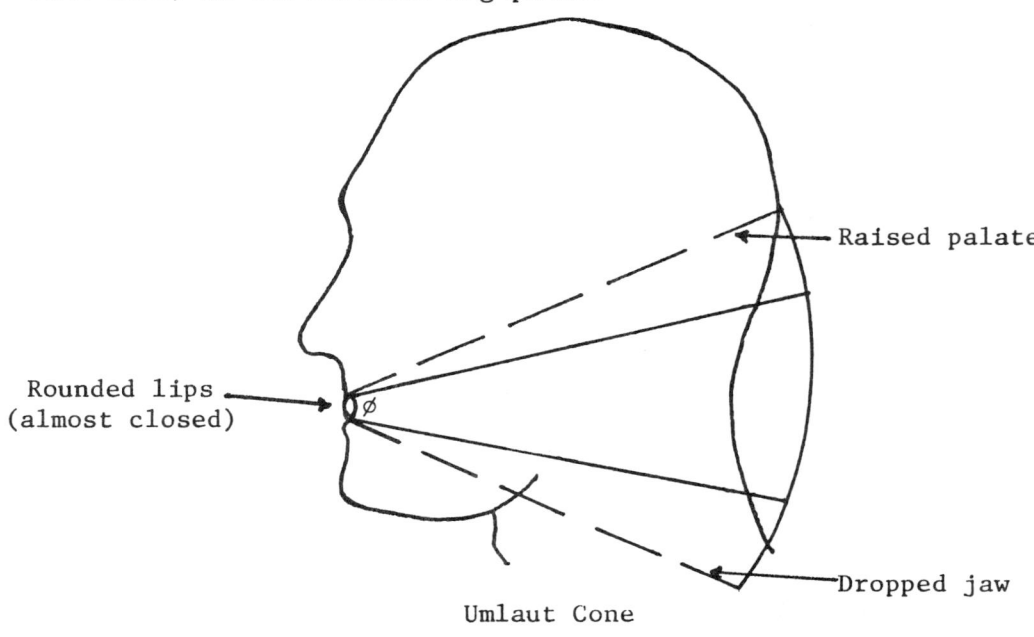

Umlaut Cone

Fig. 131

The cone gives the singer a *mold* in which the tongue moves freely, at the command of the brain. The Umlaut keeps the tongue forward, even when other vowels take precedence. The physical sensation is one of "gathering the resonance at the lips." The broken lines above and below the cone represent the cone's growth as the notes go higher or as they crescendo. This growth, of course, is acheived by the rising palate and dropping jaw, neither of which should become rigid. However, *the student should not confuse rigidity with strength!* The muscles for lifting the palate and dropping the jaw should be tremendously strong, yet they must remain flexible. They must not share in the abdominal support, but cooperate with it. If the singer feels his jaw, lips, and/or tongue are helping support the tone, he should check his abdominal muscles. They are probably either not working enough or are working incorrectly.

Pursuant to this, another aid in ventriloquizing is to imagine the words of a song or vocalise as being engraved on the belt line, epigastrium, or lower back, if articulation becomes cumbersome. Wherever the singer feels his support is most efficient is the place he should superimpose the words. He can invoke a mind-over-matter effect in doing this.

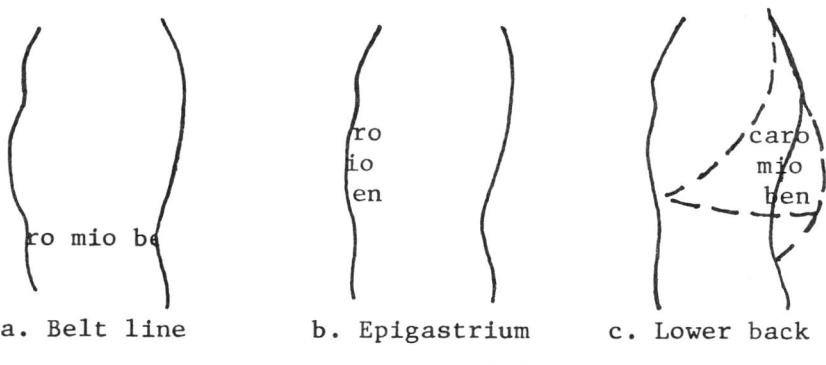

a. Belt line   b. Epigastrium   c. Lower back

Fig. 132

This approach works very well for beginning students who have learned where they feel their support. The reason for its success is probably the same as for many other aspects of vocal technique— diversion. If the singer feels that abdominal support is taking care of articulation, he can let go of the unnecessary tension that has built up in the jaw, mouth, and lips, allowing them to function more naturally.

H. Developing chromaticism

Chromatic scales are difficult for some singers. Because many songs and arias have both short and extended chromatic passages, the complete singer must learn to handle them. Chromatic figures usually group themselves in duple or triple pulses:

1. Largo   2. Moderato   3. Allegro   **mf-f**

Sing on all vowels.

Fig. 133

and

1. Largo   2. Moderato   3. Allegro   **mf-f**

Sing on all vowels.

Fig. 134

For those who do have trouble singing the chromatics accurately, Napoleon's adage "Divide and conquer," is applicable here. The singer should take one beat at a time in order to maintain control over shorter musical units. After the first beat is secure, he should perfect the second beat and then combine them, continuing in this way until the complete vocalise is mastered. He should go slowly at first in order to avoid sloppy intonation. After a *largo* tempo can be cleanly sung, he can speed up the tempo to *moderato* and then to *allegro*. Paying close attention to the rhythmic pulse can help the singer avoid getting lost from the tonal center— a frequent occurrence with beginners.

The chromatic scale is a useful technical tool for developing smooth passaggi. By using a five-tone chromatic scale, the singer can approach the passaggio, either from below or above, by half-steps. This allows a closer examination of troublesome tones that do not want to "go over" (or through"), or "turn."

I. Developing a floating tone

We have discussed the falsetto as a device used more by men than women, although women do have falsetto in their voices. This section will be devoted more to the female falsetto.

As Todd Duncan said (page 95), "I use the falsetto to give the pupil a sense of nothingness in the pharynx— weightlessness and detachment." He applies it to dark, heavy, and unwieldy voices. This is the kind of female voice that needs a falsetto concept for *remedial* purposes. But that same feeling of weightlessness is precisely what the more lyric voices need, as well, for floating the tone.

The most troublesome area for singing the floated tone is around the top of the staff and extending upward to the B♭ or B where the whistle register takes over.

Many women are unaware that they can produce these tones because they have not been asked or challenged to make the effort. About one out of three of my female students can produce this floaty sound during her first attempt— some at the beginning and some toward the end of their lessons. The sound is so light and easily produced that most of the singers who can float the voice cannot believe they are really "singing." Then I ask them to float a G at the top of the staff and to slowly crescendo the tone. A large number of them can make a beautifully smooth crescendo on the first or second attempt. Students who experience this for the first time feel as if they have discovered the "key to the universe" once they are convinced the production is not only a legitimate vocal sound, but desirable.

The group that cannot float a tone on the first few efforts should not give up. If they give it a chance and observe the progress of those who have learned to do it, it will eventually come to them. The siren sound or radar exercise is a good way to find an insight. Sometimes, asking them to imitate a male singer, singing falsetto, opens the door. A few of my students respond by singing a diminuendo portamento:

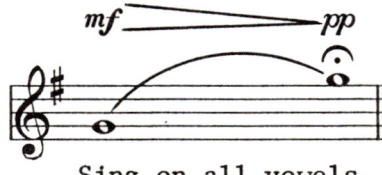

Sing on all vowels.

Fig. 135

Once the initial sensation of a floated tone is experienced, the student is motivated to apply it to her vocalises and repertoire. Stumbling blocks inevitably occur during this stage of development, but she should not be discouraged. Again, the more complex the activity, the more difficult the coordination. She will have to realize that two steps backward to gain three steps forward is progress.

Sometimes singers are so fascinated with the floated tone, once it is discovered, they try to make it work for everything. It does not! It is important that they incorporate it into the messa di voce and continue to be aware that, if the floated tone cannot be crescendoed it is not a usable tone.

Men should be encouraged to develop the floated tone, but it is much more difficult for them because they carry the heavy mechanism proportionally so much higher than women. It is a tour de force when a male singer can float the notes on either side of the passaggio secondo without resorting to the use of falsetto.

Ultimately it is not the number of vocalises a student uses, but the quality of his practice that determines the degree of artistry obtainable. Consider the story of Gaetano Caffarelli and his teacher, Niccolò Porpora.

Upon Caffarelli's agreement to follow a tedious regimen of study with him, Porpora "...wrote out on a piece of paper the diatonic and chromatic scales, ascending and descending, skips of the third, fourth, fifth, etc., for the mastery of intervals and the sustaining of tone..."[1] The single piece of paper also contained trills, turns, appoggiaturas, and vocalises which occupied Caffarelli for six years. During this time he did not deviate from these exercises, although he frequently asked his teacher if he could "graduate" to something more demanding. Until the sixth year, Porpora's answer was "No." But, at the end of that time, he is purported to have said to Caffarelli, "Go, my son, you have no more to learn. You are the premier singer of Italy and of the world." And so he was!

The readers of this text are given considerably more freedom of choice about their vocalises than Caffarelli. Some of the tempo and dynamic markings in the preceding exercises are only suggestions for the first time around. The singer may wish to set his own pace, choose his own volume levels, phrase *al dente*, and sing the vowels and consonants of his choice. The singer should select his best key or keys, as well.

Everything is interchangeable and, eventually, should be interchanged. The guideline for the student is to know what he is striving to acheive with each exercise at the time he is singing it. This principle will serve him well when he is ready to interpret the repertoire— knowing what he wants to portray with music and text.

---

[1] Pleasants, Henry; *THE GREAT SINGERS*; A Fireside Book, published by Simon and Schuster, Rockefeller Center, 1230 Avenue of the Americas, New York, New York 10020; 1966; p. 67.

CHAPTER XII
THE APPOGGIAMETER

I mentioned in chapter II the often quoted phrase, "He who breathes well sings well." In the ensuing chapters we have seen that this rather simplistic phrase actually encompasses a vast number of complexities. Breathing well for singing involves standing (and sitting and lying) well, phonating well, resonating well, articulating well, and interpreting well. After all these factors are brought under control individually and then coordinated into a united whole, then breath support and breath control still loom prominently in all technical considerations.

The collective term for breath support and breath control is *breath management*. We have seen that the "supported tone" manifests itself in a variety of ways, including emphasis on *back-breathing, epigastrium support (le point d'appui), beltline support,* and/or *pubic bone support*. All these varieties of support may be experienced by a given individual, depending on the demands of the performance. Some individuals elect to adopt only one of the above "systems" on which to focus their attention. This selection, however, does not mean that the other factors do not occur. It could mean that the singer who elects to concentrate only on one aspect of support wishes to simplify this important technical process; or it could mean that he really believes there is one best way to support. The important thing is that, whatever point of emphasis he elects, it works for him.

On the most basic level, breath support occurs when the muscles for inhalation and exhalation cooperate. In our discussion of this process, we have emphasized sensations of *direction of support* as being down and backward (back-breathing) and down and forward (first to the belt line and then to the pubic bone). Eventually, it is desirable that all elements of vocal technique be simplified so the singer's mind can be cleared for concentration on communication of music and text.

In order to accomplish this, he must relegate most of his technical concepts to his subconscious mind in such a way that, if technical problems should arise in performance, the subconscious mind will alert the singer so a solution to the problem can be affected. Much of this simplification can be accomplished if the singer can find a way to synthesize the diverse aspects of abdominal and diaphragmatic cooperation into one basic act. One of the most common methods used by teachers for doing this is to have their students lift a weight, either real or imagined, while singing. When done properly, this indicates to the singer exactly where to feel the sensations of support.

Probably the most convenient weight to be found in voice studios is the piano. Before a singer tries lifting the piano and singing, he must be cautioned about two things:
1. When he takes a big breath before trying to lift the piano, he should feel absolutely no pressure beneath the glottis! All pressure should stop at the bottom of the sternum.
2. The singer should not actually lift the piano off the floor, nor should he strain himself by *any* excessive lifting.

Locking the breath at the glottis is precisely the reason why singers are not encouraged to practice weight lifting. However, if they can learn to lift without pressure at the glottal level, it can be quite rewarding.

A good preliminary exercise before actually lifting "at" the piano while singing is for the student to take a big breath and imagine lifting about 30 lbs. of the piano's weight. While my students do this, I have them speak softly. If the pressure is at the glottal level, either they cannot speak at all or they speak with obvious strain. When they prove they can speak easily while lifting 30 lbs., I ask them to increase the weight, gradually, to about 50 lbs. as they continue to speak. If they find themselves at a loss for something to say, I have them recite the "Pledge of Allegiance" or something that does not require much intellectual concentration. Next, I have the students go to the piano and try to apply the same 30 to 50 lbs. lift to the piano as they continue to speak. The amount of weight can be varied according to need.

After I am convinced the singers can apply the weight of the piano, without strain, in speech, I have them do a phrase from their repertoire that goes to f^2. If they have no such repertoire, I have them do an exercise such as the one in Fig. 113 on page 138 (singing with eighth notes, rather than sixteenths, so they have more time to feel what is happening). As they ascend the scale, they increase the amount of weight.

It has been my experience that, in a group of ten singers who follow this procedure, seven will show immediate improvement in both sound and ease of vocal production. After having the singers repeat the exercise once or twice, I have them stand away from the piano and try to produce the same effect by only imagining the lift. Of these seven singers, about four will succeed the first time, and the others usually follow suit with a few more tries.

Now, let us observe the three singers who showed no improvement while lifting the piano. More often than not, the problem occurs when the singer tries to make the "lift go to the voice," rather than have the "voice come to the lift." In other words, these singers do not allow the voice to show the influence of the energy of lifting, but maintain the two concurrent activities, separately.

Before going any further, I should say that all ten singers should not lift at the piano at the same time. Otherwise, the instrument might levitate. Also, a grand piano is much more practical than an upright because there are so many more places to find a grip. Upright pianos can be gripped on the sides (under the keyboard section) or by the handles at the back.

Because of the problems involved in working with awkward weights, the thought occurred to me that a set of scales with side grips and handles, with a raised meter (so the singer will not have to look down at his feet) might be a solution. Such an instrument needs a name, so I dubbed it the "Supportameter." However, this name not only seemed awkward, but lacked "Klang." Then the idea came to me: The Italian word for support, *appoggio*, would be perfect. Thus, *The Appoggiameter!*

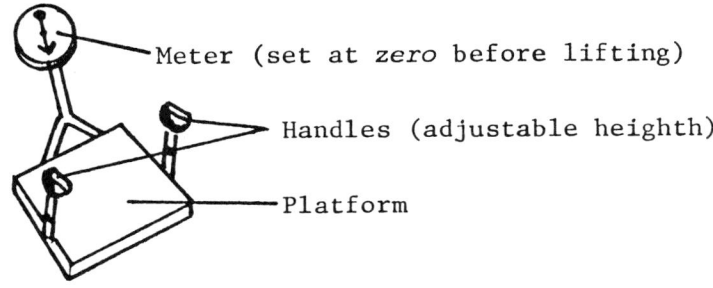

The Appoggiameter

Fig. 136

150 VOCAL DEVELOPMENT THROUGH ORGANIC IMAGERY

A crude, but functional version of the appoggiameter, as illustrated in Fig. 137, is an ordinary bathroom scales and a long leather belt or webbed strap. A rope could also be used as long as it is not so thick as to tilt the scales. A special platform with a rope trough could be devised to circumvent the problem caused by a thick rope.

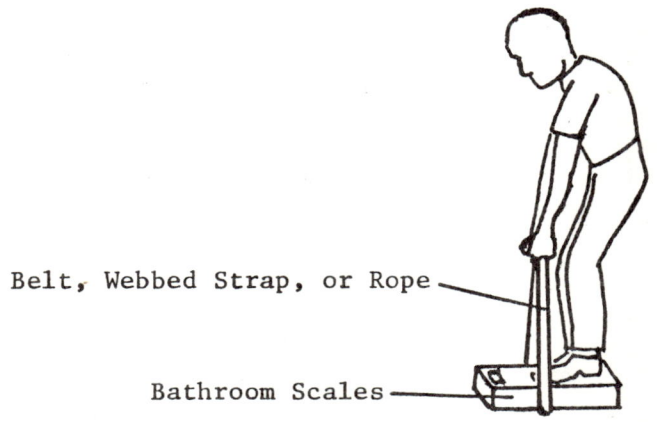

The Appoggiameter (Primitive Model)

Fig. 137

Three disadvantages mar this version, however:

1. The meter on these scales is at the level of the feet, which necessitates looking down while singing.
2. The singer has to be a mathematician in order to subtract his weight from the pulled weight to know how much weight he has pulled. Also, many singers do not care to reveal their weight if observers should be present.
3. A belt or webbed strap does not have handles to provide an easy grip. The singer has to wrap the strap around his hands or wrist in order to secure the grip. In this respect, a rope would be the superior choice, as it could be tied to wooden handles.

A belt of adjustable length with handles would make the primitive version of this appoggiameter much more practical. Almost everyone has a bathroom scales at his disposal, so some form of the appoggiameter is available to everyone. When using the appoggiameter, the singer must bend at the knees. Otherwise, when a singer lifts to his maximum weight, his shoulders would have to go too high, interfering with his breathing.

The advantages of using the appoggiameter extend beyond showing a singer just where the sensations of support occur most efficiently. The instrument also indicates precisely how much weight he pulls in order to sing a given pitch at a given dynamic level. I have my students pull a considerable amount of weight (up to 80 or 100 lbs. for the stronger students) while singing high pianissimo tones. The singers who could only "float" these tones, previously, or who could not sing softly at all above the staff, suddenly realize how much richer and more controllable these tones are with adequate support.

Although much research is needed to discover just how many uses the appoggiameter may have for training the voice, I have discovered, personally, that it is a marvelous voice conditioner. As a baritone, high B♭ is getting toward the top of my range. When I first experimented with the appoggiameter, I found I lifted 120 lbs. in order to sing that note.

After two weeks it took only 40 lbs. I suspect that it will eventually take less weight, because I can now sing high B♮ as easily, and for longer duration, than I could sing the B♭ four weeks before using the appoggiameter. And, for the first time in my life, I can reach high C (if only for a second or two). In addition to extending my range upward, it is also extending it lower. Whereas I used to sing a fairly comfortable low C (but not with enough volume to inflict on the public), I can now vocalize to the G below it, and, on a clear day, to the F♯.

An obvious and legitimate question to arise from all this is, "How well does using the appoggiameter apply to singing without it?" The answer varies from singer to singer— depending, principally, on their coordination. As I do not perceive a "concert model" of the appoggiameter as a likely success, it is incumbent on the user to become independent of the device in performance.

Most singers whose voices improve while lifting the piano or by using the appoggiameter can realize the same advantages by imagining they are lifting. For those who are less coordinated, a certain "residue" of the lifting sensation remains only dimly at first; but, with perseverance, they too can make the transfer. Eventually, of course, just the thought of lifting should trigger the proper engagement of the support muscles for all singers. Ultimate refinement in this process should eliminate the necessity of any sensation of excessive lifting.

One other word of caution should be given: *The singer must eventually transfer the muscle tension of the hands and arms to the abdominal muscles when not actually lifting weight*, even though it is often helpful for singers, at first, to flex their arm muscles (biceps) when not lifting the actual weight; but this should be done only as a reminder during the transitional period. *It should not become a habit!*

Once the singer has established where his sensation of the center of support is located, he can visualize it as a rectangular column.

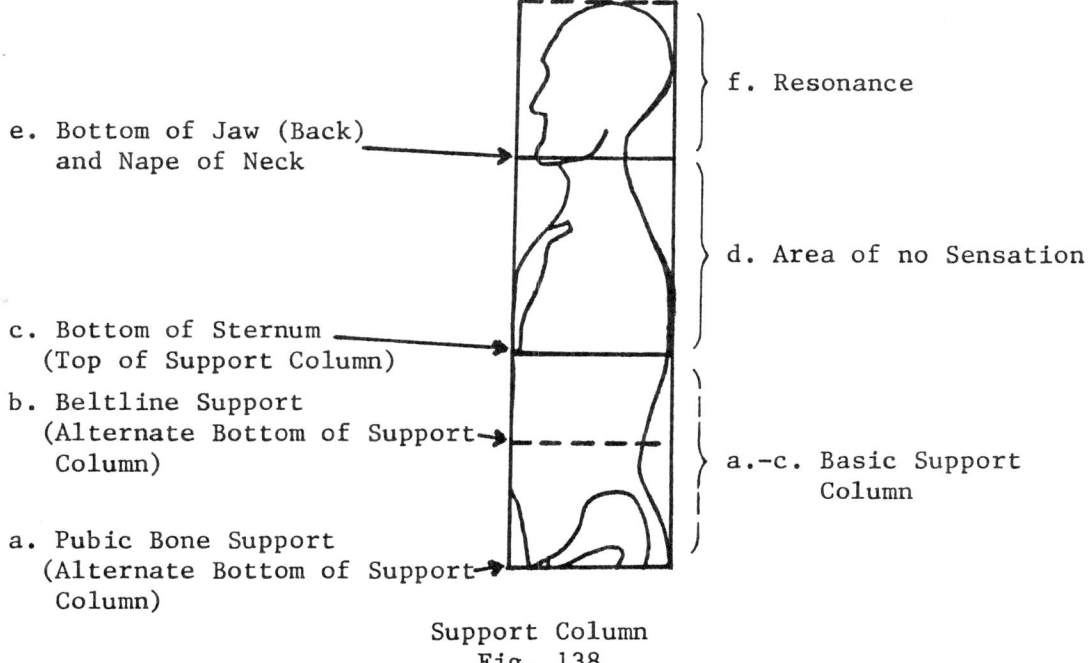

- e. Bottom of Jaw (Back) and Nape of Neck
- c. Bottom of Sternum (Top of Support Column)
- b. Beltline Support (Alternate Bottom of Support Column)
- a. Pubic Bone Support (Alternate Bottom of Support Column)

- f. Resonance
- d. Area of no Sensation
- a.–c. Basic Support Column

Support Column
Fig. 138

The bottom of this column begins, most frequently, either at the belt line or at the pubic bone and extends upward to the bottom of the sternum. This area comprises the basic support column. Between the top of the column (c) and the bottom of the jaw (e) is "no man's land" where nothing seems to happen (except the sensation of back expansion).

If the singer can identify with this imagery, so far, he is ready to apply still another use of the support column— *the stabilized jaw.*

Although there is no feeling of compression or of support between c and e, the singer can condition himself to feel as if the bottom of his jaw (which is on the level of the nape of the neck) rests firmly against the top of the support column! Obviously, this requires some imagination. Once this is accomplished, the singer will feel another platform of strength. The lowered and stabilized jaw can be the source of energy and control for articulation of vowels and consonants. The jaw will feel strong, but without being stiff and inflexible. In addition, the effectiveness of the inverted megaphone and mask resonance can be greatly enhanced. At this point, variations of the inverted megaphone can be quite helpful to many singers.

For example, a rectangular megaphone may be more beneficial than a conical one.

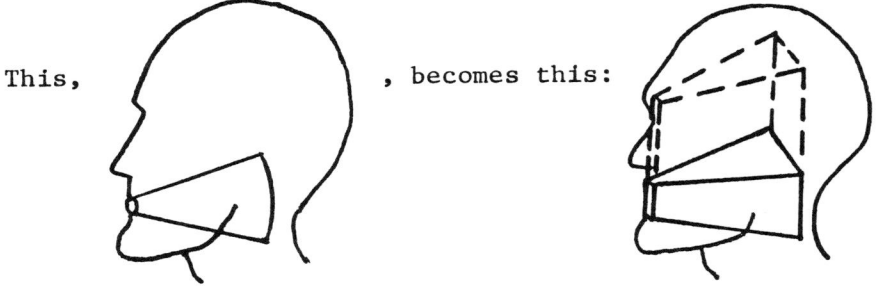

a. Conical Megaphone   b. Rectangular Megaphone

Fig. 139

The transformation of Fig. 139b contributes greater ease of vertical elongation of the mouth and mask resonators. A strong, lowered jaw, which seems to rest on top of the support column, makes the transformation possible. From the front of the mouth to the back of the throat, the base of the megaphone feels like a pie-shaped wedge (conforming to the shape of the jaw). The widest part of the wedge (backward portion) sits more firmly on the top of the support column than the narrow (frontal) part.

In order to help a student "prime" the sensation of a narrow elongated mouth, it is often helpful to have him sing a tone and, while sustaining it, press each hand on the sides of his face (as in figure 140 on the following page).

If his jaw is properly low, and resting on the support column, the student will feel the mask resonance "gather" between the hands and become more vibrant. However, just as he must learn to recall the sensation of weight-lifting at the appoggiameter, mentally, so must he learn to recreate the sensation of frontal facial elongation without the use of his hands. And, once more, he must check himself in front of a mirror after removing his hands from his face, in order to see that it is not contorted from the physical manipulation. The once outward contortion must become habitual *inner posture.*

Fig. 140

The reader may recall that, in chapter II (page 17, last ¶), I stated, "...seventy-five to eighty per cent of a singer's effort does not require such strong support..." That paragraph also included the phrase, "...in the beginning of vocal training..."

I believe young beginning singers should tread lightly, at first, in the area of developing and strengthening the abdominal muscles. It is a consistently good and safe policy for teachers to assign repertoire to their students that does not over-tax their current vocal resources in *any* way— especially songs that demand strenuous support. As the singer matures, both physically and technically, he will "grow into" more demanding material, much of which may very well require more support for a greater per cent of his singing time. Vocal stamina is another principal factor which has to be considered when a singer is deciding to which voice category he is best suited. (See Appendix III, Voice Classification)

It is often strategically advantageous for a young singer to begin his training one vocal category lower than he will ultimately adopt. It is sometimes difficult to apply that policy, however, because singers frequently do not know which is their proper category until *after* they learn to sing well. Even professional singers frequently change voice categories at the beginning, or later, in their careers.

In the last analysis, the best policy, in any situation, is to start the singer where he best fits at that given time. His individuality will manifest itself during his development. This will best determine the direction toward which he should direct his efforts. Everyone grows at a different rate, in different areas, but toward a common goal: artistic performance.

None of the foregoing suggestions for organic imagery is "carved in granite." The images are only ideas that have helped many of my students, but which do not always work for everyone. Even the ideas that work well may be only transitory as the singer goes from one vocal plateau to the next. All the images are capable of variation. As no two singers are alike, I encourage my students to look for improved variations that best fit their particular needs and to work toward simplification.

Good luck in your vocal pursuits.

APPENDICES

    I INTERNATIONAL PHONETIC ALPHABET I............. 155

   II INTERNATIONAL PHONETIC ALPHABET II............ 156

  III VOICE CLASSIFICATION........................ 159

   IV VOWEL FOCUS EXERCISES....................... 163

    V VOWEL MIGRATION CHARTS...................... 165

   VI HOW TO STUDY A SONG......................... 166

  VII IMPOSTO..................................... 167

 VIII REGISTER COORDINATION EXERCISES............. 168

   IX THE BLIND MEN AND THE ELEPHANT.............. 170

APPENDIX I
INTERNATIONAL PHONETIC ALPHABET[1]

THE INTERNATIONAL PHONETIC ALPHABET
(Revised to 1979)

	Bilabial	Labiodental	Dental, Alveolar, or Post-alveolar	Retroflex	Palato-alveolar	Palatal	Velar	Uvular	Labial-Palatal	Labial-Velar	Pharyngeal	Glottal
Nasal	m	ɱ	n	ɳ		ɲ	ŋ	ɴ				
Plosive	p b		t d	ʈ ɖ		c ɟ	k g	q ɢ		k͡p g͡b		ʔ
(Median) Fricative	ɸ β	f v	θ ð s z	ʂ ʐ	ʃ ʒ	ç ʝ	x ɣ	χ ʁ		ʍ	ħ ʕ	h ɦ
(Median) Approximant		ʋ	ɹ	ɻ		j	ɰ		ɥ	w		
Lateral Fricative			ɬ ɮ									
Lateral (Approximant)			l	ɭ		ʎ						
Trill			r					ʀ				
Tap or Flap			ɾ	ɽ				ʀ				
Ejective	p'		t'				k'					
Implosive	ɓ		ɗ				ɠ					
(Median) Click	ʘ		ʇ									
Lateral Click			ʖ									

(pulmonic air-stream mechanism) CONSONANTS (non-pulmonic air-stream)

DIACRITICS

- ̥ Voiceless n̥ d̥
- ̬ Voiced s̬ t̬
- ʰ Aspirated tʰ
- ̤ Breathy-voiced b̤ a̤
- ̪ Dental t̪
- ̫ Labialized t̫
- ̡ Palatalized t̡
- ̴ Velarized or Pharyngealized ɫ, t̴
- ̩ Syllabic n̩ l̩
- ͡ or ‿ Simultaneous sf (but see also under the heading Affricates)

- ̇ or ˙ Raised e̊, e̝, e̝ ẉ
- ̣ or ˌ Lowered e̞, ẹ, e̞ β̞
- ̟ Advanced u̟, ɪ̟, t̟
- ̠ or ˗ Retracted i̠, i̠-, t̠
- ̈ Centralized ë
- ̃ Nasalized ã
- ˞ ɚ, ɝ r-coloured aʴ
- ː Long aː
- ˑ Half-long aˑ
- ̯ Non-syllabic ŭ
- ̹ More rounded ɔ̹
- ̜ Less rounded y̜

OTHER SYMBOLS

ɕ, ʑ Alveolo-palatal fricatives
ʃ̡, ʒ̡ Palatalized ʃ, ʒ
ɹ Alveolar fricative trill
ɺ Alveolar lateral flap
ʄ Simultaneous ʃ and x
ʃ̣ Variety of ʃ resembling s, etc.
ɪ = ɩ
ʊ = ɷ
ɜ = Variety of ə
ɚ = r-coloured ə

VOWELS

	Front		Back	
Close	i	ɨ	ɯ	u
Half-close	e	ɘ	ɤ	o
Half-open	ɛ	ɜ	ʌ	ɔ
Open	a	ɐ	ɑ	ɒ

Unrounded | Rounded

	Front		Back	
Close	y	ʉ		u
Half-close	ø	ɵ		o
Half-open	œ			ɔ
Open	ɶ			ɒ

Rounded

STRESS, TONE (PITCH)

ˈ stress, placed at beginning of stressed syllable; ˌ secondary stress; ˉ high level pitch, high tone; ˊ high rising; ˋ high falling; ˏ low rising; ˎ low falling; ˆ rise-fall; ˇ fall-rise.

AFFRICATES can be written as digraphs, as ligatures, or with slur marks; thus ts, tʃ, dʒ; t͡s t͡ʃ d͡ʒ; t͜s t͜ʃ d͜ʒ.
ɕ, ʝ may occasionally be used for tʃ, dʒ.

[Reproduced by permission of the International Phonetic Association]

APPENDIX II
INTERNATIONAL PHONETIC ALPHABET[11]
ENGLISH, ITALIAN, GERMAN, FRENCH, AND SPANISH

IPA Symbols	English	Italian	German	French	Spanish
[i]	eat [it]	si [si]	viel [fil]	fils [fis]	chico [tʃiko]
[ɪ] [ᴜ]	it [ɪt]	–	bis [bɪs]	–	–
[e][1]	date [deɪt]	che [ke]	leben [lẹbɛn]	chez [ʃẹ]	queso [kẹso]
[ɛ]	set [sɛt]	bello [bɛllo]	des [dɛs]	tête [tɛːt]	cerca [θɛrka]
[æ]	rat [ræt]	–	–	–	–
[a]	lamb [lam]	–	–	glace [ɡlas]	–
[ɒ][2]	hot [hɒt]	–	–	–	–
[ɚ]	after [æftɚ]	–	–	–	–
[ɝ]	hurt [hɝt]	–	–	–	–
[ɑ]	father [fɑðɚ]	amare [amaɾɛ]	paar [pɑːr]	âme [ɑːm]	caro [kaɾo]
[u]	food [fud]	pura [pur]	tun [tuːn]	fou [fu]	mucho [mutʃo]
[ʊ] [ɷ]	book [bʊk]	–	Mund [mʊnt]	–	–
[o]	both [boθ]	voce [votʃe]	so [zoː]	faux [fo]	adobe [adobe]
[ɤ]	jovial [dʒɤvɪəl]	–	–	–	–
[ɔ]	ball [bɔl]	cosa [kɔza]	Morgen [mɔrgɛn]	coq [kɔk]	corro [kɔro]
[ə]	above [əbʌv]	–	habe [hɑbə]	le [lə]	–
[ʌ]	up [ʌp]	–	–	me [mʌ]	–
[y]	–	–	fühlen [fylɛn]	une [yn]	–
[ʏ]	–	–	Hütte [hʏtə]	–	–
[ɥ] [y̆]	–	–	–	depuis [dəpɥi]	–
[ø]	–	–	Goethe [gøtə]	boeufs [bøf]	–
[œ]	–	–	öffnen [œfnɛn]	seul [sœl]	–
[ɔ̃][3]	–	–	–	don [dɔ̃]	–
[ɑ̃][3]	–	–	–	camp [kɑ̃]	–

[1]The [e] in German and French is spoken with a slightly higher and more forward tongue position and could, more accurately, be written as [ẹ].
[2][ɒ] open, lip-rounded; used only in British English.
[3]See footnote [1] on page 131 for more about [ɔ̃] and [ɑ̃].

INTERNATIONAL PHONETIC ALPHABET

IPA Symbols	English	Italian	German	French	Spanish
[ɛ̃]	–	–	–	faim [fɛ̃]	–
[œ̃]	–	–	–	un [œ̃]	–
[w]	witch [wɪtʃ]	uomo [wɔmo]	–	oui [wi]	puerta [pwɛrta]
[ʍ] [hw]	which [ʍɪtʃ]	–	–	–	–
[j]	you [ju]	ieri [jɛri]	ja [ja]	hier [jɛːr]	hoyo [ɔjo]
[ʎ]	–	gli [ʎi]	–	fille [fiʎə]	llamar [ʎamaɾ]
[l]	law [lɔ]	la [la]	legen [lẹgɛn]	les [lɛ]	lado [laðo]
[r]*	raw [rɔ]	ricco [rikko]	reiten [raɪtɛn]	robe [rɔb]	roca [roka]
[ɹ]	same	┕────────The above [r]s are trilled────────┙			
[ɾ]	–	amore [amoɾe]	–	–	pero [peɾo]
[aʊ]	now [naʊ]	causa [kaʊza]	Haus [haʊs]	–	causa [kaʊsa]
[oʊ]	no [noʊ]	–	–	–	–
[eɪ]	day [deɪ]	pei [peɪ]	–	–	–
[ɔɪ]	boy [bɔɪ]	poiche [pɔɪkɛ]	Feuer [fɔɪʊ]	–	–
[aɪ]	lie [laɪ]	mai [maɪ]	Zeit [tsaɪt]	–	–
[h]	hop [hap]	–	hat [hat]	–	–
[ʔ]	uh oh! [ʔʌʔo]	–	ach [ʔax]	–	–
[p]	pat [pæt]	pasta [pasta]	passen [passɛn]	pas [pa]	padre [padre]
[b]	bit [bɪt]	basta [basta]	Bett [bɛt]	bête [bɛt]	banco [baŋko]
[t]	two [tu]	tempo [tɛmpo]	Tal [tal]	ton [tɔ̃]	tarde [tardɛ]
[d]	do [du]	dente [dɛnte]	des [dɛs]	du [dy]	duerme [duɛrmɛ]
[k]	class [klæs]	che [ke]	kleben [klɛbɛn]	que [kə]	cantar [kantaɾ]
[g]	glass [glæs]	golfo [golfo]	gabe [gabə]	guide [gid]	guerra [gwɛra]
[ç]	–	–	ich [ʔɪç]	–	yo [ço]
[x]	–	–	ach [ʔax]	–	jarro [xarɔ]
[ɣ]	–	–	waren [vaɣɛn]	–	rogar [roɣaɾ]

*Note: For convenience, we shall use the [r] interchangeably for the American *fricative* [ɹ] and the European *trilled* and *apical* (tip of the tongue) [r]; [ɾ] is singly flipped.

IPA Symbols	English	Italian	German	French	Spanish
[f]	fife [faɪf]	facile [fatʃile]	fahren [faːrɛn]	femme [fam]	fuerte [fuɛrtɛ]
[v]	five [faɪv]	verso [vɛrso]	was [vas]	vous [vu]	vista [vistɑ]
[β]	—	—	—	—	hablar [haβlaɾ]
[θ]	bath [bæθ]	—	—	—	cinco [θɪnko]
[ð]	bathe [beɪð]	—	—	—	lado [lɑðo]
[s]	sue [sju]	si [si]	das [dɑs]	ses [sɛ]	seguro [seguɾo]
[z]	zoo [zu]	casa [kɑzɑ]	Seele [zeːlə]	zele [zeːl]	isla [izlɑ]
[ʃ]	mission [mɪʃən]	facisti [faʃisti]	Spass [ʃpas]	crèche [krɛːʃ]	—
[ʒ]	vision [vɪʒən]	—	Charge† [ʃarʒə]	agilité [aʒilite]	—
[tʃ]	church [tʃɝtʃ]	cera [tʃera]	Klatsch [klatʃ]	—	chico [tʃiko]
[dʒ]	judge [dʒʌdʒ]	gente [dʒɛnte]	—	—	—
[ʃt]	rushed [rʌʃt]	—	standen [ʃtandɛn]	—	—
[ʒd]	rouged [ruʒd]	—	—	—	—
[m]	mow [mou]	prima [primɑ]	Mutter [mʊtɒ]	mon [mɔ̃]	madre [mɑdre]
[n]	no [nou]	vano [vɑno]	nun [nuːn]	non [nɔ̃]	andar [andaɾ]
[ŋ]	sung [sʌŋ]	vengo [vɛŋgo]	Finger [fɪŋɒ]	—	banco [bɑŋko]
[ɲ]	onion [ʌɲɪn]	agnelli [ɑɲɛllɪ]	—	montagne [mɔ̃tɑɲə]	pequeño [pɛkeɲo]
[ř]*[ʀ]	—	—	rot [řot]	liberté [liběřté]	—

Diacritical Marks

~ Nasalized Vowel
ː Lengthened Vowel (previous)
ˇ Uvular Trill

†C is not a genuine German letter and occurs only in borrowed foreign words.
*The uvular [ř] or [ʀ] is used, generally, only by French cabaret singers and their imitators. Legitimate singers avoid it.

APPENDIX III
VOICE CLASSIFICATION

Voice classification is a necessary evil in vocal music, due primarily to opera and oratorio. In these works, specific keys have been designated for particular characters.

Voice specifications have also been made for various orchestrally accompanied vocal solos. In addition to these, certain Lieder or art songs have been written in specific keys which defy transposition— at least, radical transposition— because of certain composers' desires for particular keys and voice qualities in particular songs. (See p. 108, e. Range)

The singer who attempts this repertoire must be able to sing the music effectively and safely, *as written*. He must be in the correct "Fach" or voice category. This is *voice classification*.

The standard voice classifications in America are relatively simple. In the simplest form they range, from highest to lowest, as follows:

a. Soprano
b. Contralto (Alto)
c. Tenor
d. Bass

This is the standard voicing for the basic choral works. As choral music increases in complexity, the four voices above double into:

a. 1st Soprano
b. 2nd Soprano
c. Mezzo-Soprano (1st Alto)
d. Contralto (2nd Alto)
e. 1st Tenor
f. 2nd Tenor
g. Baritone (1st Bass)
f. Bass (2nd Bass)

In America, the above categories cover every contingency. But in Europe— especially in Germany, Switzerland, Austria, and Italy— there are voice categories to stagger the imagination.

It is my personal conviction that the following groups of voice categories have evolved, partially, because of vocal incompetencies. Because of vocal limitations of range, power, and/or quality, it has apparently been found necessary to accommodate immature, worn out, or badly trained singers in roles which require a relatively small portion of a singer's vocal potential. The better singers are capable of performing well in three to four different voice categories.

The following "Fachs," as I shall call them henceforth (the actual plural for this word is *Fächer*), are divided into two basic groups for *theatrical reasons*:

1. Serious Fach - Roles which require earnest, serious types. Usually cast with lyric, youthful voices.

2. Character and Comic Fach - The Character Fach requires heavy, dramatic voices of great quality and depth; The Comic Fach requires excellent actors who may, or may not, have good voices.

Each of the above two divisions can be further sub-divided into two more distinct groups for *vocal* reasons, briefly mentioned above.

1. Lyric Voice - usually involves younger singers, but not always. From a technical standpoint, the younger singer is vocally oriented more toward the light mechanism. There is often a hint of immaturity in his vocal production, but with promise of greater things to come.

2. Dramatic Voice - is usually found in singers who are more mature, either in age or in vocal development. These singers are oriented predominantly toward the heavy mechanism. Young singers who sound mature must be especially careful not to overload their voices by assuming roles which demand their particular timbre, but, which also demand stamina which they have not yet acquired. They must be patient.

The following list of operatic voice Fachs will proceed in groups from the highest to the lowest ranges. They will be arranged under two major groups: I *Serious Fach* and II *Character-Comic Fachs*. Each of these groups will include, as sub-divisions, *General Fach*, *Specific Fach*, *Character* (role), *Opera*, *Composer*, *Aria*, and *representative singers* who are currently available on recordings and/or who belong in that particular Fach.

I Serious Fach

  A. Soprano

1. Dramatic Coloratura - Queen of the Night (*Magic Flute*) Mozart - "O zittre nicht" - Wilma Lipp; Joan Sutherland
2. Lyric - Pamina (*Magic Flute*) Mozart - "Ach, Ich fühl's" - Hilde Gueden; Kiri Te Kanawa
3. Young Dramatic (Spinto) - Donna Elvira (*Don Giovanni*) Mozart - "Ah, fuggi il traditor" - Carla Cavazzi; Martina Arroyo; Mirella Freni
4. Dramatic - Leonora (*La forza del destino*) Verdi - "Pace, pace mio dio" - Leontyne Price; Zinka Milanov; Monserrat Caballé
5. High Dramatic - Isolde (*Tristan und Isolde*) Wagner - Conclusion of Act II - Kirsten Flagstad; Helen Traubel; Birgit Nilsson

  B. Mezzo-Soprano

1. Lyric Mezzo-Soprano - Cherubino (*Le nozze di Figaro*) Mozart - "Non so più" - Frederika von Stade; Janet Baker; Judith Forst
2. Dramatic Mezzo-Soprano - Eboli (*Don Carlos*) Verdi - "O don fatale" - Elena Nicolai; Christa Ludwig; Fiorenza Cossotto; Marilyn Horne

  C. Contralto
1. Dramatic - Azucena (*Il Trovatore*) Verdi - "Stride la vampa" - Fedora Barbieri; Jean Madeira; Risë Stevens
2. Deep Alto - Dame Quickly (*Falstaff*) Verdi - "Guinta all' Albergo della Giarrettiera" - Amalia Pini; Regina Resnik; Giulietta Simionato

D. Tenor

1. Lyric - Almaviva (*Barber of Seville*) Rossini - "Ecco ridente in cielo" - Cesare Valletti; Luigi Alva; Nicolai Gedda
2. Lyric-Spinto - Rodolfo (*La Boheme*) Puccini - "Che gelida manina!" - Jussi Bjoerling; Luciano Pavarotti; Jerry Hadley
3. Young Helden Tenor (Spinto) - Alvaro (*La forza del destino*) Verdi - "La vita è inferna all' infelice" - Richard Tucker; Franco Corelli; Placido Domingo
4. Helden Tenor - Siegmund (*Die Walküre*) Wagner - "Winterstürme wichen dem Wonnemond" - Lauritz Melchior; Wolfgang Windgassen; James McCracken; Jon Vickers

E. Baritone

1. Lyric - Silvio (*Pagliacci*) Leoncavallo - "E allor perche" - Marcello Rossi; Richard Stilwell
2. Cavalier - Enrico (*Lucia di Lammermoor*) Donizetti - "Cruda, funesta smania" - Ettore Bastiannini; Leonard Warren; Sherrill Milnes; Pablo Elvira
3. Helden (High Bass) - Wotan (*Die Walküre*) Wagner - "Leb' wohl, du kühnes, herrliches Kind!" - George London; Walter Berry; Theo Adam; Thomas Stewart

F. Bass

1. Basso Cantante - King Philip (*Don Carlos*) Verdi - "Ella giammai m'amò!" - Boris Christoff; Hans Sotin; Nicolai Giaurov; Cesare Siepi; Paul Pliska; Jan Opalach
2. Basso Profundo - Sarastro (*Magic Flute*) Mozart - "O Isis und Osiris" - Kurt Boehme; Jerome Hines; Jeff Morris

II Character and Comic Fach

A. Soprano

1. Lyric-Coloratura - Rosina (*Barber of Seville*) Rossini - "Una voce poco fa" - Roberta Peters; Judith Blegen; Kathleen Battle
2. Soubrette - Marzelline (*Fidelio*) Beethoven - "O wär' ich schon mit dir vereint" - Reri Grist; Anneliese Rothenberger; Lucia Popp
3. Character - Tosca (*Tosca*) Puccini - "Vissi d'arte" - Renata Tebaldi; Zinka Milanov; Renata Scotto; Mirella Freni

B. Contralto

1. Comic Alto - The Witch (*Hänsel und Gretel*) Humperdinck - Maureen Forrester; Gisela Litz

C. Tenor

1. Tenor Buffo - Beppe (*Pagliacci*) Leoncavallo - "O Colombina" - Salvatore Di Tommaso; Peter Schreier
2. Character - Spalanzani (*Tales of Hoffman*) Offenbach - "La! Dors en paiz" - Michel Sénéchal; Gino del Signore.

D. Baritone

1. Buffo - Gianni Schicchi (*Gianni Schicchi*) Puccini - "Si corre dal notaio" - Giuseppe Taddei; Tito Gobbi
2. Character - Tonio (*Pagliacci*) Leoncavallo - "Prologo" - Leonard Warren; Robert Merrill; Giuseppe Taddei; Enzo Mascherini

162 VOCAL DEVELOPMENT THROUGH ORGANIC IMAGERY

E. Bass

1. Buffo - Leporello (*Don Giovanni*) Mozart - "Notte e giorno faticar" - Italo Tajo; Fernando Corena
2. Character - Sparafucile (*Rigoletto*) Verdi - "Signor... Ne'il chiesi..." (Duet) - Ivo Vinco; Norman Treigle
3. Heavy Basso-Buffo - Basilio (*Barber of Seville*) Rossini - "La calunnia" - Giorgio Tozzi; Cesare Siepi

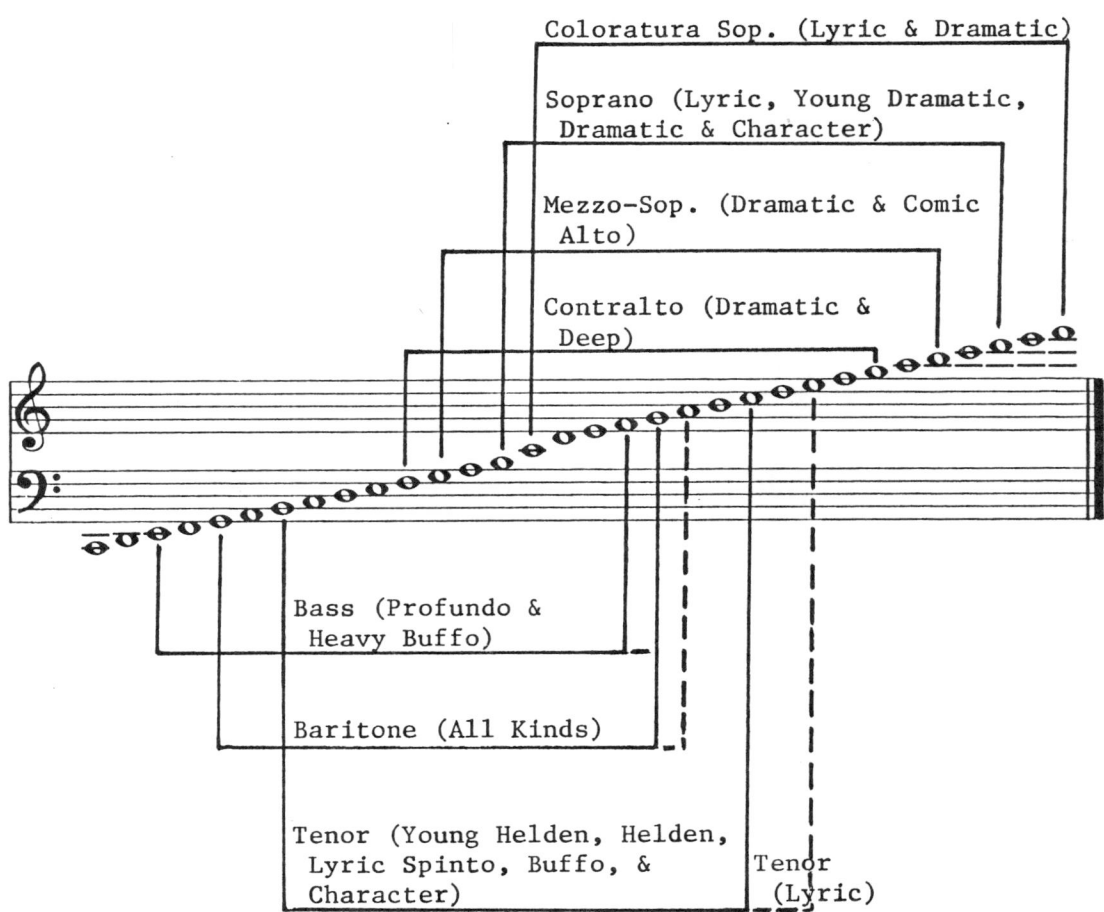

Approximate functional ranges of the various voice categories

Fig. 141

APPENDIX IV
VOWEL FOCUS EXERCISES

These exercises help the singer coordinate the *quality vowel* with the *identity vowel*. They are prerequisite to Vowel Migration (Appendix V). (See p. 46, Vowel Dualism)

Each of the exercises on the following page is to be done in three stages:

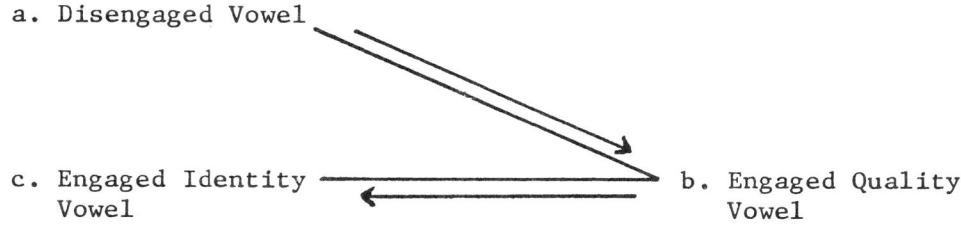

Fig. 142

a. Beginning on middle C for women and one octave lower for men, sing the disengaged (unfocused) vowel (a.) at the mezzo forte dynamic level. The tone should have no intensity, whatsoever. If it is sung too well the rest of the exercise will be ineffective.

> The disengaged vowel is sung breathily, with a high larynx, closed throat, and *no* heavy mechanism.

Sustaining the disengaged vowel, carry it to b.

b. The instant b. (engaged quality vowel) is reached, the throat should spring open; the larynx should lower and the chest voice (heavy mechanism) should become dominant. All breathiness should disappear. The vowel will migrate, as indicated, from a. to b. The singer will feel he has just become Superman at b., whereas he was only Clark Kent at a.

c. After b. is firmly established, allow the vowel to retain its quality at b. and move on to c. (engaged identity vowel) with as little movement of the tongue and/or jaw as possible. The singer should note that although the vowels at a. and c. are the same, the vowel at c. will no longer have the light, colorless quality of the vowel at a. The singer will feel the strength of the quality vowel sustain the integrity of the identity vowel. He will have a built-in stereo system of vowels. The quality vowel keeps the throat open and should always be present while the more closed identity vowels are sung. This constant presence also facilitates ease of the first vowel migration, as it is already there.

All vowels under Group I migrate. None of the vowels under Group II migrates during the first migration because each is a stable vowel.

164 VOCAL DEVELOPMENT THROUGH ORGANIC IMAGERY

The following vowel focus exercises correspond, generally, with first stage vowel migrations, but not in every case:

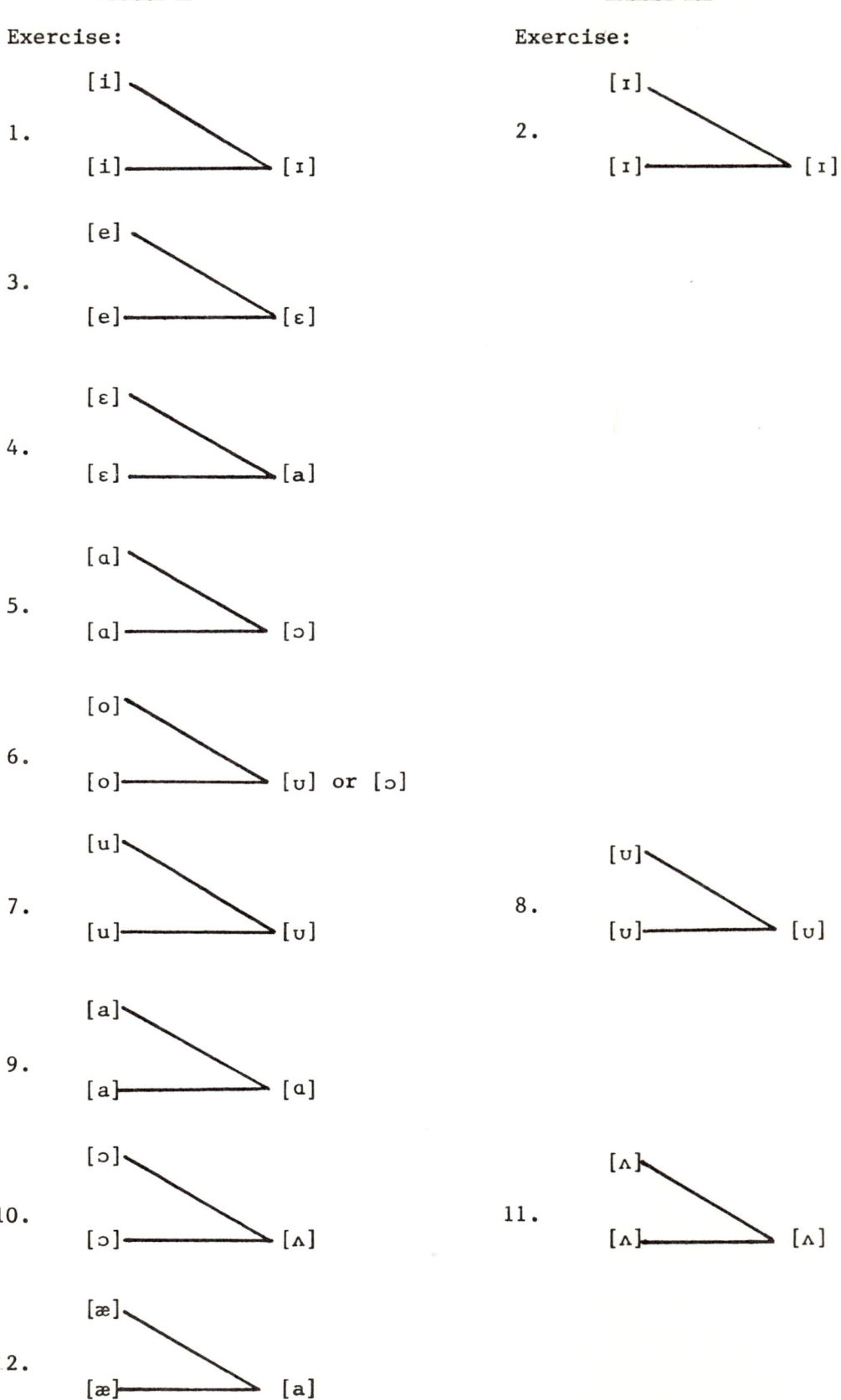

APPENDIX V
VOWEL MIGRATION CHARTS

As the singer ascends the scale or as he crescendos a tone on a single pitch, the vowel is slightly and gradually altered. The converse is true, but the changes do not always occur at the same pitch levels on descension or at the same volume levels on the diminuendo:

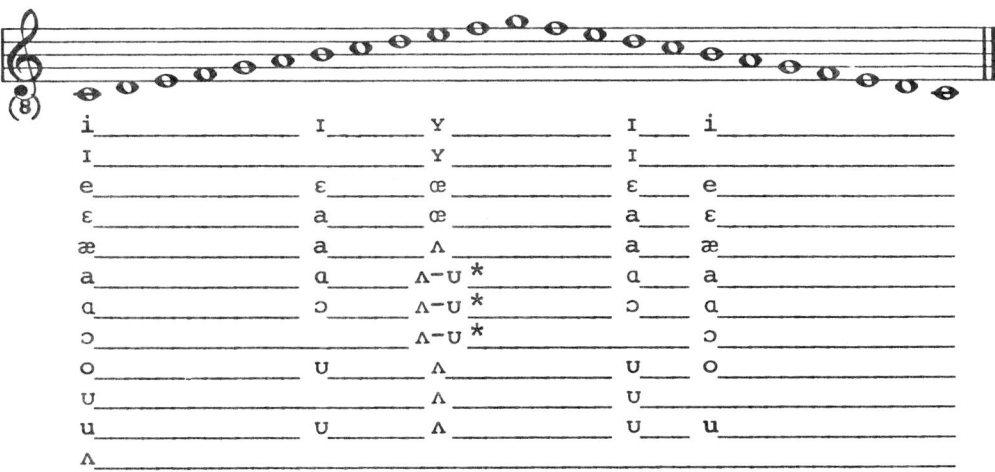

i	ɪ	ʏ	ɪ	i
ɪ		ʏ	ɪ	
e	ɛ	œ	ɛ	e
ɛ	a	œ	a	ɛ
æ	a	ʌ	a	æ
a	ɑ	ʌ-ʊ *	ɑ	a
ɑ	ɔ	ʌ-ʊ *	ɔ	ɑ
ɔ		ʌ-ʊ *		ɔ
o	ʊ	ʌ	ʊ	o
ʊ		ʌ	ʊ	
u	ʊ	ʌ	ʊ	u
ʌ				

Fig. 143

i	ɪ	ʏ	ɪ	i
ɪ		ʏ		ɪ
e	ɛ	œ	ɛ	e
ɛ	a	œ	a	ɛ
æ	a	ʌ	a	æ
a	ɑ	ʌ-ʊ*	ɑ	a
ɑ	ɔ	ʌ-ʊ*	ɔ	ɑ
ɔ		ʌ-ʊ*		ɔ
o	ʊ	ʌ	ʊ	o
ʊ		ʌ		ʊ
u	ʊ	ʌ	ʊ	ʌ
ʌ				

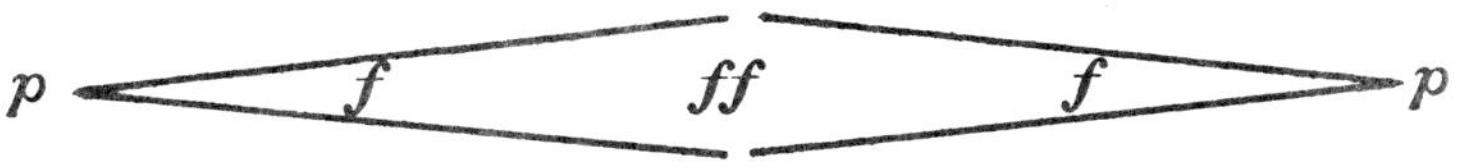

Fig. 144

*Indicates a choice of one vowel or the other. For example, ʌ-ʊ means the singer can migrate to [ʌ] or to [ʊ] on that pitch or intensity level.

Note: The reader should realize that the vowel migrations given above might not necessarily be particularly applicable to him. He should be prepared to compensate by a tone or semitone if that pitch level should prove more efficient, and he should modify the vowel color as needed. The charts should work for *most* singers as presented here, however.

APPENDIX VI
HOW TO STUDY A SONG

The most efficient method for learning new song material is not usually the approach taken by most students. They are impatient to "get on with" singing the song, and they by-pass the proper method. This occurs, occasionally, out of necessity; but, more often than not, it happens from sheer slovenliness or ignorance.

A method which has proved to be most effective with serious amateurs and professional singers is as follows:

1. Isolate the text from the music and read it for content (that is, understanding).

2. Read the text as poetry, emphasizing its dramatic value.

3. Memorize the text.

4. Read the text in the rhythm of the music.

5. Without the text, sing the melody by *marking** on a neutral syllable of your choice.

6. After the melody is *securely* learned by marking, sing it in full voice.

7. Memorize the melody.

8. Sing the melody with the text, marking at first, then in full voice.

9. Study the accompaniment.

10. Put it all together with an accompanist and sing by memory.

---

*Marking is the technique of singing an octave lower (if it is easier) or in falsetto or half-voice (if it is easier), while studying a song or rehearsing a stage production, in order to save the voice from being over-taxed.

APPENDIX VII
IMPOSTO

Some of the great teachers of the Bel Canto era used the term, *imposto*, to describe the sensation of mask resonance. Imposto, then, may be considered synonomous with such terms as *forward placement, mask resonance, nasal resonance, resonance focus,* and other similar terms which describe the position and sensations a singer feels at the base of the juncture of the hard and soft palates and around the nasal arch. As I prefer to use the word *focus* in terms of phonation, it would be ambiguous to use it for resonance as well. *Imposto* is an ideal term for *resonance focus*. The Italian word, *impostare*, means *to place* or *lay foundations*. In reality, we know that this "placement" is an effect and not a cause; nevertheless, the sensation is critical in freeing the voice. The following organic images will aid the singer in activating these sensations.

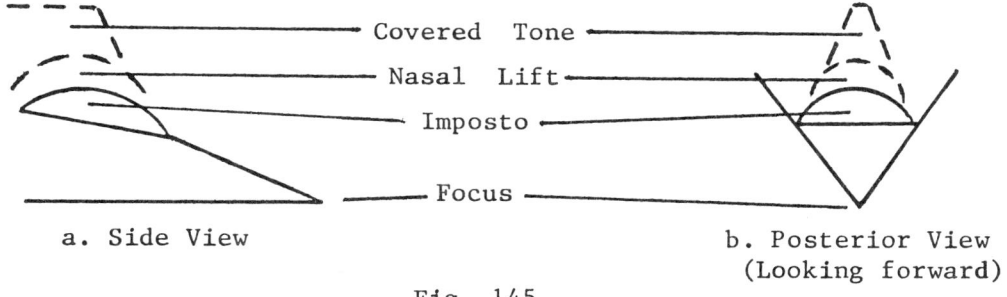

a. Side View   b. Posterior View
(Looking forward)

Fig. 145

In Fig. 145, the basic position for Imposto is represented by the lower arch. It will aid the singer to think of *aiming* the tone through that arch. As he sings higher or more loudly, the arch should rise (Nasal Lift). When the singer reaches his *cover* note (Covered Tone), the arch will rise even higher and become more pointed. For the anterior view of this image, see page 93 (2) Covered Tone - Registration.

Imposto will enable the singer to feel as if he is leading the tone through the nose, although the nasal port will be closed when this is done properly. If the singer gently pinches the nostrils closed while singing anything but nasal vowels and consonants, this will indicate if the tone is produced correctly. If the tone and sensation remain unaltered, the tone is properly produced. (See "Wee, wee, wee" exercise, p. 41)

WARNING: There is a distinct danger that the sensation of imposto will feel so good to the singer that it may lure him into the trap of letting go of the other suspensory mechanisms which keep the throat open and the focal point intact. This may not happen within the first few days. Be on guard!

Another variation of the image for imposto and for the inverted megaphone (Fig. 139a on p. 152) is the "keyhole" megaphone, which allows the singer to feel vertical narrowness at the lips, and round maskiness around the nasal arch:

Fig. 146

APPENDIX VIII
REGISTER COORDINATION EXERCISES

The following general rule will aid the singer in understanding the various adjustments necessary for singing the different registers:

> When singing softly, the singer should have the *sensation* of inhaling; when singing loudly, the singer should have the sensation of exhaling. However, any inhaled tone must be converted to an exhaled tone at some point during a crescendo, and, vice-versa.

As the singer progresses up and down the scale, through the various registers, the dynamic levels are exceedingly important for particular segments of those registers. For example, if the singer sings a two octave scale at the dynamic level of mezzo forte, the points at which he "inhales" the tone will be different than when he sings the same scale at the forte or piano dynamic level.

When the singer inhales the tone, he will feel an inward and upward "tuck" from the bottom of the sternum to the top of the pubic bone (Fig. 147a). At the same time, he will be more aware of back breathing (Fig. 147c), which is necessary for supporting the inhaled tone.

Conversely, when the singer exhales the tone, he will feel an outward and downward thrust from the bottom of the sternum to the top of the pubic bone (Fig. 147b). While he will still be aware of the back breathing muscles, he will become increasingly aware of frontal support, downward toward the pubic bone, as he gives more support required by a crescendo or higher range. This support is often accompanied by an inward flex of the buttocks (Fig. 147d).

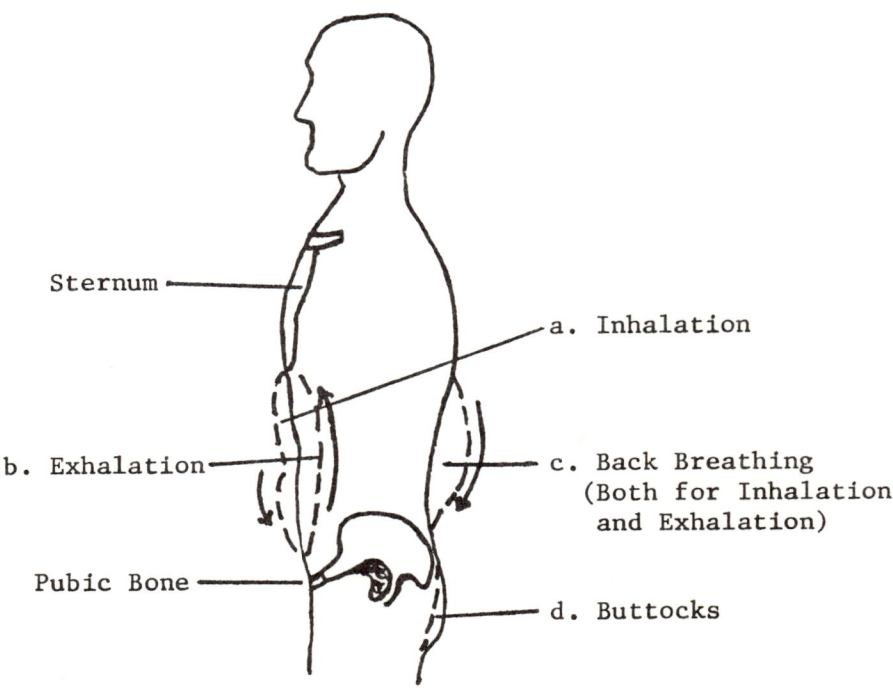

Fig. 147

REGISTER COORDINATION EXERCISES

The middle vocal register (*voix mixte* or *coordinated register*) requires special handling. The following exercise has proved to be most effective in aiding singers in conceptualizing this sensitive coordinative process:

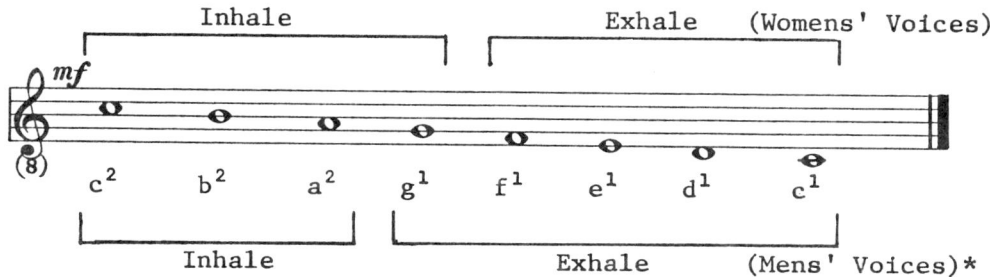

*[Men sing one octave lower than the pitches indicated above]

Fig. 148

In descending the scale from c^2 through g^1 (women) or from c^2 through a^2 (men), the singer should inhale the tone in a yawning position. He must be careful to *maintain focus*, however, as the inhaled yawn can become muffled or "woofy" quite easily. After reaching f^1 (women) or g^1 (men), the singer should convert the sensation of inhaling to one of exhaling, *while maintaining focus* and *the yawning position*. In ascending the scale, he should reverse the process, first exhaling, then inhaling at the designated tone. The yawn and focus will allow a smooth transition from one register to another.

If, while descending the scale, the singer does not convert from the inhaling to the exhaling sensation at the designated note, he will carry a disproportionate amount of the light registration (head voice) too low; and the tone will not have adequate power or vibrancy.

On the other hand, if, while ascending the scale, the singer does not convert from the exhaling to the inhaling sensation at the designated note, this and successive tones in that series will become progressively heavier and forced. These tones will be uncomfortable to produce, unpleasant to hear, and will allow only limited extension into the upper range.

When he ascends the scale, the back breath support must gradually increase; or the open throat, which is facilitated by the yawn, will close. When he descends the scale, gradually less back breath support is needed; but the yawn position must be maintained. The yawn should be a deep one, felt at the bottom, sides, and back of the rib cage. There should be absolutely no upward or inward compression, which can be felt in the throat or upper chest.

The singer should realize that the breath-lift exercise (Fig. 148) is only a voice primer. It is designed to acquaint him with the changing sensations of registration at a specific range and dynamic level. By mastering this coordinated octave, he will learn the directions required for applying the general rule given on the previous page (¶ 1).

APPENDIX IX
THE BLIND MEN AND THE ELEPHANT*
A HINDOO FABLE
John Godfrey Saxe

It was six men of Indostan
  To learning much inclined,
Who went to see the Elephant
  (Though all of them were blind),
That each by observation
  Might satisfy his mind.

The *First* approached the Elephant
  And happening to fall
Against his broad and sturdy side,
  At once began to bawl:
"God bless me! but the Elephant
  Is very like a wall!"

The *Second*, feeling of the tusk,
  Cried, "Ho! what have we here
So very round and smooth and sharp?
  To me 'tis mighty clear
This wonder of an Elephant
  Is very like a spear!"

The *Third* approached the animal,
  And happening to take
The squirming trunk within his hands,
  Thus boldly up and spake:
"I see," quoth he, "the Elephant
  Is very like a snake!"

The *Fourth* reached out an eager hand,
  And felt about the knee.
"What most this wondrous beast is like
  Is mighty plain," quoth he;
"Tis clear enough the Elephant
  Is very like a tree!"

The *Fifth* who chanced to touch the ear,
  Said: "E'en the blindest man
Can tell what this resembles most;
  Deny the fact who can,
This marvel of an Elephant
  Is very like a fan!"

The *Sixth* no sooner had begun
  About the beast to grope
Than, seizing on the swinging tail
  That fell within his scope,
"I see," quoth he, "the Elephant
  Is very like a rope!"

And so these men of Indostan
  Disputed loud and long,
Each in his own opinion
  Exceeding stiff and strong,
Though each was partly in the right,
  And all were in the wrong!

MORAL

So oft in theologic wars,
  The disputants, I ween,
Rail on in utter ignorance
  Of what each other mean,
And prate about an Elephant
Not one of them has seen!

(before 1887)

*[See page 118, Chapter IX, *The Whole Elephant*, for a vocal pedagogical paraphrase of this poem.]

BIBLIOGRAPHY

Numbers in brackets [ ] indicate pages in this volume on which quotations or references were given.

Apel, Willi; *HARVARD DICTIONARY OF MUSIC*; Harvard University Press; Cambridge, Mass.; 1944 (eleventh printing 1958); [82] [109]

Appelman, D. Ralph; *THE SCIENCE OF VOCAL PEDAGOGY*; Indiana University Press; Bloomington; Second printing, 1974. [47] [142]

Bach, Richard; *JONATHAN LIVINGSTON SEAGULL*; The Macmillan Company, pub.; 866 Third Ave., New York; 1970. [120] [121]

Baer, Hermanus; "Establishing A Correct Basic Technique For Singing"; *THE NATS BULLETIN*; Chicago, Illinois; Vol. XXVIII, No. 4, May/June 1972. [23] [28]

Bates, William H., M.D.; *BETTER EYESIGHT WITHOUT GLASSES*; Holt, Rinehart and Winston; 1940 and 1943; Pyramid Books (Paper back), 919 Third Ave., New York, N.Y. 10022; eighth printing; 1975. [124]

Coffin, Berton; *OVERTONES TO BEL CANTO - Phonetic Basis of Artistic Singing*; The Scarecrow Press; Metuchen, New Jersey and London, England; 1980. [129]

Coffin, Berton; Errolle, Ralph; Delattre, Pierre; and Singer, Werner; *PHONETIC READINGS OF SONGS AND ARIAS*; Pruett Publishing Company; Boulder, Colorado; 1964. [128]

Coffin, Berton; Vocal Pedagogy Classics: "Sbriglia's Singing Method", Margaret Chapman Byers; *THE NATS BULLETIN*, Vol. 40, No. 3, Jan./Feb. 1984. [105]

Corbett, Margaret Darst; *HELP YOURSELF TO BETTER SIGHT*; Prentice - Hall, Inc.; Englewood Cliffs, New Jersey; 1949; Wilshire Book Company (Paper back edition), 12015 Sherman Road, North Hollywood, Calif. 91605; 1974. [125]

Delattre, Pierre and Howie, John; "An Experimental Study of the Effect of Pitch on the Intelligibility of Vowels"; *THE NATS BULLETIN*, Oct. 1958; Reprinted in *CONTRIBUTIONS OF VOICE RESEARCH TO SINGING* (See Large, John, below). [44]

Duncan, Todd; "The NATS Bulletin Interviews"; *THE NATS BULLETIN*, Vol. 37, No. 5, May/June 1981. [95]

Engel, Lehman; *GETTING THE SHOW ON*; Schirmer Books; New York; Collier Macmillan Publishers, London; 1983. [xi]

Garcia, Manual; *HINTS ON SINGING*, Translated by Beata Garcia; E. Ascherberg and Co., Publishers; London; 1894. [110]

Gollobin, Laurie Brooks and White, Harvey; "Voice Teachers On Voice, Part 2"; *MUSIC EDUCATORS JOURNAL*, Vol. 64, No. 6, Feb. 1978. [83]

Herbert-Caesari, Edgar F.; *THE SCIENCE AND SENSATION OF VOCAL TONE*; Crescendo Publishing Co.; Boston; Fifth printing, 1971. [23]

Hines, Jerome; *GREAT SINGERS ON GREAT SINGING*; Doubleday and Company, Inc.; Garden City, New York; 1982. [40] [63] [92]

Holland, Bernard; "A Very Special Soprano"; *THE NEW YORK TIMES MAGAZINE*, Section 6; Nov. 17, 1985. [102]

Husler, Frederick and Rodd-Marling, Yvonne; *SINGING: THE PHYSICAL NATURE OF THE VOCAL ORGAN*; October House, Inc.; New York; 1965. [122]

Jones, Daniel; *THE PHONEME - ITS NATURE AND USE*; W. Heffer & Sons, LTD.; Cambridge, England; 1950. [127]

Klein, Joseph J.; *SINGING TECHNIQUE (How To Avoid Vocal Trouble)*; D. Van Nostrand Company, Inc.; Princeton, New Jersey, Toronto, London; 1967; [57]

Ladefoged, Peter; *A COURSE IN PHONETICS*; Harcourt Brace Jovanovich, Inc.; New York - Chicago - San Francisco - Atlanta; 1975. [127]

Lamperti, Francesco; *THE ART OF SINGING*, translated by J.C. Griffith; G. Schirmer, Inc.; New York. [3] [107]

Lamperti, Giovanni Battista; *VOCAL WISDOM*, Transcribed by William Earl Brown; Taplinger Publishing Company; New York; 1931. [106]

Large, John, editor; *CONTRIBUTIONS OF VOICE RESEARCH TO SINGING*; College Hill Press; Houston, Texas 77035; 1980. [21]

Large, John and Patton, Robert; "The effects of Weight Training and Aerobic Exercise On Singers"; *JOURNAL OF RESEARCH IN SINGING*, Vol. IV, No. 2, 1981. [135]

Lawrence, Van, M.D.; Laryngoscope: "Post-Nasal Drip"; *THE NATS BULLETIN*, Vol. 39, No. 1, Sept./Oct. 1982. [115]

Lawrence, Van, M.D.; Laryngoscope: "When All Else Fails Read The Instructions"; *THE NATS BULLETIN*, Vol. 39, No. 3, Jan./Feb. 1983. [115]

Leyerle, William D.; Pedagogical Opinion: "Organic Imagery and Technical Vocal Priorities"; *THE NATS BULLETIN*, Vol. 37, No. 5, May/June, 1981. [35]

Leyerle, William D.; Point Counterpoint No. 17: "Certain female voices make successful use of the flageolet range"; *THE NATS BULLETIN*, Vol. 41, No. 1, Sept./Oct., 1984. [43]

Marchesi, Mathilde; *BEL CANTO: A THEORETICAL AND PRACTICAL VOCAL METHOD*; Unabridged republication by Dover Publications, Inc.; New York; 1970. [59] [80]

Miller, Richard; *ENGLISH, FRENCH, GERMAN AND ITALIAN TECHNIQUES OF SINGING: A Study In National Tonal Preferences and How They Relate to Functional Efficiency*; The Scarecrow Press, Inc.; Metuchen, New Jersey; 1977. [60] [63]

Miller, Richard; sotto voce: "Have You Read The Literature?"; *THE NATS JOURNAL*, Vol. 42, No. 2, Nov./Dec., 1985. [119]

Miller, Richard; sotto voce: "Woofy Baritones and Tinny Tenors"; *THE NATS BULLETIN*, Vol. 39, No. 5, May/June, 1983. [89]

Moses, Elbert R., Jr.; *PHONETICS - HISTORY AND INTERPRETATION*; Prentice-Hall, Inc.; Englewood Cliffs, New Jersey; 1964; [126] [128]

Pleasants, Henry; *THE GREAT SINGERS*; A Fireside Book; Simon and Schuster; Rockefeller Center, 1230 Avenue of the Americas; New York, N.Y. 10020; 1966. [147]

Rose, Arnold; *THE SINGER AND THE VOICE*; St. Martin's Press; New York; 1962, 1967. [31]

Seabury, Deborah; Voice Teachers II: "The Singer's World" (The second of a two-part article); *OPERA NEWS*, Vol. 43, No. 8, Dec. 16, 1978. [122]

Vennard, William; *SINGING, THE MECHANISM AND THE TECHNIC*, revised ed. 1967; Carl Fischer, Inc.; New York. [3] [24] [68]

Wolfsohn, Alfred; *VOX HUMANA*; Folkways Records Album No. FPX 123; 1956. [63] [83]

INDEX

abdominal muscles, 12, 17, 105, 145; Fig. 8, 9, 10, 11, 36, 95, 97, 98, 103, 132, 138, 147
abdominal support, 35, 53, 94, 99, 105, 111, 118, 144, 148-152, 168
abduction, 66-68
adduction, 66-68
afflictions, 114-115
affricatives, 76, 155
alignment of spine, 1
alphabet, international phonetic, 43, 48, 126-134, 155, 156-158; Fig. 47, 51
alveolar, 127, 155
alveolar ridge, 73-74; Fig. 77
alveoli, 10; Fig. 4
amplitude, 101
appoggiameter, 148-153, Fig. 136, 137
articulation, 73-79, 118, 143-145; Fig. 129, 130, 131, 132
articulators, 73-75; Fig. 80
arytenoid cartilage, 20-22, 66-68; Fig. 20, 21, 22, 69
arytenoid muscles, 66; Fig. 69
aspirant attack, 45
atlas, Fig. 7
attack, 45-46, 68; Fig. 48
axis, Fig. 7

back breathing, 15-18, 31-35, 85-89, 106, 168-169; Fig. 12, 13, 14, 15, 16, 17, 18, 29, 30, 31, 32, 36, 56, 57, 91, 95, 98, 132d, 147
baritone, 59-61, 65, 108, 159-162; Fig. 61, 62, 64, 68
bass, 59-61, 108-109, 159-162; Fig. 61, 62, 64
bell register (see *whistle register*)
belty voice, 92; Fig. 92
Bernoulli, Daniel, 21
Bernoulli effect, 21, 45
bi-labial, 74, 155
blade of tongue, 73; Fig. 80
body migration, 52, 87, 134
bottled, 31, 57
breaking voice, 90
breast bone (see *sternum*)
breath, 6, 122
breath control, 12-18, 65, 104-106, 109, 122, 139, 148, 169; Fig. 18, 148
breath flow, 15, 104
breathiness, 68, 91, 163
breathing, 6-18; Fig. 4, 5, 6, 12, 13, 14, 15, 16, 17, 18, 29, 30, 31, 32, 36, 57, 91
breath management, 148

breath support, 12-18, 30-35, 53, 104-106, 109, 144-145, 148-152, 168-169; Fig. 31, 32, 36, 57, 138, 147
breath triangle, 14-18; Fig. 12, 13, 14, 18
bronchi, 10; Fig. 4
bronchioles, 10; Fig. 4

Caffarelli, Gaetano, 147
catarrh, 115
cervical vertebrae, 4, 8; Fig. 3, 7
channels, 10
characterization, 84, 88, 122, 159-162
chest register, 55, 57-66; Fig. 58, 59, 60, 61, 62, 63, 64, 65, 66, 67, 68
chesty voice, 92; Fig. 92
chiaro-oscuro, 84; Fig. 88
chin, 3
chord of nature, 81
classification of voice, 108-109, 159-162; Fig. 162
clavicle, Fig. 7
coccyx, Fig. 7
colds, 115
coloration, 80-89; Fig. 82, 83, 84, 86, 88, 89, 90, 91
coloratura, 63, 160-162; Fig. 141
compression, 35, 81, 94, 148-152; Fig. 36
condyle of the mandible, 27; Fig. 36
confidence, 116
consonants, 73-79, 126-129, 131-133, 155
contralto, 109, 159-162; Fig. 61, 86, 88, 89, 90, 91
conus elasticus, Fig. 20
coronoid process, Fig. 24
coupling, 45
Courtenay, Jean Badouin de, 126
covered tone, 92-93, 167
covering, 92-93
cranial flex, 4; Fig. 3
cricoid cartilage, 19-22; Fig. 19, 20, 21, 22
cricoarytenoid muscles, 66; Fig. 69

dental, 127, 155
depressed larynx, 23
depressed tongue, 25, 26
diaphragm, 10-12, 105; Fig. 4, 5, 6
diet, 112-113
disengaged vowel, 163-164; Fig. 142
dorsal vertebrae, Fig. 7
dropped jaw, 27, 52, 79, 88, 144, 152;

Fig. 24, 55, 57, 131
dualism of vowel, 46-47, 163; Fig. 49, 142

ego, 116
elation 16-17; Fig. 15
engaged vowel, 163-164; Fig. 142
enthusiasm, 116, 123
epigastrium, 105, 107, 144, 148; Fig. 97, 132b
epiglottis, 25-26; Fig. 19, 23
equalized scale (see *tempered scale*)
esophagus, 24, 38; Fig. 5, 37
ethmoidal sinus, Fig. 37
excitement, 116
exhalation, 6
expiration, 6, 12-18; Fig. 14c
expiratory muscles, 12; Fig. 8, 9, 10, 11
external intercostals, 11-12; Fig. 5
external oblique, Fig. 9

Fach, 60, 159-160
Fächer, 159
falsetto, 55, 94-95, 138, 146
falsetto register, 55
fear, 117
feet, placement of, 1; Fig. 1
flageolet register (see *whistle register*)
flared nostrils, 40; Fig. 42
floating ribs, 14; Fig. 7
floated tone, 146-147; Fig. 135
flow, breath, 15, 104
focus, 28-35, 70, 103, 163-164; Fig. 25, 26, 28, 73, 74, 75, 76, 142
  blunted, 33; Fig. 34, 35a
  detached, 33; Fig. 34, 35b
formants, 82
frequency, Fig. 83-84
fricatives, 76, 155, 157
frontal bone, Fig. 7
frontal sinus, Fig. 37
fundamental tone, 81; Fig. 82, 83

glides, 76, 129
glissando, 138; Fig. 114, 115
glottal attack, 45, 67-68, 132
glottis, 66-68, 75, 132, 155; Fig. 80
goat (or sheep) bleat exercise, 67-68
grip, 67-68
growl register (see *Stroh register*)

hands, position of, 4-5
hard palate, 40, 74, 104; Fig. 23, 43, 80

head register, 55-57, 64-65; Fig. 67, 68, 77
head resonance, 42-44; Fig. 46, 57
head voice, 55-57, 64-65
health, 112-117
  physical, 112-115
  psychological, 115-117
heavy mechanism, 55-58, 92, 163; Fig. 58, 59, 60, 92
Helmholtz octave system, xi
hooking, 92-93
humming, 106-107
hung-ah exercise, 97
hyoid bone, Fig. 7, 19

identity vowel, 47, 163-164; Fig. 142
iliac crest, Fig. 7
imagery 14
  organic (see *organic imagery*)
imagination, 88, 123-125
impingement (approximation), 28 (also see *adduction*)
imposto, 167
inferior horn of thyroid cartilage, 21; Fig. 19, 22
inhalation, 6
inspiration, 6, 11-12
inspiratory muscles, 11-12; Fig. 4, 5, 6
intensity, 100-103
intercostal muscles, 10-12; Fig. 5
internal oblique, Fig. 8
international phonetic alphabet, 43, 48, 126-134, 155, 156-158; Fig. 47, 51
intevertebral disc, Fig. 7
intonation, 95-97

jaw, 3, 27, 38, 51, 64, 66, 76, 84, 97, 152; Fig. 24, 55, 57, 88, 138, 152
  dropped, 27, 51, 64, 84, 144, 152; Fig. 24, 55, 57, 88, 131
  loose, 22, 85, 97
Jonathan Livingston Seagull exercise, 120, 140; Fig. 106, 119
Jones, Daniel, 127

Kempelen, Baron Wolfgang von, 126
King Kong, 83
Kruszewski, 126

large voice, 102-103
laryngo-pharynx, 36; Fig. 37
larynx, 10, 19, 35, 38, 54, 85; Fig. 4, 7, 19, 20, 21, 22, 25, 37, 69
  high, 24, 94, 107, 163
  low, 22-25, 28, 85, 107, 163

INDEX

lateral crico-arytenoid muscles, 21, 66; Fig. 21, 69
lethargy, 116
lift, breath, 169; Fig. 148
lift, palatal, 26-27, 39, 51, 88, 167; Fig. 41, 55, 67, 77, 145
light mechanism, 55-58, 67, 92; Fig. 58, 59, 60, 92
lingua-alveolar, 74-75
lingua-dental, 74
lingua-palatal, 74
lingua-velar, 74
lips, 38, 49-50, 74, 77, 84, 88, 107-108, 144, 156, 167; Fig. 51, 80, 88, 91, 131, 146
loose jaw, 22, 85, 97
lowered palate, 39, 97; Fig. 41
low register, 54-58, 61, 64-65, Fig. 58, 59, 60, 67, 68
lumbar vertebrae, Fig. 7
lungs, 10-18, 89; Fig. 4, 12, 13, 14, 15, 16, 17, 18, 91

maladies, 114-115
mandible, 27; Fig. 7, 24
marking, 107, 166
mask resonance, 39-42, 51, 104, 167, Fig. 42, 43, 44, 45, 145
mastoid process, Fig. 7
maxillary bone, Fig. 7
maxillary sinus, Fig. 37
megaphone image, 38, 89, 144, 152; Fig. 38, 39, 91, 131, 139, 146
messa di voce, 68-70, 95, 143, Fig. 71, 72
metaphysical concepts, 120-122; Fig. 106
mezzo-soprano, 64-65, 159-160; Fig. 61, 62, 63, 65, 67, 141
middle register, 55-61
migration of vowel, 47-53, 101, 163-165; Fig. 47, 49, 52, 53, 55, 67, 68, 77, 78, 96, 142
mirrors, 24, 123, 152
morality, 112, 114
motivation, 116
mouth, 10, 36-38; Fig. 37
mouth resonance, 36-38; Fig. 37

nasal arch, 167
nasal bone, 40; Fig. 7, 42, 43
nasal cavity, 37-40; Fig. 37, 41, 42
nasal consonants, 37, 40, 76, 155, 167
nasality, 41-42, 90, 97; Fig. 44
nasal lift, Fig. 145
nasal port, 37, 39, 76, 97; Fig. 41
nasal resonance, 39

nasal vowel, 37, 40, 76, 131, 133, 155
naso-pharynx, 36; Fig. 37
natural scale, 81-82; Fig. 83
Nefertiti's hat resonance, 42-44; Fig. 46, 47, 67, 77
nervousness, 16, 113, 117
nodules (nodes), 91

oblique arytenoid muscles, 21, 66; Fig. 69
occipital bone, Fig. 7
octaves (Helmholtz), xi
open throat, 22-28, 44, 53, 85, 89, 163; Fig. 23, 24, 91
organic imagery, 14-35, 38, 40, 46, 47, 52-53, 70-71, 83-89, 111, 144-145, 151-153, 163-164, 167-169; Fig. 12, 13, 15, 16, 17, 18, 25, 26, 28, 29, 30, 31, 32, 35, 36, 38, 39, 40, 42, 44, 46, 48, 49, 56, 57, 66, 73, 74, 75, 76, 77, 81, 87, 88, 89, 90, 91, 93, 95, 98, 103, 114, 115, 131, 132, 138, 139, 142, 145, 146
oro-pharynx, 36, 44; Fig. 37
overtone series, 81-83; Fig. 83

palatal lift (see *lifted palate*)
palate, 26-27, 51, 74, 85, 144; Fig. 23, 41, 43, 55, 67, 77, 80, 131
parietal bone, Fig. 7
partials, 82, 118; Fig. 84, 85, 86
passaggio, 58-65; Fig. 61, 62, 64, 65, 66, 67, 68
   intermèdia, 59, 60; Fig. 64, 65
   primo, 59-61; Fig. 61, 64, 65
   secondo, 59, 62; Fig. 62, 64, 65
pharyngeal resonance, 37
pharyngeal wall, 39, 75; Fig. 23, 41, 80
pharynx, 10, 36-44; Fig. 37, 38, 39, 49, 57
phlegm, 115
phonation, 19-35, 38, 47, 118; Fig. 25, 26, 28, 29, 30, 31, 32, 33, 35, 36, 39, 49, 57
phonetic alphabet (see *international phonetic alphabet*)
physical health, 112-114
physical training, 112-114, 135-136
placement of feet, 1; Fig. 1
plosives, 76, 155
point d'appui, 105-106, 148; Fig. 97, 98
polyps, 91
Porpora, Niccolò, 147
position, 107-108
   hands, 4-5

posterior cricoarytenoid muscles, 66; Fig. 69
posture, 1-5; Fig. 1, 2, 3
problems, 90-117
  health, 112-117
  technical 90-111
projection, 101-103
promiscuous migration, 52
psychological health, 115-117
pubes, Fig. 7
pulsation drills (see *pulsation exercises*)
pulsation exercises, 141; Fig. 126, 127, 128

quality vowel, 46-47, 163-164; Fig. 49, 142

radar vocalise, 138; Fig. 114, 115
raised palate (see *lift, palatal*)
range, 108-109; Fig. 141
rarefaction, 81
recorders, 123
recordings, 123
rectus abdominus, 105; Fig. 11
registration, 54-72, 168-169; Fig. 58, 59, 60, 61, 62, 63, 64, 65, 66, 67, 68, 77, 147, 148
resonation, 36-53; Fig. 37, 38, 39, 40, 41, 42, 43, 44, 46, 49, 57
resonators, 36-38; Fig. 37
respiration, 6-18; Fig. 4, 5, 6, 8, 9, 10, 11, 12, 13, 14, 15, 16, 17, 18
rest, 112
ribs, 10-12, 14; Fig. 5, 6, 7
root of tongue, Fig. 80

sacrum, Fig. 7
scapula, Fig. 7
Schnarregister (see *Stroh register*)
self-image, 116
shoulders, position of, 3
singer's formant, 82
sinuses, 38; Fig. 37
small voice, 102-103
smiling back, Fig. 15
Snerdometer, 86-89; Fig. 89, 90
Snerd, Mortimer, 85-86, 89
Snerd synthesizer, 85, 88-89
soft palate, 26-27, 51, 74; Fig. 55, 80
soprano, 43, 59, 110, 159-161; Fig. 61, 62, 63, 141
sore throat, 115
spine (vertebrae), 1; Fig. 7
stage-fright, 16
steel-wire exercise, Fig. 25
sternum (breast bone), 148, 152, 168; Fig. 6, 7, 36, 97, 138, 147
stridency, 97-98
Stroh bass, 54, 63; Fig. 68
Stroh register, Fig. 68
superior horn of thyroid cartilage, Fig. 19
Sweet, Henry, 127
sympathetic vibration, 38, 40, 42, 66

tape recorders, 119, 123
technical problems, 90-111; Fig. 92, 93, 95, 96, 102, 103
teeth, 74 (see *dental*)
tempered scale, 81-82
temporal bone, Fig. 7
tenor, 40, 60, 61, 108, 159, 161-162; Fig. 61, 62, 64, 141
tessatura, 108
throat, 22-27 (also, see *pharynx*)
thyro-arytenoid muscles, Fig. 21
thyrohyoid membrane, Fig. 19
thyroid cartilage, 20-21; Fig. 19, 20, 21, 22
timbre, 80, 89, (also, see *coloration*)
timing, 109
tone color, 80 (also, see *coloration*)
tone quality, 80 (also, see *coloration*)
tongue, 22, 25-26, 38, 47, 49-50, 52, 73-74, 76, 77, 97, 107, 112 (also, see all *lingua-* prefixes)
trachea, 6; Fig. 4
tracheal cartilage, Fig. 19
transverse abdominus, Fig. 10
transverse arytenoid muscle, 21, 66; Fig. 69
tremolo, 98, 100
trill, 109-112
  ornamental 109-111
  phonetic 109, 112

umlaut cone, 144; Fig. 131
uvula, 74, 77, 132, 155, 158; Fig. 80
uvular trill, 77, 132

velum (velar) (also, see *soft palate*), 39, 74, 97, 132, 155; Fig. 41, 80
ventriloquization, 78, 85, 144
vertebrae, 10-11, Fig. 7
vibrato, 98-100
Vinci, Leonardo da, 126
violin-viola-cello exercise, 84; Fig. 87
vocal cords (folds), 19-22, 66; Fig. 20, 21, 22, 23, 69
vocal ligaments (see *vocal cords*)

vocalises (see *vocalization*)
vocalization, 135-147; Fig. 107, 108, 109, 110, 111, 112, 113, 114, 115, 116, 117, 118, 119, 120, 121, 122, 123, 124, 125, 126, 127, 128, 129, 130, 133, 134, 135
vocal problems, 90-117
voice classification, 108-109, 159-162
voiced consonants, 75, 132
volume, 100-101
vowel:
  circle, 49; Fig. 53
  dualism (see *dualism of vowel*)
  focus, (see *focus*)
  identity (see *identity vowel*)
  migration (see *migration of vowel*)
  quadrangle, 48-50; Fig. 51, 52, 54
  quality (see *quality vowel*)
  triangle, 47; Fig. 50

wee-wee-wee exercise, 41-42; Fig. 44
wind pipe, 24
wobble, 100
woofiness (see *woofy tone*)
woofy tone, 85-89, 169

yawn, 23-26, 169; Fig. 67, 68, 77, 148
yawn-sigh exercise, 136
zona intermèdia, 59; Fig. 64, 65
zygomatic bone, (cheek bone) 108; Fig. 7

ABOUT THE AUTHOR:

William Leyerle, who has performed as principal baritone soloist in Germany, Switzerland, and Denmark, and in major cities on the West Coast and in New York, is also active as a performer in Lieder recitals and oratorio. He teaches studio and class voice at the State University of New York, College of the Arts and Science at Geneseo, where he has been for eleven years.

His present position and his first book have their roots in his first voice lesson, at the age of fourteen, in the small cotton and soya bean farming community of Cardwell, Missouri. His teacher was Jane Rauls Washington. The interest generated by Mrs. Washington led to undergraduate study in music with J. Clyde (Doc) Brandt at Southeast Missouri State University and graduate study in voice at Millikin University at Decatur, Illinois, with Hubert Norville. Next, he did post graduate study at the University of Illinois with Ludwig Zirner, Paul Ulanowsky, and William Miller. In addition, he did other post graduate work at the famed Akademie für Musik und darstellende Kunst in Vienna, where he studied voice privately with Baron Hans Karg-Bebenburg.

After formal institutional study ended, he continued in private study with Hazel Arth in Washington, D.C., Ivan Rassmussen in Tacoma, Washington, Farrold Stephens in San Diego, Mario Chamlee in Hollywood, Enzo Mascherini in Zurich, and in New York City with Armen Boyajian, Oren Brown, Lili Wexberg, and Carmine Gagliardi.

Other preparation includes coaching with George Trovillo, Hans Willi Häuslein, Otto Guth, Kurt Adler, and Thomas Martin. He has also worked with stage directors, Matthew Farruggio, William Adams, William Ball, Alfred Schönolt, Frank Corsaro, Lotfi Monsouri, Michael Hampe, James Lucas, and Henry Butler.

Although Mr. Leyerle sang for nine years as a tenor, his professional career did not start moving until he converted to baritone, on the advice of Mario Chamlee. While he was a tenor, he was a finalist in two Metropolitan Opera Regional Final Auditions in Chicago and Los Angeles (the latter, for which he received an honorable mention and a financial scholarship from the Metropolitan Opera Studio). He also won a San Francisco Opera Regional Final Audition in San Diego and participated two summers in the San Francisco Opera's Merola Opera Program.

After changing to baritone, he participated for one year at the Zurich Opera's International Opera Studio in Switzerland, during which time he was awarded a grant from the Martha Baird Rockefeller Fund for Music, Inc., after an audition in Munich, Germany. This grant enabled him to make an audition tour in Germany, where he secured his first full-time European opera engagement in Flensburg, Germany.

Interspersed throughout most of his years of study and performance, Mr. Leyerle has been active as a vocal or instrumental music teacher from first grade through the college level in the states of Missouri, Illinois, California, and New York. He served two years as State Chairman in Voice for the New York State School Music Association (NYSSMA) and has given numerous voice clinics and workshops throughout the state.

He is a member of the National Association of Teachers of Singing, Pi Kappa Lambda, Actors Equity Association, and the American Guild of Musical Artists.

Mr. Leyerle has consolidated these experiences as student, performer, and teacher, and the result is *VOCAL DEVELOPMENT THROUGH ORGANIC IMAGERY*. After the publication of the first edition in 1977, he organized Leyerle Publications, which has published three song collections, co-edited by his wife, Anne, and himself.

MORE ABOUT THE IPA AND OTHER AIDS FOR SINGERS AND TEACHERS

LEYERLE PUBLICATIONS is a company dedicated to bringing innovative and highly useful vocal music books and collections to all who are involved directly or indirectly with singing. High on our list of priorities is helping the student of voice become as self-sufficient as possible.

To this end, we have begun producing song anthologies which include both the word-for-word translations and the International Phonetic Alphabet (IPA) spelling of the foreign language texts. In *SONG ANTHOLOGY ONE* and *SONG ANTHOLOGY TWO*, we have included English singing translations as well. The foreign language songs, included in one or more volumes, are French, German, Italian, Spanish, Russian, and Basque. Songs originally written in English are also included. As an extra bonus, in *FRENCH DICTION SONGS*, which includes Ravel's "Five Greek Folk Songs", we have added lead sheets for these songs with the Greek language and the IPA spelling and the word-for-word translations. In *FRENCH DICTION SONGS*, we have placed the IPA spelling of the French texts directly beneath the French words on the actual music pages.

All the measures in our anthologies are numbered for easy reference by teacher and student. Commentary about the songs and/or composers is provided in the appendix of each book, along with helpful suggestions for efficient use of the IPA.

Quality and economy are also important factors high on our priority list. We use 70 pound paper for effective opacity of pages, and we bind the anthologies either with plastic combs (which allow the books to stay open easily on the piano or music stand) or with sewn signatures. Smyth-sewn books take a bit more "conditioning" to stay open, but are even more durable than the plastic comb bindings; and, they do not fall apart after two or three months use, as do the euphemistically named "Perfect Bindings."

Concerning economy, one does not have to look far to contrast our prices favorably with other comparable volumes. For example, Ravel's "Five Greek Folk Songs" cost almost as much, in the cheapest available edition, as all twenty-five songs in *FRENCH DICTION SONGS*.

The four volumes, listed in complete detail on the following two pages, can be ordered directly from LEYERLE PUBLICATIONS, Box 384, Geneseo, New York 14454, or through your local music store. If you order directly, add $1.50 for postage and handling (4th class book rate). New York residents add 7% for sales tax. Telephone orders are accepted between 4 and 7 P.M., Eastern Time (except for the months of July and August, and the last two weeks of December). Call (716) 658-2193.

For all orders of ten or more books or music, in any combination, we extend a 25% discount— the same as for retail stores. For LIBRARIES, we extend a 20% discount for any number of books.

LEYERLE PUBLICATIONS

SONG ANTHOLOGY ONE
Edited by Anne and William Leyerle
Third Revised Edition, Enlarged and Improved

CONTENTS

Ah! Mio Cor	G.F. Handel
Ah! Mon Berger!	J.-B. Weckerlin
Après Un Rêve	G. Fauré
Arise, Sweet Messenger Of Morn	T.A. Arne
Bist Du Bei Mir	J.S. Bach
Black Is The Color Of My True Love's Hair	W. Leyerle
Blow, Blow, Thou Winter Wind	T.A. Arne
Caro Mio Ben	G. Giordano
Come Again, Sweet Love	J. Dowland
Come Unto These Yellow Sands	H. Purcell
Deep River	(Arr.) A. Leyerle
Der Leiermann	F. Schubert
Die Nacht	R. Strauss
Du Ring An Meinem Finger	R. Schumann
Élégie	J. Massenet
Ev'ry Time I Feel The Spirit	(Arr.) A. Leyerle
Fare You Well	(Arr.) A. Leyerle
Greensleeves	(Arr.) A. Leyerle
I Attempt From Love's Sickness To Fly	H. Purcell
In Haven	E. Elgar
Joshua Fit The Battle Of Jericho	(Arr.) A. Leyerle
Kommt Dir Manchmal In Den Sinn	J. Brahms
Lou Baïlèro	J. Canteloube De Malaret
Madrigal	V. D'Indy
Mandoline	C. Debussy
Nel Cor Più Non Mi Sento	G. Paisiello
Nur Wer Die Sehnsucht Kennt	R. Schumann
Ombra Mai Fù	G.F. Handel
O Mistress Mine	Mrs. H.H.A. Beach
Rapsodia Primaverile	R. Leoncavallo
Romance	C. Debussy
Rule Britannia	T.A. Arne
Schlagende Herzen	R. Strauss
Shenandoah	(Arr.) A. Leyerle
Sigh No More, Ladies	W.A. Fisher
Un Moto Di Gioja	W.A. Mozart
Vado Ben Spesso	S. Rosa
Villanelle	H. Berlioz
Vittoria Mio Core	G. Carissimi
Volksliedchen	R. Schumann
Wayfaring Stranger	(Arr.) A. Leyerle
Where Corals Lie	E. Elgar

159 Pages   Comb-Binding   Medium Range
ISBN 0-9602296-3-9 $10.95

"....This is a most valuable and unique anthology. It should find wide acceptance, especially in the areas of class voice and beginning vocal study.... The anthology is heartily recommended."

James Wainner
The NATS Bulletin, March/April 1981

SONG ANTHOLOGY TWO
Edited by Anne and William Leyerle

CONTENTS

ENGLISH:
Take, O Take Those Lips Away	Mrs. H.H.A. Beach
The Lass That Loves A Sailor	C. Dibdin
The Minstrel Boy	(Arr.) A. Leyerle
The Treasure Chest	W. Leyerle
Now Sleeps The Crimson Petal	R. Quilter
Bright Is The Ring Of Words	R. Vaughan Williams

BASQUE:
Ten Old Spiritual Basque Songs	C. Bordes
Haur Gaixua Lo Eta, Lo	(Arr.) A. Leyerle

FRENCH:
Quand Li Roussignol Joli	C. De Coucy
Fuis, Séducteur	F. Couperin
Lamento	H. Duparc
Pholoé	R. Hahn
Buvons Bien	V. D'Indy
La Bergère Avisée	V. D'Indy
Sur L'Herbe	M. Ravel

GERMAN:
Der Kuss	L. Beethoven
Nur Ein Gesicht Auf Erden Lebt	J. Brahms
Lob Der Faulheit	J. Haydn
Liebst Du Um Schönheit	G. Mahler
Verborgenheit	H. Wolf

ITALIAN:
L'Immago Tua	E. Astorga
Maledetto	P.F. Cavalli
Tu Fai La Superbetta	W. Defesch
Lascia Ch'Io Pianga	G.F. Handel
Nebbie	O. Respighi
Star Vicino	S. Rosa

RUSSIAN:
Царкосельская Статуя	C. Cui
Если Жизнь Тебя Обманетъ	C. Cui
Сомнѣние	M.I. Glinka
Классикъ	M. Moussorgsky
Как Небеса, Твой Взор Блистает	N. Rimsky-Korsakov
Весна	P.I. Tchaikowsky

SPANISH:
Del Salón En El Ángulo Oscuro	I. Albéniz
Canto De La Trilla	J. Inzenga
Seguidillas Manchegas	(Arr.) A. Leyerle
Amor, Que Tan Bien Sirviendo	L. Milán
El Curro Marinero	S. Yradier

159 Pages CombBinding Medium to High Range
ISBN 0-9602296-4-7 $10.95

"... the Leyerles have published another excellent collection of songs... a welcome expansion of available literature. ..great for most teaching studios... This collection of 46 songs is a real bargain!"

Walter Martin
The NATS Bulletin, May/June 1985